WORLDWIDE WARD COOKBOOK

SECRET RECIPES!

More Than 280 Recipes from Around the Globe

Design copyrighted 2011 by Covenant Communications, Inc.
American Fork, Utah

Copyright 2011 by Deanna Buxton
All food imagery © istockphoto.com
Worldwide Ward Cookbook Series Covers and books designed by Christina Marcano, © 2011 Covenant Communications, Inc.

Printed in China
First Printing March 2011

16 15 14 13 12 11 10   10 9 8 7 6 5 4 3 2 1

ISBN: 978-1-60861-211-6

WORLDWIDE WARD COOKBOOK

SECRET RECIPES!

More Than 280 Recipes from Around the Globe

Deanna Buxton

Right to left: Deanna's oldest son, Scott Buxton, and his new wife, Charelle; Deanna's oldest daughter, Erin Miner, with her husband, Adam, and their baby, Milo; Deanna's youngest son, Sam Buxton, and her youngest daughter, Lani Buxton; and Deanna with her husband, David Buxton.

I find such pleasure in a really good secret. Like the secret fort my brothers and I built in the haymow among the bales of straw when we were little—the fort where we hid and from which we went to faraway imaginary places. Or like my secret crush in high school that only my best friend knew about. Or like when my son Scott confided that he was going to ask his girlfriend, Charelle, to marry him—and the resulting deliciously excruciating quest to keep the secret for an entire month while he waited for the ring to be made. Or like knowing before the rest of world that my firstborn grandbaby would be a boy (not to mention that just being able to know such things seems secretly magical).

There are also dreadful secrets that I learned the hard way—like the fact that fresh lime juice turns bitter very quickly, and that squeezing the lime juice in advance only results in a ruined recipe instead of saving time. But there's also glee—like learning that the secret to preventing lime juice from turning bitter is as simple as a sprinkle of salt!

There are the secrets I learned from my mother in the kitchen—like the fact that a fresh slice of bread in the cookie jar with cookies that have become hard will make them turn soft again. The same secret holds for hard brown sugar, too: Put the bread right in the bag of brown sugar, and *voila!* Magically soft brown sugar. And speaking of brown sugar, just a teaspoon added to a plain jar of commercial spaghetti sauce makes a world of difference in the bite of the tomatoes.

What delicious pleasure now in learning secrets from wonderful people around the globe. Like sweet little Kadie, who hides a different kind of candy bar each time in the cookies she makes for her daddy. What delight she gets—not just from making Kadie's Kookies for him, but in keeping the secret from him and letting him guess the surprise. Or Natalie, who uses her Yummy Caramel Chip Bars as her secret weapon to get her husband to do whatever she wants. Or Elizabeth, who knows that the secret to really great Crab Pasta Salad is lime mayonnaise. Or Ryan, who happened to find out his mother-in-law's closely guarded secret recipe for Lemon Bar Trifle and who shared it with all of us because, as he says, "the secret is way too good to keep."

Some secrets really are just too good to keep—begging the question, What is more delicious? Knowing the secret or sharing the secret?

—Deanna Buxton

If you would like to be included in the next Worldwide Ward Cookbook, go to www.worldwidewardcookbook.blogspot.com and submit your recipe!

Adjustments for Altitude

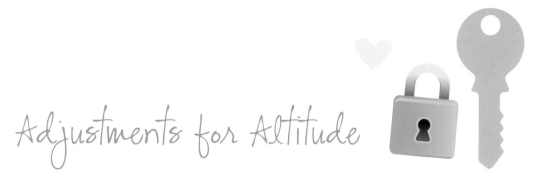

Because the recipes in this cookbook have been submitted by people from throughout the world, it's important to compare the altitude where you live to the altitude where the recipe originated. Keep in mind that many recipes originated in Utah, which has an elevation of 3,500 feet and higher.

If the recipe comes from an area similar in altitude to yours, no changes are necessary.

If you are at a higher altitude than where the recipe originated, keep the following in mind:

- Water boils at a lower temperature at high altitudes, so foods take longer to cook. If you're making stews or braised meats, add 1 hour for every 1,000 feet above sea level. Beans may take twice as long to cook. Pasta needs to cook at a hard boil for a longer period. When making baked goods, increase your oven temperature by 15–25 percent at elevations of 3,500 to 6,500 feet; you may also need to increase baking time.

- Air pressure is lower at higher elevations, so baked foods rise faster. Don't use self-rising flour at high elevations; it will overexpand. Watch yeast breads; don't let them rise to more than double in size.

- Too much leavening in baked goods will cause them to rise too fast and then fall, resulting in dry or tough foods. At higher altitudes, reduce the amount of baking powder or baking soda in a recipe by 25 percent.

- Liquids evaporate more rapidly at higher elevations, so candies and cooked frostings will get harder faster. Decrease cooking time.

- Flour gets drier at higher altitudes and will absorb more of the liquid in a recipe; increase liquid by 2–4 tablespoons for every cup of flour used in the recipe.

- At higher altitudes, use eggs at room temperature. Beat them less; beat egg whites only to soft-peak consistency.

- Fill pans for cakes, cupcakes, muffins, and other baked goods only half full, not two-thirds full.

- Cakes and other baked goods stick more at higher altitudes, so grease pans more heavily and dust the greased pans with flour.

If you're at a significantly lower altitude from where the recipe originated, simply reverse the directions above!

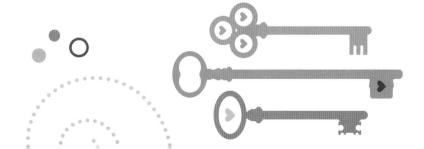

Table of Contents

{ APPETIZERS }

Three may keep a secret, if two of them are dead.

{ Benjamin Franklin }

Thanksgiving Cheese Ball

1 8-oz. pkg. cream cheese
4 oz. sharp cheddar cheese
2 oz. bleu cheese, crumbled
2 Tbsp. onion, grated

1 clove garlic, minced
4 dashes Worcestershire sauce
1 2.25-oz. can green olives
½ C. pecans, chopped

In a food processor, mix the cream cheese, cheddar cheese, bleu cheese, onion, garlic, and Worcestershire sauce. Process until well blended. Add olives and pulse into small chunks. Shape the mixture into a ball; roll in the chopped pecans to coat. Wrap in plastic and chill at least 4 hours in the refrigerator. Serve with crackers. (Cracked Pepper and Olive Oil Triscuits are amazing with this!) Makes 8–10 servings.

Sarah Jane Clayton
Providence 5th Ward
Providence Utah South Stake
Providence, Utah

For as long as I can remember this cheese ball has been on the table for the hour or two before the turkey is done on Thanksgiving Day. My mom got it out of a little no-name cookbook and it is the must-have for Thanksgiving. The secret ingredients in this are the bleu cheese and the Worcestershire, which make this cheese ball unforgettable. About ten years ago, after my mom had made this for more than twenty-five years, my dad asked if we could have something different, because he just doesn't like this one. We were dumbfounded, especially considering the amount of it he had eaten over the years! But instead of having something different, we just made a second one, and the rest of us still got our fix!

O-ee Kimchee

1 o-ee (English cucumber)
1 tsp. kosher salt
¼ C. red onion, chopped
2 tsp. dark sesame oil

2 Tbsp. rice vinegar
2 tsp. honey
¼ tsp. red pepper flakes

Cut the cucumber into thin slices. Sprinkle with salt and mix well. Let sit in a colander in the sink for 30 minutes to drain. Rinse the cucumber slices, wrap in paper towels, and squeeze out any water. Combine cucumber slices with onion, sesame oil, rice vinegar, honey, and red pepper flakes. Cover and refrigerate until ready to serve. Makes 4 servings.

Lee Yong Hee
Yuseong Ward
Daejeon Stake
Daejeon City, South Korea

The secret to good cucumber kimchee is waiting to eat it. The longer you wait, the better it gets.

World's Best Pimiento Cheese

4 Tbsp. mayonnaise

1 3-oz. pkg. cream cheese, softened

3 cloves garlic, minced

Handful of fresh parsley

Several vigorous shots of Tabasco sauce

1 C. pecans

1 small jar diced pimientos, undrained

12 oz. sharp cheddar cheese

In a food processor, combine the mayonnaise, cream cheese, garlic, parsley, and Tabasco sauce. Puree until smooth. Pour into a bowl. Put pecans in the same food processor; process just until coarsely chopped. Add pecans and pimientos with juice to mayonnaise mixture. Grate the cheese. (I do this in the food processor, but by hand works well too.) Add grated cheese to the remaining ingredients. Stir well to combine. Refrigerate at least 1 hour, but it is best if served the next day. Makes 8 servings.

Andreevsky Cakir
Helsinki 3rd Ward
Tampere Finland Stake
Helsinki, Finland

I love pimiento cheese sandwiches or pimiento cheese and crackers. This is my secret recipe, and it is divine.

Dilly Beans

4 pts. young, tender green beans

4 heads dill

4 cloves garlic

1 tsp. red pepper, diced

2 C. cider vinegar

2 C. water

¼ C. salt

Wash and stem green beans. Pack in 4 sterilized pint-size glass jars. Place 1 head dill, 1 clove garlic, and ¼ tsp. red pepper in each jar. In a medium saucepan, boil the vinegar, water, and salt; pour over the beans. Seal jars. Makes 4 pints.

Patti Call
Pleasant Grove Utah 9th Ward
Pleasant Grove Utah Stake
Pleasant Grove, Utah

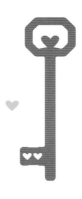

I first remember Mom making dilly beans when my sisters and I were little girls. She sent us outside to play so she could work uninterrupted. We were giddy with excitement that day, and couldn't wait until she was finished. When we came inside from playing, imagine our disappointment when we saw jars of vegetables sitting on the counter—we thought she said she was making JELLY beans. The dilly beans were delicious, though, and have been a favorite ever since. Did Mom know we thought she was making jelly beans? She isn't telling!

BBQ Shrimp Orleans

Barbecue Butter:

1 lb. butter, softened at room temperature

Scant 2 tsp. black pepper

Scant ¼ tsp. cayenne pepper

1½ tsp. paprika

1 tsp. salt

½ tsp. whole dried rosemary leaves (measured, then finely chopped)

2 oz. (¼ C.) garlic, finely chopped

2 tsp. Worcestershire sauce

1 tsp. Tabasco sauce

1½ tsp. water

Shrimp:

1 Tbsp. plus 1 tsp. olive oil

1 lb. (16–20 count) cleaned, peeled, and deveined shrimp

¼ C. green onions, chopped

½ C. white grape juice

Barbecue Butter: In a mixing bowl, combine all ingredients. Whip on high speed 3 minutes or until thoroughly blended. Refrigerate. The following shrimp recipe will use 1 C. of the butter; reserve extra for another use. Makes about 2½ cups.

Shrimp: Pour olive oil in a hot sauté pan. Add shrimp to the sauté pan and cook on one side for 1–2 minutes. (Don't crowd; if necessary, use 2 pans. A 12-inch pan will accommodate 1 pound of shrimp.) Reduce heat to medium, turn shrimp, and add the chopped green onion. Cook for an additional 1–2 minutes. Add white grape juice and cook until grape juice is reduced to ¼ C. Stir in 1 C. cold Barbecue Butter, reduce heat to low, and cook and stir frequently until shrimp are just done (white throughout, moist, and tender), approximately 1½ minutes. Take care not to overcook the shrimp. Serve immediately in a warm bowl. Makes 4 servings.

Kristi Craft
Newport Ward
Providence Rhode Island Stake
Portsmouth, Rhode Island

This shrimp tastes just like Ruth's Chris Steakhouse BBQ shrimp. We love sitting at home eating this incredible shrimp. We usually double it and eat it as a main dish because it's just that yummy!

Turkish Pastry

4 C. flour
½ tsp. baking soda
1 C. plus 2 Tbsp. butter
½ C. sour cream

2 C. walnuts, crushed
¾ C. sugar
1 egg, separated

Preheat oven to 375. Sift flour and baking soda together. Cut in butter and sour cream until dough can be molded into a ball (dough should not be too wet). Separate dough into four balls and roll each into a circle. Cut each circle into five parts (like slicing pie). Mix walnuts, sugar, and egg white. Place a small amount of walnut mixture in the middle of each triangle and roll up. Pinch together any openings and place on a baking sheet. Brush with egg yolk to make the pastries pretty and golden. Bake for 20–25 minutes. Makes 20 pastries.

My friend from Azerbaijan (near Iran) gave me this recipe while we were both living in Washington. We were neighbors in our apartment complex, and she was learning English. It was very difficult for her to translate the recipe for me, so I had her come and show me how to make it. I learned her secrets by watching her.

Mandy Jack
Monticello 3rd Ward
Monticello Utah Stake
Monticello, Utah

Ranch Chicken Cheese Dip

1 pkg. dry ranch dressing mix (not the dip)
1 can chicken

1 C. cheese, shredded
2 8-oz. pkgs. cream cheese, softened

Mix all ingredients; serve with crackers, chips, or veggies. Can also be formed into two balls and rolled in nuts or cheese for a traditional cheese ball. Makes 12 servings.

Heather Hawkins
Syracuse Utah 7th Ward
Syracuse Utah Stake
Syracuse, Utah

This is a recipe I made up after going to parties and gatherings and not ever really liking any of the dips! I take this to every party, potluck, or get-together, and it's always the first to go. It doesn't have a secret ingredient, but it is definitely the secret to a successful party!

Crab Cheese Dip

1 C. buttery round crackers (Ritz), crushed

½ C. Parmesan cheese, grated

¼ C. margarine or butter, melted

2½ tsp. Old Bay seasoning, divided

3 8-oz. pkgs. cream cheese

½ C. sour cream

4 eggs

1¼ C. cheddar cheese, shredded

¼ tsp. lemon juice

½ tsp. Worcestershire sauce

¼ green pepper, minced

1 lb. lump crab meat (pick through and remove any shell pieces)

Preheat oven to 350. Mix crushed crackers, Parmesan cheese, melted margarine, and ½ tsp. Old Bay seasoning. Press mixture into the bottom of a 9-inch springform pan and up the sides about an inch. Beat cream cheese until soft and fluffy. Slowly beat in sour cream. Beat in eggs one at a time. Stir in cheddar cheese, 2 tsp. Old Bay seasoning, lemon juice, Worcestershire sauce, and green pepper. Gently fold in crab meat. Pour mixture into crust. Bake 50–55 minutes or until set. Remove dip from oven and let sit for 15 minutes. Carefully loosen and remove springform pan. Set warm dip on a serving plate with assorted crackers. Makes 12–15 servings.

This is a must-have at parties. I love how it looks like cheesecake! The buttery cracker crust goes so well with the crab and cream cheese. It's divine.

Beatrix Guntherson
Iowa City 2nd Ward
Iowa City Iowa Stake
North Liberty, Iowa

Hearts of Palm Dip

1 14.25-oz. can hearts of palm, drained and chopped

1 C. mozzarella cheese, shredded

½ C. Parmesan cheese, grated

1 C. green onion, chopped

¼ C. sour cream

¾ C. mayonnaise

Preheat the oven to 350. Lightly grease a glass pie plate. In a medium bowl, mix all ingredients; spread into the greased pie plate. Bake uncovered for 20 minutes, or until light brown and bubbly. Serve with crackers or Melba rounds. Makes 10 servings.

Move over artichoke and spinach dip—this stuff ROCKS! When I married my wife I didn't even know what hearts of palm were. That quickly changed when she made this dip one day. Her sister, Liz, is actually the one who introduced it to my wife, so I have to give credit to her. It's so easy any guy could throw it together. My wife is always asked to bring her dip for all ward functions, so I figured I might as well share it with everyone.

JonRyan Reed
Seaford Ward
Wilmington Delaware Stake
Millsboro, Delaware

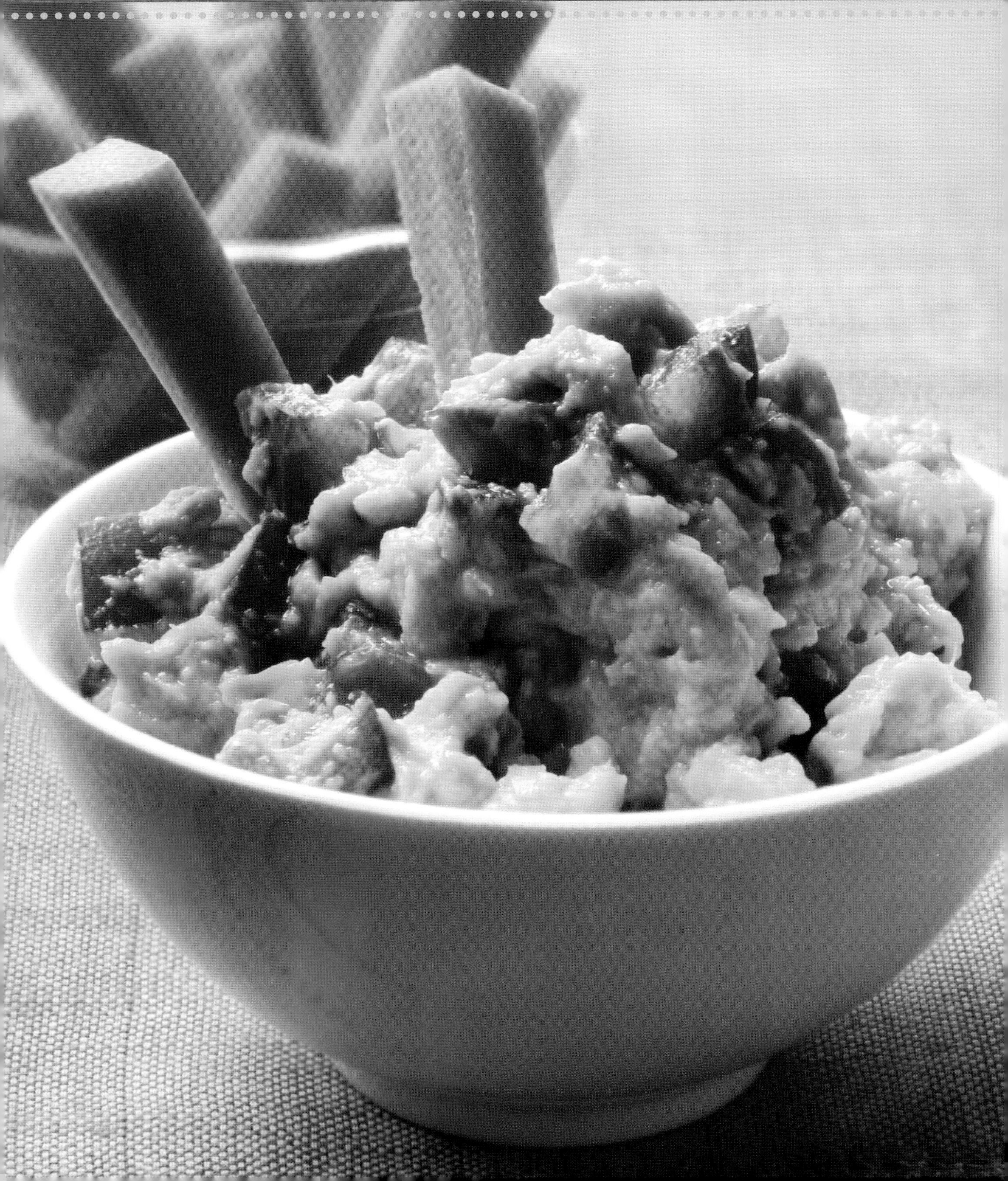

Tucson Guacamole

4 avocados, peeled, pitted, and diced
1½ Tbsp. sour cream
2 3-oz. pkg. cream cheese, softened
2 Tbsp. salsa
1 Roma tomato
¼ C. red onion, chopped (optional)
2–3 Tbsp. cilantro, chopped (or more)

Splash of lime juice
1 pinch salt
1 dash ground black pepper
1 dash garlic salt
1 dash onion powder

In a blender, mix the avocados, sour cream, cream cheese, salsa, tomato, onion, cilantro, and lime juice. Blend to desired consistency. In a small bowl, mix the salt, pepper, garlic salt, and onion powder. Stir into the avocado mixture. Cover and chill in the refrigerator half an hour before serving. Makes 6 servings.

Amanda De Boise
Santa Fe Ward
Santa Fe New Mexico Stake
Santa Fe, New Mexico

This is my favorite way to make guacamole. It is perfect for those who don't like the traditional guacamole. It is so creamy and yummy. I call it "Tucson Guacamole" because I discovered the recipe at a small cafe in Tucson while on vacation. I love that I can have my favorite guacamole whenever I want and I don't have to travel to Tucson to get it!

Maryann's Sinful Fruit Dip

1 tub Philadelphia Cheesecake Filling
2–3 C. light brown sugar

1 12-oz. pkg. toffee chips or 3 Heath bars, crushed

In a large bowl, mix cheesecake filling and brown sugar until smooth. Fold in toffee chips. Serve with fruit, pretzel sticks, or graham cracker sticks. Makes 15 servings.

Maryann Hanberg
Marsh Creek Ward
Antioch California Stake
Brentwood, California

This dip is so good. The secret is that it looks like onion dip, and some people pass it up at first. Once they taste it, the bowl empties quickly—there is never any left over! The original recipe called for plain cream cheese. I was in the grocery store to buy the ingredients and passed by the cheesecake filling and thought I'd try it instead of plain cream cheese. Now I can't make it any other way! The secret ingredient is the toffee chips.

Southwest Egg Rolls and Cool Avocado Dip

2½ C. chicken, cooked and shredded

1½ C. Mexican cheese blend, shredded

⅔ C. frozen corn, thawed

⅔ C. canned black beans, rinsed and drained

5 green onions, chopped

¼ C. fresh cilantro, minced

1 tsp. salt

1 tsp. ground cumin

1 tsp. lime peel, grated

¼ tsp. cayenne pepper

20 egg roll wrappers

Oil for deep-fat frying

1 C. ranch salad dressing

1 medium ripe avocado, peeled and mashed

1 Tbsp. fresh cilantro, minced

1 tsp. lime peel, grated

In a large bowl, combine the first 10 ingredients. Place ¼ C. chicken mixture in the center of one egg roll wrapper. (Keep remaining wrappers covered with a damp paper towel until ready to use.) Fold bottom corner over filling. Fold sides toward center over filling. Moisten remaining corner with water; roll up tightly to seal. Repeat. In an electric skillet or deep-fat fryer, heat oil to 375 degrees. Fry egg rolls, a few at a time, for 2 minutes on each side or until golden brown. Drain on paper towels. Meanwhile, combine dressing, avocado, 1 Tbsp. minced cilantro, and 1 tsp. grated lime peel. Serve with egg rolls. Makes 20 egg rolls.

Johana Keough
Harper's Ferry Ward
Winchester Virginia Stake
Charlestown, West Virginia

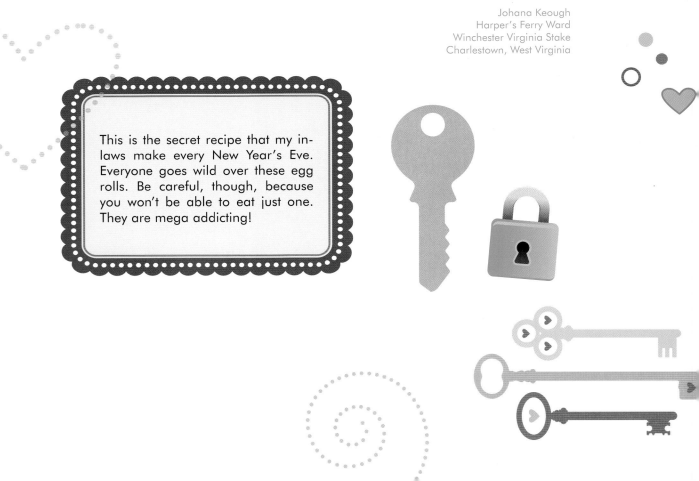

This is the secret recipe that my in-laws make every New Year's Eve. Everyone goes wild over these egg rolls. Be careful, though, because you won't be able to eat just one. They are mega addicting!

Million-Dollar Spinach Dip

1 C. mayonnaise

1 16-oz. container sour cream

2 pkgs. vegetable soup mix (Lipton)

1 4-oz. can water chestnuts, drained and
chopped

1 10-oz. pkg. frozen chopped spinach,
thawed and squeezed dry

1-lb. round loaf sourdough bread

In a medium bowl, mix mayonnaise, sour cream, dry soup mix, water chestnuts, and chopped spinach. Chill in the refrigerator at least 6 hours, preferably overnight. Remove top and interior of sourdough bread. Fill hollowed loaf with mayonnaise mixture. Tear removed bread chunks into pieces for dipping or serve with tortilla chips. Makes 10 servings.

Rayetta Mickle
Little Valley 7th Ward
St. George Utah Little Valley Stake
St. George, Utah

This is the BEST dip! It's so simple that anyone can throw this together. The secret is how simple and quick this really is. It tastes like a million bucks!

Avocado Mango Salsa

1 mango, peeled, pitted, and diced

1 avocado, peeled, pitted, and diced

4 medium tomatoes, diced

1 jalapeño pepper, seeded, and minced

½ C. fresh cilantro, chopped

3 cloves garlic, minced

1 tsp. salt

2 Tbsp. fresh lime juice

¼ C. red onion, chopped

3 Tbsp. olive oil

In a medium bowl, combine mango, avocado, tomatoes, jalapeño, cilantro, and garlic. Stir in salt, lime juice, red onion, and olive oil. Refrigerate for about 30 minutes before serving to allow the flavors to blend. Makes 6 servings.

Melissa Stehling
Miami 4th Ward
Miami Florida South Stake
Miami, Florida

This is my secret salsa recipe that until now has never been given out. I get asked at church all the time to bring my "salsa stuff." It's very addicting!

Melodee's Chili Con Queso

¼ C. butter or margarine

½ C. onion, chopped

1 16-oz. can tomatoes, undrained

2 4-oz. cans green chiles, drained, chopped

Salt to taste

1 lb. Monterey Jack cheese, cubed

½ C. heavy cream

In a medium skillet, heat butter; sauté onion in butter until tender. Add tomatoes, chiles, and salt. Mash tomatoes with a fork. Simmer, stirring occasionally, for 15 minutes. Add cheese cubes, stirring until cheese is melted. Stir in cream. Cook for 2 minutes, stirring constantly. Remove from heat and let stand for 15 minutes. Serve with veggies or corn tortilla chips. Makes 10 servings.

Melodee Finch
Lake Norman Ward
Gastonia North Carolina Stake
Mooresville, North Carolina

Manhattan Meatballs

2 lbs. ground beef

2 C. soft bread crumbs

2 eggs

½ C. onion, chopped

2 Tbsp. parsley, chopped

2 tsp. salt

2 Tbsp. butter

1 8–10-oz. jar pure apricot preserves

½ C. barbecue sauce

Preheat oven to 350. In a large bowl, combine meat, bread crumbs, eggs, onion, parsley, and salt. Mix lightly and shape into medium-size meatballs. Brown meatballs in butter. Place in a shallow dish. Combine preserves and barbecue sauce; pour over meatballs and bake for 30 minutes. Makes 12 servings.

Kestin Gruhn
Carthage Ward
Joplin Missouri Stake
Carthage, Missouri

These are very good. The secret is how easy they are to make! Most people assume that making your own meatballs is time-consuming, but these are a lot easier than you might think. I have been asked for this recipe more times than I can count. It's a crowd favorite!

Queso Especial

1 small can evaporated milk

1 10.75-oz. can cream of chicken soup

1 env. (2 Tbsp.) ranch dressing mix

1 4-oz. can diced green chiles

1 large jar pimientos

1-lb. loaf processed American cheese (Velveeta)

In a large saucepan, stir milk, soup, dressing mix, chiles, and pimientos together over low heat. Cut cheese in cubes and stir in. Heat until cheese is melted and all ingredients are blended well.

This is top secret in the Pena family. After my son was baptized, we had a big luncheon with the ward. Everyone brought so much delicious food, but this dip was the best. It was so good! One of the missionaries in the ward, Elder Raspersonm, made it and gave me the recipe. My whole family oohs and ahhs over this and it has become a tradition, especially around holidays and, of course, during football season. I can't thank that missionary enough for this awesome queso. I think of him every time I make this.

Chandra Pena
Valencia Ward
Los Lunas New Mexico Stake
Belen, New Mexico

Rozlynn's International Bean Dip

1 15-oz. can refried beans

4 oz. cream cheese

12 oz. sour cream

1 bunch green onions, very finely chopped

¾ C. salsa

1 env. taco seasoning

½ 4-oz. can diced green chiles

Dash oregano

Salt and pepper to taste

1 C. Monterey Jack or cheddar cheese, grated

In an ovenproof dish, combine all ingredients except grated cheese. Sprinkle top with grated cheese. Bake at 300 for 1 hour. Makes 15 servings.

Rozlynn Peterson
Cedar Rapids 3rd Ward
Cedar Rapids Iowa Stake
Cedar Rapids, Iowa

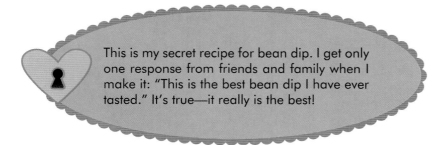

This is my secret recipe for bean dip. I get only one response from friends and family when I make it: "This is the best bean dip I have ever tasted." It's true—it really is the best!

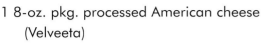

Slow-Cooker Seafood Dip

1 8-oz. pkg. processed American cheese (Velveeta)

2 Tbsp. reduced-fat cream cheese

1½ C. sour cream

½ C. small shrimp, cooked

½ C. crab meat, cooked and flaked

½ C. lobster meat, cooked and flaked

2 tsp. seafood seasoning (Old Bay)

1 tsp. Worcestershire sauce

1 loaf French bread, sliced and lightly toasted

In a slow-cooker, combine processed cheese food, cream cheese, sour cream, shrimp, crab, and lobster. Cover and cook on low heat until cheese is melted, about 1 hour, stirring occasionally to break up lumps. Once the cheese is melted, stir in seafood seasoning and Worcestershire sauce. Serve with toasted French bread or in a hollowed-out bread bowl. Makes 10 servings.

Elizabeth Mortonsen
Charleston 1st Ward
Charleston South Carolina Stake
Folly Beach, South Carolina

When we lived in Seattle we learned how to make a lot of really great seafood dishes; this recipe was given to us by a member of the ward about twenty-five years ago, when I was a baby. We love it and make it for any parties or gatherings we have. It is delicious. Some people in my family like only crab, so sometimes we add more crab and leave out the shrimp and lobster. We sometimes also hollow out round loaves of bread and pour the dip into them. We cube the pieces from the hollowed-out bread and use it to dip.

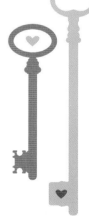

Raleigh House Dressing

1 qt. mayonnaise

½ C. plus 2 Tbsp. ketchup

⅛ tsp. garlic powder

⅓ tsp. dry mustard

¾ C. evaporated milk

Mix all ingredients well by hand with a whisk or a mixer. Pour dressing back into the jar the mayo came out of; you'll also need a smaller jar for the remainder. It keeps for months in the refrigerator. Makes 5¼ cups.

Natalia Stegall
Harvest Hills Ward
Rexburg Idaho East Stake
Rexburg, Idaho

This is the secret, highly guarded house dressing recipe from where I once waited tables. The restaurant was known for its Raleigh House Dressing. This dressing is great with fish, hamburgers, hot dogs, shrimp, fries, and lots of other things. It's not salad dressing—it's more of a sauce, and is wonderful stuff. I promise if you make this one time, it won't be your last.

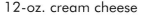

Dream Fruit Dip

12-oz. cream cheese

1 C. powdered sugar, unsifted

1 C. sour cream

1 7-oz. jar marshmallow cream

2 tsp. vanilla extract

2 tsp. almond extract

2 tsp. cinnamon

In a small bowl, stir the cream cheese until soft and smooth. Add powdered sugar and beat until well blended. Add the rest of the ingredients, and blend just until well combined. Cover and refrigerate several hours before serving. Serve with a variety of fresh fruit (bananas, strawberries, cherries, grapes, pineapple, honeydew, apples). Makes 12 servings.

I love when my wife gets invited to a baby or wedding shower because she always makes this—but she doubles it and leaves half at home for us to munch on. I love this stuff!

Daniel Kimber
West Maple Ward
Omaha Nebraska Stake
Omaha, Nebraska

Crafting Angels' Taco Salad Dip

1 16-oz. can refried beans

2 8-oz. containers avocado dip

1 16-oz. container sour cream

1 env. (2 Tbsp.) taco seasoning mix

2 medium to large tomatoes, diced

1 can sliced black olives, drained

About 1 C. lettuce, shredded

1 16-oz. pkg. cheddar cheese, shredded

Spread refried beans on bottom of a 9 x 13-inch dish. Top with avocado dip. Combine sour cream and taco seasoning mix. Spread over avocado dip. Top with tomatoes, olives, lettuce, and cheese. Use tortilla chips to scoop up the dip and enjoy! Makes 12 servings.

I used to make this for our "Crafting Angels" (humanitarian group) potluck lunch. It was always a hit, especially with the full-time seminary teachers who joined us each month! Every month our group assembled newborn kits for UMC hospital in Las Vegas, made loom knit hats, and so much more!

Bev Qualheim
Logandale 4th Ward
Logandale Nevada Stake
Logandale, Nevada

{ BEVERAGES }

Secrets are made to be found out with time.

{ Charles Sanford }

Mormon Mojitos

3 C. water, divided

1½ C. sugar

2 C. fresh mint leaves, chopped (about 2 pkgs.)

2 C. lime sherbet

1 C. lime juice

8 C. club soda

Lime slices for garnish

In a microwave-safe bowl, combine 2 C. water and sugar; microwave on high for 5 minutes. Stir in mint leaves; let stand for 5 minutes. In a large pitcher, combine sherbet, remaining water, and lime juice; mix well. Pour mint water mixture through a strainer into the pitcher so all mint leaves are strained out. Mix well. Add club soda and mix until well blended. Serve over ice cubes. Enjoy! Makes 10 servings.

Tim Channing
South Royalton Ward
Montpelier Vermont Stake
Woodstock, Vermont

I enjoyed this drink at a birthday party, and asked for the recipe because I'd never seen an alcohol-free version of Mojitos. My kids love it, and I try to make it for most holidays. The mint leaves are the secret ingredient that makes this really refreshing without being too sweet.

Lemon Sherbet Punch

4 C. lemon sherbet

1 C. frozen lemonade concentrate, thawed

3 C. warm water

Ice cubes

Lemon slices

Place sherbet in punch bowl. Using mixer on low, add lemonade concentrate and water. Mix well for 5 minutes. Refrigerate. Serve in tall glasses with ice; garnish with lemon slices. Makes 8 servings.

Charles Wells
Terenure Ward
Dublin Ireland Stake
Dublin, Ireland

We usually don't allow our children to drink many sweet drinks, but occasionally I like to whip up a batch of this tart and tangy punch. It beats anything you will find at the markets here in Ireland, and it has become my claim to fame in the Terenure Ward.

Peppermint Punch

1 gal. peppermint ice cream, in scoops
2 qt. eggnog
2 qt. ginger ale

2 C. heavy cream, whipped
1 C. peppermint candies, crushed

Put first three ingredients in punch bowl. Top with cream, then sprinkle with candy. Makes 18 servings.

Natalia Stegal
Harvest Hills Ward
Rexburg Idaho East Stake
Rexburg, Idaho

Kids love this punch! It still reminds me of home and the holidays. Unfortunately, peppermint ice cream and eggnog are available only during the fall and winter seasons, so I can't enjoy this punch as much as I would like to. My family has made this for so many holiday ward and block parties that friends have come to expect it. The one year my mom didn't make it, she never heard the end of it from the ward members. This is holiday punch at its finest!

The Perfect Pink Punch

1 10-oz. pkg. frozen strawberries with syrup
½ gal. pineapple sherbet

1 2-liter bottle cherry 7-Up, icy cold

Partially thaw berries until slushy. Put in punch bowl and add sherbet in chunks. Stir in cherry 7-Up. Serve immediately. Makes 18 servings.

Anastasia Upton
Falls Lake Ward
Raleigh North Carolina Stake
Raleigh, North Carolina

Frosty Lime Punch

2 liters pineapple juice

2 env. unsweetened lime drink powder (Kool-Aid)

1 liter lime sherbet

2 liters ginger ale or lemon-lime soda

In a large punch bowl, combine pineapple juice and drink powder. Stir. Add sherbet in scoops. Slowly add ginger ale or lemon-lime soda. Let stand 15 minutes, until sherbet froths. Makes 20 servings.

My nephew's favorite color is green, and since we were throwing a Shrek party for his fifth birthday, it was only fitting to find a green punch that tasted great. Our neighbor uses this punch for Christmas and St. Patrick's Day, and it was PERFECT! Since then, we've made it for Christmas and Easter; it's simply the best punch ever. There's never a drop left.

Chelsea Harden
San Antonio 8th Ward
San Antonio Texas North Stake
San Antonio, Texas

Haitian Banane Grage

4 green bananas

4 C. water

1 tsp. nutmeg

2 tsp. vanilla

1 12-oz. can evaporated milk

2 C. sugar

Choose very green bananas and wash them well. Dice the bananas, with the peel on, into very small pieces. Puree in a blender (don't worry—it's supposed to be gray). In a large saucepan, combine banana puree and remaining ingredients. Cook over medium heat until the bananas turn a pretty pink. (Yes, they will turn pink!) Serve warm. I love to add a little more milk to thin it so I can drink it, but I also like to eat it from a bowl with a spoon, much as I would hot cereal. Makes 4 servings.

Variola Sanon
Deschapelles Branch
Port-au-Prince Haiti Stake
Delmas, Haiti

FOR YOUR EYES ONLY

The Harden Family Cinnamon Punch

3 C. cranberry juice
2½ C. orange juice
1 C. lemon juice
42 oz. lemon-lime soda (7-Up)

2 C. water
1½ C. sugar
4 cinnamon sticks
Ice cubes

Chill fruit juices and soda. In a medium saucepan, combine water, sugar, and cinnamon sticks; simmer for 10 minutes. Set aside for several hours to allow the mixture to develop a deep cinnamon flavor. When ready to serve, remove the cinnamon sticks from the sugar syrup. In a large punch bowl, combine the sugar syrup, cranberry juice, orange juice, and lemon juice. Slowly pour in the soda. Add ice cubes and garnish with lime slices, if desired. Makes 20 servings.

This is the most delicious punch! My sisters and I used to look forward to holiday gatherings where my mom used to serve this punch—and we could never get enough! The cinnamon syrup provides the unique flavor, and it's the part of the punch that requires advance preparation. Mom often made the syrup days in advance and stored it in the refrigerator.

Chelsea Harden
San Antonio 8th Ward
San Antonio Texas North Stake
San Antonio, Texas

Josie Punch

1 qt. pineapple juice
1 qt. cranberry juice
1¼ C. sugar

Ice
2 qt. ginger ale

Mix the pineapple juice, cranberry juice, and sugar; stir until sugar dissolves. Right before serving the punch, add ice; slowly add ginger ale so the punch will be fizzy when served. Makes 16 servings.

Emerson Jeter
Kihei 1st Ward
Kahului Hawaii Stake
Kihei, Hawaii

My old roommate Josie made this scrumptious punch ALL the time. She sold Tupperware products, so she threw promotional parties almost every week; she always included this punch because it was a favorite in her family—and it was easy. I have served this punch ever since for any event that required a beverage. I usually don't like the bitter taste of cranberries, but this punch is so refreshing, and there's no bitter taste at all. I recommend making twice the amount you think you'll need, because it goes fast!

Tropical Party Punch

6 C. water

3–4 C. sugar

1 46-oz. can pineapple juice

1 12-oz. can frozen orange juice concentrate

1 6-oz. can frozen lemonade concentrate

½ tsp. almond extract or vanilla extract

1 2-liter bottle lemon-lime soda

In a large saucepan, bring the water and sugar to a light boil. Cook and stir for 2 minutes, then pour into a large container. Add pineapple juice, orange and lemonade concentrates, and almond or vanilla extract. Cover and freeze for at least 24 hours. Remove from freezer 1–2 hours before serving. The drink should be slushy, so don't let the mixture thaw completely. Just before serving, mash the mixture with a potato masher and stir in lemon-lime soda. Makes 12 servings.

Josiah Brenner
Forest Lake Ward
Centenary Australia Stake
Brisbane, Australia

This punch has been served at every birthday I've celebrated with my kids; it brings back wonderful memories of all the birthdays we have celebrated throughout the years. My wife gets asked for this recipe constantly, so I knew it was one I wanted to share. You can also freeze the mixture in a couple of freezer bags.

Mom's Hot Chocolate Mix

1 20-qt. box powdered milk

2 56-oz. containers instant chocolate mix for milk

1 32.5-oz. container instant chocolate mix for milk

1 2-lb. bag powdered sugar

2 44-oz. containers instant creamer powder

Put one large garbage bag inside a second; turn them inside out because some are perfumed on the inside. Pour all ingredients into the inside bag; twist toward the end of the bags to hold them shut (twist the inside and outside bags separately, but hold both in your hands). Toss around and around on a table or the counter until you think the ingredients are mixed. Store the mix in a 5-gallon food-grade bucket. Tip the bag upside-down into the bucket. Carefully pull the bag off, or the powder will go everywhere. To serve: Mix a heaping ⅓ C. chocolate mix with 1 C. hot water. Serve with whipped cream or marshmallows. Makes 100 servings.

Amanda Silverhorn
Snowflake 2nd Ward
Snowflake Arizona Stake
Snowflake, Arizona

My mother-in-law makes this hot chocolate mix every year and gives some to all of her children. The secret to making a lot of the mix at the same time is using garbage bags to mix it in. I found 5-gallon food-grade buckets at Walmart. This is a great mix to make up and then put into festive containers and give as a homemade gift!

Sparkle Punch

3 large oranges, thinly sliced
2 lemons, thinly sliced
1 6-oz. can frozen lemonade concentrate, thawed

1 liter seltzer water
2 750-ml. bottles sparkling apple cider
1 Tbsp. sugar
2 trays ice cubes

Place the orange and lemon slices in a large punch bowl; pour in the lemonade concentrate. Gently stir in the seltzer water and the sparkling apple cider. Stir in sugar to taste; add ice cubes. Makes 15 servings.

My best friend sells Pampered Chef, so she has a lot of parties. We were in a hurry before one of her parties and invented this punch by throwing together everything we had on hand. It quickly became a favorite of everyone. I also served it at my wedding reception, and even though we tripled the amount based on expected guests, there was still not enough. People were going back for four or five refills! The secret is adding the frozen lemonade to the sparkling cider. I never would have thought to mix the two, but they are delicious together.

Kori Simmons
Barton Creek Ward
Austin Texas Oak Hills Stake
Austin, Texas

Lion's Froth

4 C. sugar
6 C. water
1 6-oz. can frozen orange juice, mixed with 2 cans water

½ C. fresh lemon juice
2 46-oz. cans pineapple juice
6 ripe bananas, mashed
6 1-qt. bottles ginger ale

In a large pan, combine sugar and water; bring to a boil. Cool. In a large bowl, combine all the juices and the mashed bananas. Stir the mixture into the cooled sugar water. Freeze in quart containers or in gallon freezer bags. When ready to serve, defrost slightly and break up frozen mixture with a fork. Add 1 bottle ginger ale to each quart of frozen mixture; punch will be slushy. Makes 50 servings.

When I was in a student ward, I had a roommate whose mom was a super chef (and super at everything else, actually!). She sent us lots of party recipes from her time as Young Women camp director, and this punch was one of them. It's so addictive that I keep a stash in the freezer most of the time. Then all I have to do is buy a bottle of ginger ale, and I can make this punch on the spot. It's so quick and easy once you've prepared the concentrate.

Natalia Stegall
Harvest Hills Ward
Rexburg Idaho East Stake
Rexburg, Idaho

Coconut Tropics

½ gal. vanilla ice cream, softened
1 20-oz. can crushed pineapple (blend in a blender for fewer chunks)
1 8-oz. can cream of coconut

1 46-oz. can pineapple juice
2 C. coconut milk
1 2-liter bottle lemon-lime soda

In a large plastic container, combine ice cream, crushed pineapple, cream of coconut, pineapple juice, and coconut milk. Mix well; slowly stir in the lemon-lime soda. Freeze for about 2 hours or until slushy. Makes 15 servings.

Karsyn Prevara
Boynton Beach Ward
Pompano Beach Florida Stake
Boynton Beach, Florida

I live and breathe anything coconut or tropical—and this is my most-requested punch. It reminds me of walking along the Florida coast or enjoying get-togethers with friends and family on our boat . . . bringing to mind the salty ocean smell carried on every breeze and the sound of the seagulls soaring overhead. Pure paradise!

Spiced Cider Punch

3 C. water
1 C. sugar
½ tsp. nutmeg
2 C. grape juice

3 C. cider
4 C. ginger ale
3 lemons, thinly sliced

Boil water, sugar, and nutmeg for 5 minutes. Cool. Add remaining ingredients. Chill before serving. Makes 16 servings.

Tracy Nordell
Bozeman 3rd Ward
Bozeman Montana Stake
Bozeman, Montana

I grew up near Lancaster, Pennsylvania, and love the Amish recipes I have gradually collected over the years. When I went back to visit my parents a few years ago, I ran across a huge goldmine of recipes at an estate sale. This is one of the recipes from that bunch. It's a wonderful drink, especially as the fall weather begins.

{ BREAKFASTS }

What is told into the ear of a man is often heard a hundred miles away.

{ Chinese Proverb }

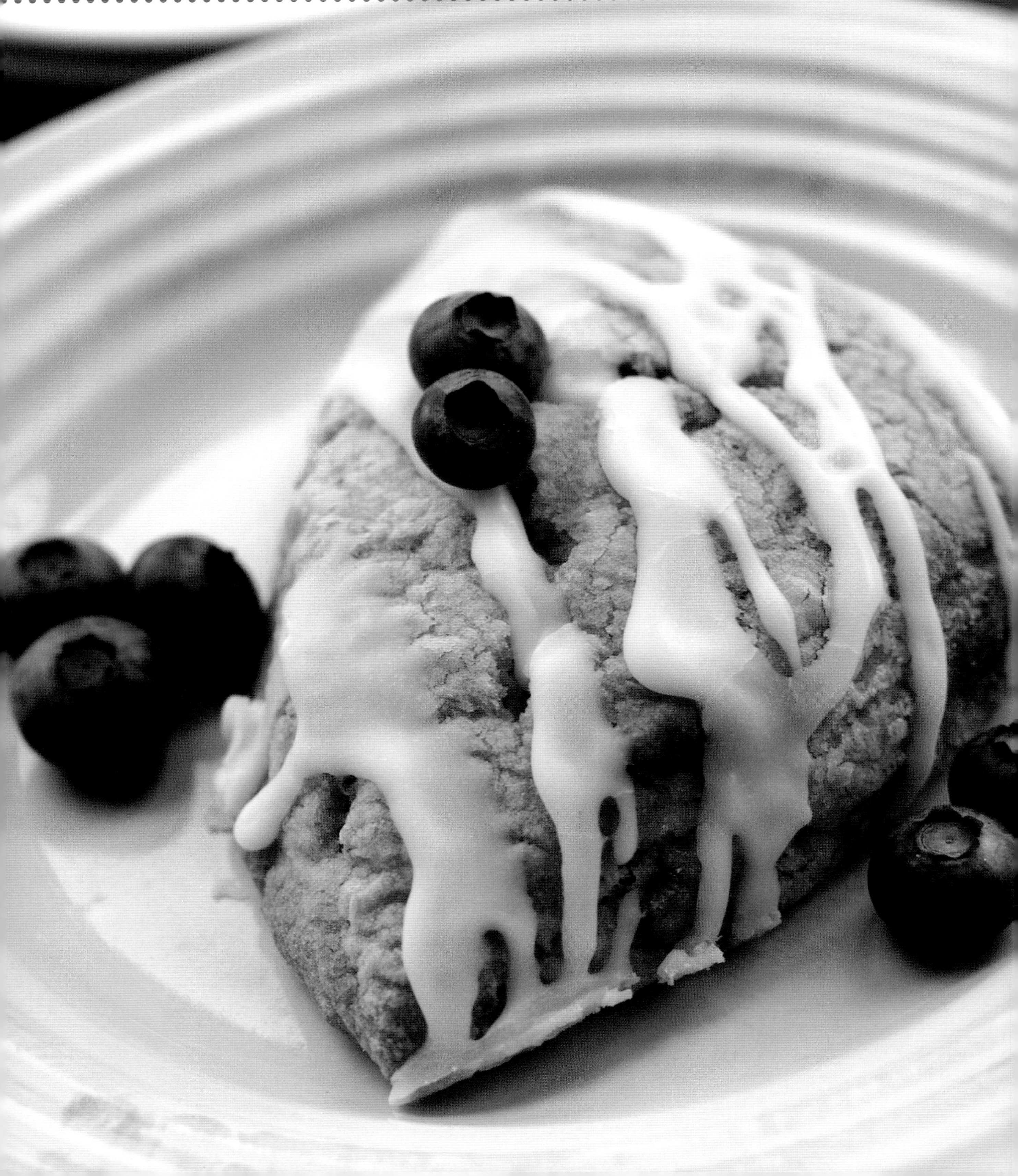

Giant Blueberry Sour Cream Scones

Scones:

1 C. sour cream

1 large egg, slightly beaten

½ tsp. vanilla

½ tsp. almond or vanilla extract (total of 1 tsp. vanilla extract)

1 tsp. baking soda

4 C. flour

1 C. sugar

2½ tsp. baking powder

¼ tsp. cream of tartar

1 tsp. salt

½–1 tsp. cinnamon (optional)

1 C. very cold butter (cut into small cubes)

1 C. fresh blueberries

Vanilla glaze (optional)

Vanilla Glaze:

2 C. powdered sugar, sifted

¼ C. heavy cream

1½ tsp. vanilla or almond extract

Scones: Preheat oven to 350. Lightly grease or line a baking sheet with parchment paper. In a small bowl, blend sour cream with egg, vanilla extract, almond extract, and baking soda; set aside. In a large bowl, mix the flour (measure 4 C. exactly), sugar, baking powder, cream of tartar, salt, and cinnamon (if desired). Using a pastry blender, cut in cold butter cubes. Add the sour cream mixture; mix just until moistened. Gently fold in the fresh blueberries. Roll or pat the dough into a 1- to 1½ -inch-thick round. Cut dough into 12 even wedges. Place the wedges onto the prepared baking sheet about 2 inches apart. Bake for 12–15 minutes, or until the bottoms are browned. Drizzle the top of each warm scone with Vanilla Glaze, if desired, or dust the cooled scones lightly with powdered sugar.

Vanilla Glaze: Whisk all ingredients in a bowl, adding additional cream until desired texture is achieved (do not make it too thin, or it won't stick on the scones). Makes enough to glaze 12 scones.

Daria Abraham
Palmerston North Ward
Palmerston New Zealand North Stake
Palmerston, New Zealand

This recipe was my grandma's best-kept secret; she wouldn't even give her recipes to her own children, but decided to share them just before she died. This scone recipe is one of her most popular. We miss her so much, and I'm glad she finally decided to leave us with her cherished recipes to remember her by.

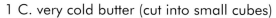

Tropical Coffee Cake

Cake:

1 C. sugar

½ C. vegetable oil

2 eggs

1 C. sour cream

1½ C. flour

2 tsp. baking powder

½ tsp. salt

1 8-oz. can crushed pineapple, drained

Topping:

½ C. flaked coconut

3 Tbsp. sugar

½ tsp. ground cinnamon

In a mixing bowl, blend the sugar and oil. Add eggs, one at a time, beating well after each addition. Beat in sour cream. In a separate bowl, combine the flour, baking powder, and salt; add to the sour cream mixture. Stir in pineapple. Transfer to a greased 9-inch square baking dish. In a small bowl, combine coconut, sugar, and cinnamon; sprinkle over batter. Bake at 350 for 35–40 minutes or until a toothpick inserted near the center comes out clean. Cool on a wire rack. Makes 8 servings.

I got this recipe while on a cruise years ago. I loved the coffee cake so much and mentioned to the waitress that I would love the recipe. I saw her later that evening, and she had written the recipe out for me. What a doll! I have made this delicious coffee cake many times since.

Daria Abraham
Palmerston North Ward
Palmerston New Zealand North Stake
Palmerston, New Zealand

Baked Eggs with Three Cheeses

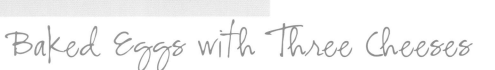

7 eggs, beaten

1 C. milk

2 tsp. sugar

1 lb. small-curd cottage cheese

4 oz. cream cheese, cubed

1 lb. Monterey Jack cheese, shredded

⅔ C. butter or margarine, melted

½ C. flour

1 tsp. baking powder

Beat together eggs, milk, and sugar. Add cheeses and melted butter; mix well. Mix in flour and baking powder, then pour into a 3-quart baking dish sprayed with nonstick coating. Bake at 350 for 45–50 minutes or until knife inserted in the center comes out clean. Cut into rectangles and serve. Makes 6 servings.

Whoever thought you could bake your eggs in the oven! These are our "secret eggs," and everyone who visits loves to eat them. They are so easy, and can be made ahead of time; just store, covered, in the refrigerator. If you pop them into the oven straight from the fridge, increase the cooking time to 60 minutes. We have been making these for years. They're awesome!

Audrey Bullock
Ken Caryl Ward
Columbine Colorado Stake
Littleton, Colorado

Mayfield Ward Breakfast Casserole

1 lb. sliced bacon or 1 lb. breakfast sausage

1 medium sweet onion, chopped

6 eggs, lightly beaten

4 C. frozen shredded hash brown potatoes, thawed

2 C. cheddar cheese, shredded

1½ C. small-curd cottage cheese

1¼ C. Swiss cheese, shredded

In a large skillet, cook bacon and onion until bacon is crisp; drain and crumble bacon. In a bowl, combine the remaining ingredients; stir in bacon mixture. Transfer to a greased 9 x 13-inch baking dish. Bake uncovered at 350 for 35–40 minutes or until set and bubbly. Let stand for 10 minutes before cutting. Makes 8 servings.

Once a month the Relief Society posts a recipe in the bulletin, and that's where I got this recipe. (My mom has a whole recipe book stuffed full of ward recipes from years of saving all those bulletins!) I live for those recipes—they are always sooo good. My sisters and I have marked this recipe as a favorite and have been making it for years. The secret ingredient is the Swiss cheese—or maybe it's the cottage cheese. This dish is so easy, makes a great Sunday morning breakfast, and goes great with flour tortillas and salsa.

Kara Carpenter
Mayfield Ward
Kirtland Ohio Stake
Shaker Heights, Ohio

Baked Oatmeal

½ C. oil

1 C. sugar

2 eggs

2 tsp. baking powder

1 C. milk

3 C. oatmeal (old-fashioned, not quick-cooking)

1 tsp. salt

In a large bowl, mix oil, sugar, and eggs. Add remaining ingredients. Pour into a greased 9 x 13 pan and bake at 350 for 30 minutes. Serve hot with milk. VARIATION: Instead of oil and white sugar, use ½ C. melted margarine or butter and ¾ C. packed brown sugar. Add ½ C. raisins or cinnamon apples, if desired. Makes 6 servings.

May Fitzgerald
Taos Ward
Santa Fe New Mexico Stake
Angel Fire, New Mexico

This is the only way we make oatmeal at our house. We have eight kids, so this is a time-saver and tastes much better than making oatmeal on the stove or in the microwave. The secret is definitely baking the oatmeal.

Yankee Cinnamon Buns

1¼ C. milk

1 pkg. dry yeast

¼ C. warm water

5 C. flour, sifted, divided

1½ tsp. salt

1 Tbsp. sugar

½ C. butter, softened

¾ C. sugar

2 eggs

¼ C. butter, melted

½ C. packed brown sugar

2 tsp. cinnamon

½ C. nuts, chopped

1 C. dark corn syrup, divided

½ C. raisins

2 Tbsp. citron, finely chopped

In a small saucepan, scald milk; cool to lukewarm. In a medium bowl, dissolve yeast in ¼ C. warm water; add cooled scalded milk. Make a sponge mixture by adding 2 C. flour, salt, and 1 Tbsp. sugar to liquid. Beat until smooth. Set aside in a warm place and cover with a damp cloth. In a mixing bowl, beat ½ C. butter until fluffy; beat in ¼ C. sugar. Add eggs one at a time, beating mixture thoroughly. When sponge mixture is bubbly, beat in the butter-sugar mixture. Knead in the remaining 3 C. flour. Place soft dough ball in bowl and cover with damp cloth. Let rise in a warm place until doubled in size. Roll dough out into ¼-inch thickness, in the shape of a rectangle. Spread with melted butter, and sprinkle with mixture of brown sugar and cinnamon. Drizzle ½ C. corn syrup over dough. Sprinkle with nuts, raisins, and citron. Roll dough in jelly-roll fashion and cut in slices about 1½ inches thick. Pour remaining corn syrup into buttered pan. Place rolls cut side down in prepared pan. Cover and let rise until they have doubled in size. Bake at 350 for about 45 minutes. Makes 24 servings.

I love cinnamon rolls and have tried many different recipes and versions. These buns are one of my tried-and-true recipes. These are Yankee buns, unlike traditional cinnamon rolls that include frosting or icing. But there is no need for frosting with these—the corn syrup makes a perfect glaze that is plenty sweet. Everyone who tries these oohs and ahhs over them.

Nathaly Manchaca
Yonkers Ward
Westchester New York Stake
Yonkers, New York

 # Ma's Waffles

2 C. flour

2 Tbsp. baking powder

1 tsp. salt

1 Tbsp. sugar

2 eggs

1½ C. milk

¼ C. butter, melted

Combine dry ingredients. In a separate bowl, beat eggs; add milk and butter, mixing well. Pour onto dry ingredients. Beat until smooth. Cook in a hot waffle iron. Makes 8 servings.

These yummy waffles are from my childhood. I still make these, and they are always a hit. Who doesn't love nice hot waffles for breakfast?

Tracy Nordell
Bozeman 3rd Ward
Bozeman Montana Stake
Bozeman, Montana

Grandma Webb's Famous Raised Waffles

2 tsp. yeast
½ C. warm water
2 C. whole milk
½ C. butter
1 tsp. salt

1 Tbsp. sugar
2 C. flour
¼ tsp. baking powder
2 eggs

In bowl, dissolve yeast in warm water. Set aside. In large microwave-proof bowl, scald milk by heating to 100 degrees in the microwave. Add butter, salt, sugar, flour, and baking powder. Stir in yeast and water mixture. Whisk in eggs. This batter will be really thin. Cover bowl and refrigerate at least 8 hours or as long as 2 days. Batter will rise and will need to be stirred down occasionally. Cook in a waffle iron. These waffles are delicious, light, and crisp with a very buttery flavor. The batch can be easily doubled. Serve with syrup or jam. Makes 4–5 servings.

This recipe was sent to me by my mother-in-law. The secret ingredient in these unique waffles is yeast, which is what makes them so light and crispy. After you have tried these waffles, you won't want any other kind! Yummy!

Leslie Owen
Coppell 1st Ward
Carrollton Texas Stake
Coppell, Texas

Christmas Breakfast Casserole

1 24-oz. bag frozen shredded hash browns,
    partially thawed
⅓ C. butter, melted
1 C. cheddar cheese, shredded
1 C. Swiss cheese, shredded

6 eggs
½ C. half-n-half
1 C. cooked ham, diced
½ Tbsp. seasoned salt
1 bunch green onions, sliced

Spray 9 x 13-inch pan with nonstick spray. Spread hash browns in pan. Drizzle with butter. Bake at 450 for 25 minutes or until a little golden brown. Mix other ingredients and spread over potatoes. Bake at 350 for 30–40 minutes. Makes 6–8 servings.

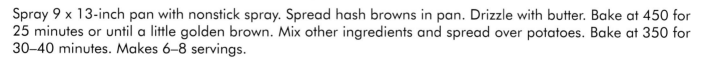

Ever since I can remember, my mom has made this casserole every Christmas morning. It almost brings as much excitement as opening presents from Santa. We received this recipe from my grandma's friend LaRae, and it has been a favorite ever since. When I have a family of my own, I plan to carry on the tradition of this Christmas Breakfast Casserole.

Amanda Chase
Herriman 2nd Ward
Herriman Utah West Stake
Herriman, Utah

Chocolate-Covered Strawberry Muffins

1¾ C. flour
½ C. sugar
2 tsp. baking powder
¼ tsp. salt
1 egg, beaten

¾ C. milk
¼ C. applesauce
⅓ C. dehydrated strawberries
⅓ C. semisweet chocolate chips

Preheat oven to 400. Lightly grease muffin tins. In a large bowl, whisk the flour, sugar, baking powder, and salt. In a separate bowl, combine egg, milk, and applesauce. Make a well in the center of the flour mixture. Pour in the applesauce mixture. Stir until all ingredients are moistened but the batter is still lumpy. Stir in berries and chocolate chips. Spoon batter into tins, filling ⅔ full. Bake 20 minutes or until golden brown. Makes 12 muffins.

This is a special recipe given to me by my sister. I make these on Valentine's Day and serve them in my candy shop. They don't last long, and customers tend to order them in bulk. Super delicious!

Lynn Churchill
Frontenac Ward
St. Louis Missouri Stake
St. Louis, Missouri

English Pancakes

Eggs (2 per serving)
1 Tbsp. flour (for each egg used)
1 Tbsp. milk (for each egg used)
Dash salt

Shortening or butter for frying
Butter
Sugar

(As an example of the ingredients, if you were making two servings of English Pancakes, you would use 4 eggs, 4 Tbsp. flour, and 4 Tbsp. milk.) Beat eggs. In a separate bowl, combine flour, milk, and salt. Stir into eggs. Heat a medium-large frying pan with butter or shortening in the bottom. Pour a thin layer of batter (⅓ to ½ C.) over the entire bottom of the pan. Cook on both sides. Layer pancakes on a large platter. As you put each pancake on the platter, top it with a few pats of butter and sprinkle it with a few teaspoons of sugar. The butter melts and dissolves the sugar, making a syrup as each new pancake is placed on stack. Slice the stack into wedges to serve. Spoon some butter syrup from the platter onto each serving. Very good, but very rich! 10–12 eggs makes enough to fill a family of six.

This recipe has been loved by our family ever since my dad was a child. He ate it for breakfast every Thanksgiving and Christmas, and we continued that tradition. Now it's a tradition enjoyed by the third generation of the family. We all live in the same area, so we still get together on those two days for this breakfast—more than 100 of us!

Lynne Fisher
Redlands 2nd Ward
Redlands California Stake
Redlands, California

Blueberry Cream Muffins

4 eggs
1¼ C. sugar
1¼ C. packed brown sugar
1 C. vegetable oil
1 Tbsp. vanilla extract
2 C. sour cream

4 C. flour
1½ tsp. cinnamon
1 tsp. salt
1 tsp. baking soda
3 C. blueberries

Preheat oven to 400. Grease 24 muffin cups or line with paper muffin liners. In a large bowl, beat eggs. Gradually add sugars while beating. Continue beating while slowly pouring in oil. Stir in vanilla and sour cream. In a separate bowl, stir together flour, cinnamon, salt, and baking soda. Stir dry ingredients into egg mixture. Gently fold in blueberries. Scoop batter into prepared muffin cups. Bake for 20 minutes. Makes 20–24 muffins.

This is a secret recipe passed down from my grandmother, and these muffins are absolutely delicious! My grandmother made blueberry muffins every time we visited her. When she passed away, all the granddaughters were given a copy of her book of recipes, which I will always cherish. These are my favorite muffins ever! There are more than twenty grandchildren, and we all make these muffins. I am sure she would be proud to know her recipe is being enjoyed by all of us.

Karoline Bradley
Washington DC 3rd Ward
Washington DC Stake
Washington, DC

Snowy Oranges

1 large orange
Spoonful of powdered sugar

Peel a large orange, then break it in half. Use a sharp knife to slice through each section. Put the orange on a small plate and sprinkle powdered sugar over the top of each piece of orange. This is excellent as a side dish served with an omelet, scrambled eggs, French toast, pancakes, or other breakfast foods. Makes 1 serving.

Teri Rodeman
Benton City Ward
Kennewick Washington Stake
Benton City, Washington

My Grandma Sarah used to fix this when my mother was growing up. My mom continued this tradition, and so have I. This is the only way I eat my oranges now. It's delicious!

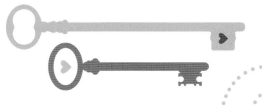

Aunt Kandy's Claim-to-Fame Cinnamon Rolls

Rolls:

1 oz. active dry yeast

1⅓ C. warm water (110 F.)

3 extra-large eggs

¼ C. butter, plus

½ C. granulated sugar

⅓ C. nonfat dry milk powder

½ tsp. salt

5 C. flour

Vegetable oil (as needed)

Filling:

¼ C. butter or margarine, melted

⅓ C. sugar

1 Tbsp. ground cinnamon

½ C. raisins

½ C. pecan pieces

½ C. miniature marshmallows

Icing:

1 lb. powdered sugar

⅓ C. evaporated milk

2 Tbsp. butter

1½ tsp. butter, melted

½ tsp. vanilla

In large mixing bowl, dissolve yeast in warm water. Add eggs and ¼ C. butter. Using dough hook of electric mixer, beat on medium speed until well blended. Add sugar, dry milk, and salt. Mix well. Add flour, 1 C. at a time, mixing until dough begins to pull away from sides of bowl. Lightly grease top of dough with oil. Cover loosely and let rise in warm place 1 hour or until doubled in size. Lightly grease baking sheet. Punch dough down. Roll out on lightly floured surface to form 10½ x 8-inch rectangle. For filling: spread ¼ C. melted butter over dough. Combine sugar and cinnamon and sprinkle evenly over butter. Sprinkle with raisins, pecans, and marshmallows. Roll up tightly starting at long edge. Pinch dough to seal seam. Cut into 1½-inch pieces. Place cut sides up on baking sheet. Let rise in warm place for 1 hour. Heat oven to 350; bake 20–22 minutes or until golden brown. For icing, whisk together all ingredients until smooth and creamy. Spread over rolls. Makes 8 servings.

Chezna Givens
Durban 1st Ward
Durban South Africa Stake
Durban, South Africa

My husband and I are currently living in Durban, South Africa; he travels for business, and we move a lot. I am so glad that Heavenly Father has blessed us to be able to travel the world and to meet so many people. We are so grateful to have our eyes opened to so many cultures. It has been humbling to see the simplicity of life in Africa. South Africa has been my favorite place we have lived outside of the United States so far. It's truly a remarkable place. As much as we ADORE the friends we have made in Durban, nothing can replace home-style Southern food—like these cinnamon rolls!

One-Gram Low-Fat Banana-Blueberry Muffins

1 C. flour
1 Tbsp. baking powder
½ tsp. baking soda
¼ tsp. salt
½–1 tsp. cinnamon
¼ tsp. nutmeg (optional)
1 C. fresh blueberries

1¼ C. ripe bananas, mashed
⅓ C. sugar or sugar substitute (increase for a sweeter muffin)
¼ C. nonfat sour cream (can use low-fat sour cream or fat-free yogurt)
1 large egg
2 tsp. vanilla

Preheat oven to 350. Grease muffin tin or line with paper liners. In a large bowl, mix flour, baking powder, baking soda, salt, cinnamon, nutmeg, and blueberries. In a separate bowl, beat bananas, sugar, sour cream, egg, and vanilla until just blended; stir into the dry blueberry mixture JUST until combined. Do not overmix! A few small lumps are fine. Spoon into the muffin cups and bake for 15–20 minutes or until the muffins test done. Do not double this recipe. Makes 12 muffins.

Katya Yakushev
Nevsky Branch
St. Petersburg Russia Stake
St. Petersburg, Russia

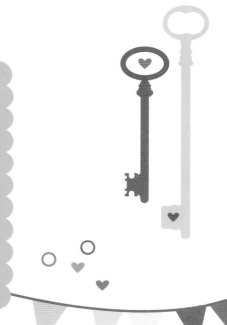

We had an American exchange student living with us for a year, and she was such an amazing little cook. She taught us how to make these tasty muffins, and they quickly became my favorite. The secret: you would never know they are low-fat, BUT THEY ARE! My children and husband devour these, which proves these muffins are five-star, because my family is a tough group to please when it comes to food. These are even better the next day, and are just as delicious without the berries. You can use regular sour cream or yogurt, and flavored yogurts add to the taste of these muffins. I like to sprinkle a sugar/cinnamon mixture on top of each muffin before baking, but that is optional.

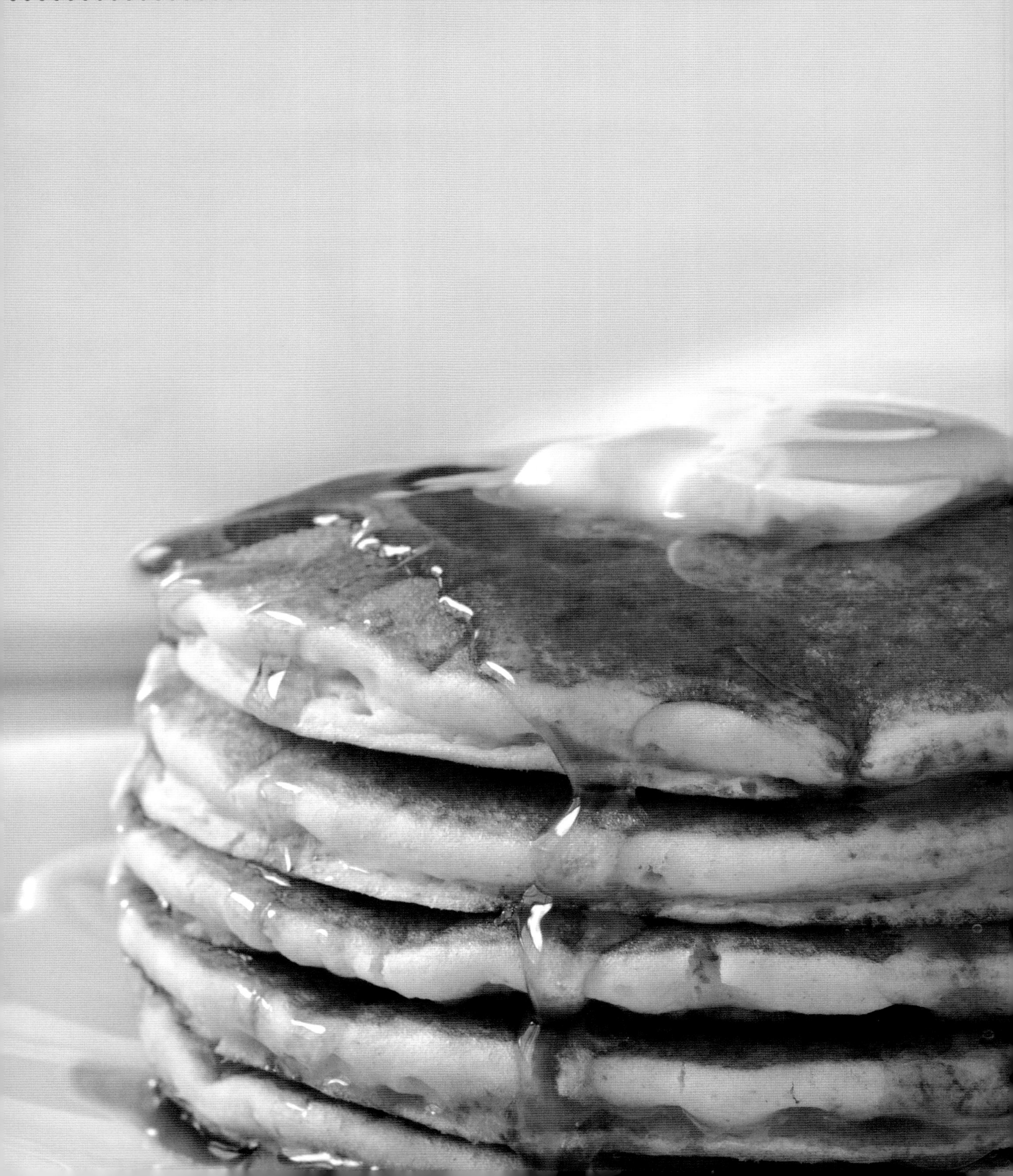

Saturday Night Pancakes

1 egg
1 C. milk
1 Tbsp. vinegar
1 Tbsp. canola oil
1 Tbsp. all-natural applesauce
1 C. flour

½ C. whole-wheat flour
1 Tbsp. sugar
1 tsp. baking powder
½ tsp. baking soda
½ tsp. salt (optional)

Beat egg, milk, and vinegar until foamy and doubled in volume. Add remaining ingredients in order while mixing continuously; don't overmix! The batter should be light and airy. Ladle ¼-C. scoops onto a hot nonstick griddle or frying pan; flip to finish cooking. Serve with peanut butter and syrup. Makes 10 pancakes (3–4 servings).

Emily King
St. Johns Ward
Lansing Michigan Stake
DeWitt, Michigan

This was a basic recipe that was passed down to me from my Nana, who lives in Boston. The original recipe calls for buttermilk, but Nana shared her secret: by adding the vinegar to the milk you get the same taste as buttermilk without the fat. The vinegar also reacts with the baking soda, giving these pancakes a very light texture. My husband perfected the technique of mixing the milk and egg until foamy to give these an even lighter, fluffier texture. He also began adding our homemade applesauce in place of half the oil, which gives the pancakes a sweeter taste. Friends can't believe the wonderful texture and taste—and are never able to guess that the secret ingredients are vinegar and applesauce. We have these pancakes every Saturday night; we triple the batch and serve the leftovers Sunday morning reheated in the toaster. This cuts down on Sunday morning prep time. We love these delicious pancakes!

TOP SECRET

Strawberry Banana Crepes

Crepes:
1 C. flour
1 Tbsp. sugar
½ tsp. ground cinnamon
1½ C. milk
2 eggs
1–2 Tbsp. butter, divided

Filling:
1 8-oz. pkg. cream cheese, softened
1 8-oz. container frozen whipped topping, thawed
½ C. powdered sugar

Topping:
2 C. fresh strawberries, sliced
2 medium-firm bananas, sliced
¼ C. sugar (optional)

In a large bowl, combine flour, sugar, cinnamon, milk, and eggs. Cover and refrigerate for 1 hour. In an 8-inch nonstick skillet, melt 1 tsp. of the butter. Stir batter; pour about 2 Tbsp. into the center of the skillet. Lift and tilt pan to evenly coat bottom. Cook until top appears dry; turn and cook 15–20 seconds longer. Remove to a wire rack. Repeat with remaining batter, adding butter to the skillet as needed. When cool, stack crepes on paper towels with waxed paper in between. In a large bowl, beat the filling ingredients until smooth. Spread 2 rounded tablespoonfuls on each crepe; roll up. In a large bowl, combine topping ingredients; spoon over crepes. Makes 8 servings.

Johana Keough
Harpers Ferry Ward
Winchester Virginia Stake
Charlestown, West Virginia

Every year while I was growing up, we had these crepes for breakfast on the first day of school. It was a real treat, since my mom was usually so busy getting everyone ready for school she rarely had time to make breakfast for all seven of us. It was usually plain ol' dry cereal. But on the first day of school, she always made us crepes from this secret recipe. We all love them and still make them to this day; my little ones look forward to them just as much as I did.

Sausage Kolache

2.25-oz. pkg. dry yeast
½ C. lukewarm water
¼ C. unsalted butter, softened
¼ C. shortening or lard
¼ C. sugar
2 egg yolks

⅔ C. milk
1 tsp. salt
4 C. flour
¼ C. butter, melted, for topping
1 16-oz. pkg. cocktail smoked sausage links

(recipe continued on next page)

(Sausage Kolache, continued)

In a small bowl, combine the yeast and water. Set aside. In a large bowl, cream the unsalted butter, shortening, and ¼ C. sugar until the mixture is light and fluffy. Mix in the egg yolks, milk, and salt, combining well. Stir in the dissolved yeast and the flour, and mix until the ingredients are thoroughly blended into a soft dough. Cover the dough with a towel and set aside to rise until about double in size, approximately 1 to 1½ hours. Grease a baking sheet. Pinch off pieces of dough about the size of a golf ball, flatten the balls slightly, and place them on the baking sheet at least 1 inch apart; brush the dough balls liberally with the melted butter. Set them aside to double in size again, about 45 minutes to one hour. Gently indent the top of the dough with your thumb, fairly deep. Place the little pinky-size smoked sausage link in the indent and fold the kolache over the sausage and seal. Bake at 425 for 10–12 minutes or until golden brown. Immediately brush butter on the top. They are best eaten as soon as they are cool enough to handle. Makes 24 servings. VARIATION: Try using spicy sausage links, or adding a little cheese and/or diced jalapeño pepper with each sausage.

These are my famous kolaches. If only I had a nickel for every person who has asked for the recipe. . . .

Liz Henwood
Stone Oak Ward
San Antonio Texas North Stake
San Antonio, Texas

Banana Poppy Seed Muffins

Muffins:

2 C. flour

1½ Tbsp. poppy seeds

2 tsp. baking powder

½ tsp. salt

2 ripe bananas, pureed (about 1 C.)

1 egg

¾ C. sugar

¼ C. oil

2 tsp. orange zest, grated

Citrus Glaze:

1¼ C. powdered sugar

¼ C. orange juice

1 tsp. orange zest, grated

1 tsp. vanilla

Preheat oven to 375. Grease 12-cup muffin tin. In large mixing bowl, combine flour, poppy seeds, baking powder, and salt. In a separate bowl, combine pureed bananas, egg, sugar, oil, and 2 tsp. orange zest. Mix well. Stir banana mixture into flour mixture. Spoon batter into muffin cups. Bake for 20 minutes or until done. To make glaze, combine powdered sugar, juice, 1 tsp. orange zest, and vanilla. Mix until smooth. Drizzle over muffins while muffins are still hot from the oven. Makes 12 muffins.

Beatrix Guntherson
Iowa City 2nd Ward
Iowa City Iowa Stake
North Liberty, Iowa

This is my secret recipe for the muffins that I snagged my hubby with. Watch out—these are dangerous!

Pumpkin Cinnamon Rolls with Caramel Frosting

Rolls:

2 Tbsp. yeast
½ C. warm water
½ C. canned pumpkin
⅔ C. sugar
½ tsp. salt
1 egg, beaten
¼ C. melted butter
¼ tsp. ground cloves
1 tsp. cinnamon
4–5 C. bread flour
2 Tbsp. butter, melted
½ C. packed brown sugar
2 Tbsp. cinnamon

Caramel Frosting:

¼ C. butter
½ C. packed brown sugar
2 Tbsp. milk
¼ tsp. vanilla
Pinch of salt
½–¾ C. powdered sugar, sifted

Rolls: Dissolve yeast in warm water. Wait 5 minutes. Add pumpkin, sugar, salt, egg, ¼ C. melted butter, cloves, and cinnamon; mix well. Slowly add flour 1 C. at a time. Scrape down sides of bowl after each addition of flour. Turn into lightly greased bowl, cover, and set in warm place until double in bulk. Punch down dough and let rest for 5 more minutes. Roll dough out into a rectangle. Brush dough with 2 Tbsp. melted butter. Combine brown sugar and cinnamon, and sprinkle over butter. Starting with long side of dough, roll up jelly-roll style. Pinch seams to seal. Using sharp serrated knife, cut roll into 12 1-inch slices. Place rolls cut side up in greased 9 x 13-inch pan. Cover and let rise until double, 30–45 minutes. Bake rolls at 350 about 20 minutes or until golden brown.

Caramel Frosting: In a small saucepan, heat butter until melted. Stir in brown sugar and milk. Cook over medium-low heat for 1 minute. Transfer to small bowl and cool mixture. Stir in vanilla, salt, and powdered sugar. Beat with electric mixer until well blended. If necessary, add more sugar for desired consistency. Drizzle caramel frosting on rolls as soon as they come out of the oven. Let cool until warm, then add the rest of the frosting. Enjoy! Makes 12 servings.

Andrea Ingleby
Fort Herriman 3rd Ward
Fort Herriman Utah Stake
Riverton, Utah

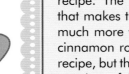

My family loves cinnamon rolls and we were so happy to discover this recipe. The pumpkin is the secret that makes these cinnamon rolls so much more wonderful than regular cinnamon rolls. This the perfect fall recipe, but they are actually splendid any time of the year.

{ BREADS }

To keep your secret is wisdom; but to expect others to keep it is folly.

{ Samuel Johnson }

Joyce Riggs' Biscuits Supreme

2 C. sifted flour

4 tsp. baking powder

½ tsp. salt

½ tsp. cream of tartar

2 tsp. sugar

½ C. shortening

¾ C. milk

¼ C. butter, melted

In a large bowl, combine flour, baking powder, salt, cream of tartar, and sugar; mix well. Cut in shortening with a pastry blender or fork until mixture is crumbly. Add milk and mix with a fork until dough is formed. Put on floured surface and form a ball. Roll out to about ½ inch thick. Cut with a biscuit cutter or other circular cutter. NOW FOR THE SECRET: Dip each biscuit into the melted butter, then double-stack the biscuits. Bake at 450 for 10–12 minutes. Makes 6 large or 9 medium-size biscuits.

Jill Saddler
Corner Canyon 6th Ward
Corner Canyon Utah Stake
Draper, Utah

Clover's Johnny Cakes

4 C. flour

6 tsp. baking powder

2 Tbsp. sugar

2 tsp. salt

1 Tbsp. mayonnaise

1 Tbsp. sour cream

2 Tbsp. milk

About 1 C. warm water

About ½ C. canola oil

In a large bowl, mix dry ingredients; add mayonnaise, sour cream, and milk. Gradually add water until you get a soft, sticky dough. You may not need a full cup. Roll the dough on a floured surface and let it rest for half an hour. Then roll the dough out until it's ¾ inch thick. Use a small glass/cookie cutter, as if you were going to cut out biscuits, and cut as many as you can. Reroll the scraps of dough to cut more. In a frying pan, pour enough oil to cover the bottom of the pan. When oil is hot, add Johnny cakes and fry on both sides until golden. Makes 6–8 servings.

Lacy Allphin
Weldon Springs Ward
St. Louis Missouri North Stake
St. Peters, Missouri

My husband attended medical school on the island of Saba in the Caribbean. We had no ward there, and we held sacrament meeting in our living room with the other student members. My husband baptized the first local. Her mother, Clover, made the best Johnny cakes on the island. She said her secret is Robin Hood flour. I haven't seen that brand of flour in the United States, but regular flour still works to make these splendid Johnny cakes.

Broccoli Cornbread

1 8.5-oz. pkg. self-rising cornmeal mix

1 tsp. salt

4 eggs

1 C. cottage cheese

1 onion, chopped

½ C. butter, melted

1 10-oz. pkg. chopped frozen broccoli, thawed and drained

4 oz. cheddar cheese, shredded (optional)

Preheat oven to 400. Lightly grease an 11 x 7-inch baking pan. In a large mixing bowl, combine cornmeal mix and salt. In a separate bowl, mix eggs, cottage cheese, onion, and melted butter. Stir into the flour mixture. Fold in the broccoli and shredded cheese, if desired. Pour batter into prepared pan. Bake for 30 minutes, or until a toothpick inserted into the center comes out clean. Makes 12 servings.

My wife introduced me to Broccoli Corn-bread a very long time ago, and I must say it is GREAT. It's also a great secret to getting some vegetables into the kiddos!

Martin Leventhral
Kungsbacka Ward
Göteborg Sweden Stake
Kungsbacka, Sweden

Hot-and-Sassy Cornbread

1 C. stone-ground yellow cornmeal

¾ C. flour

¼ C. whole-wheat flour

1 tsp. baking powder

½ tsp. baking soda

¾ tsp. salt

Dash black pepper

1 C. canned cream-style corn

½ C. fresh or frozen corn kernels (thaw if frozen)

½ C. sour cream

½ C. milk

2 eggs, lightly beaten

2 Tbsp. vegetable oil

1 Tbsp. packed brown sugar

1 jalapeño pepper, seeded and minced

Preheat oven to 400. Butter an 8-inch square pan. In a large bowl, combine cornmeal, flour, whole-wheat flour, baking powder, baking soda, salt, and pepper. In a separate bowl, combine cream-style corn, kernel corn, sour cream, milk, eggs, oil, brown sugar, and jalapeño. Stir wet corn mixture into dry ingredients, mixing until blended. Pour batter into pan. Bake for 25 minutes, or until top is lightly browned and knife inserted in center comes out clean. Makes 12 servings.

Making this recipe was my final exam for a college home economics class. That was ten years ago, and I have yet to grow tired of this cornbread. If you like spicy food, you will love the twist on this cornbread recipe. The jalapeño pepper is the secret ingredient that makes this cornbread over-the-top good.

Beatrix Guntherson
Iowa City 2nd Ward
Iowa City Iowa Stake
North Liberty, Iowa

Pina Colada Bread

Bread:

5 C. flour

¾ C. sugar

2 Tbsp. baking powder

1 tsp. cinnamon

½ tsp. nutmeg

2 tsp. salt

4 eggs

1 C. unsalted butter, melted

1 8-oz. can crushed pineapple, undrained

1 C. cream of coconut (NOT coconut milk)

⅔ C. walnuts

⅔ C. golden raisins

Topping:

2¾ C. flaked coconut, divided

⅔ C. cream of coconut

Preheat oven to 350. Spray two 9 x 5 x 3-inch pans. In a large bowl, combine flour, sugar, baking powder, cinnamon, nutmeg, and salt. In a small bowl, combine eggs, melted butter, pineapple with juice, and 1 C. cream of coconut; mix well. Pour butter mixture over the flour mixture and stir well. Toss walnuts and raisins with a handful of flour just to coat, then toss into the batter. Mix. Divide batter in half and place equal amounts in each loaf pan. Bake 35–40 minutes. Let cool. For topping, combine 1¾ C. coconut and ⅔ C. cream of coconut. Spread on top of loaves. Toast remaining coconut and sprinkle on top of loaves. Makes 2 loaves (6–8 servings per loaf).

> This is my family's favorite bread. The secret is that we think it is good enough to be dessert. Enjoy!

Katherine Hinkley
Sheridan 1st Ward
Gillete Wyoming Stake
Sheridan, Wyoming

Whole-Wheat Zucchini Bread

3 C. whole-wheat flour

1 tsp. salt

1 tsp. baking soda

¼ tsp. baking powder

3 tsp. cinnamon

3 eggs

2 C. sugar or honey

1 C. oil

2 C. zucchini, grated

Preheat oven to 350. Grease a 9 x 5 x 3-inch loaf pan. Sift flour, salt, baking soda, baking powder, and cinnamon. In a large bowl, whisk eggs, sugar or honey, and oil. Add zucchini and stir to combine. Add dry ingredients and mix well. Spread batter in pan. Bake 50–60 minutes or until toothpick inserted in center comes out clean. Makes 1 loaf.

> I like this bread very much because it is so moist and sweet. Many recipes for wheat bread are dry, but this one is not. You can't taste the zucchini, and it's a nice way to get your vegetables in for the day.

Andreevsky Cakir
Helsinki 3rd Ward
Tampere Finland Stake
Helsinki, Finland

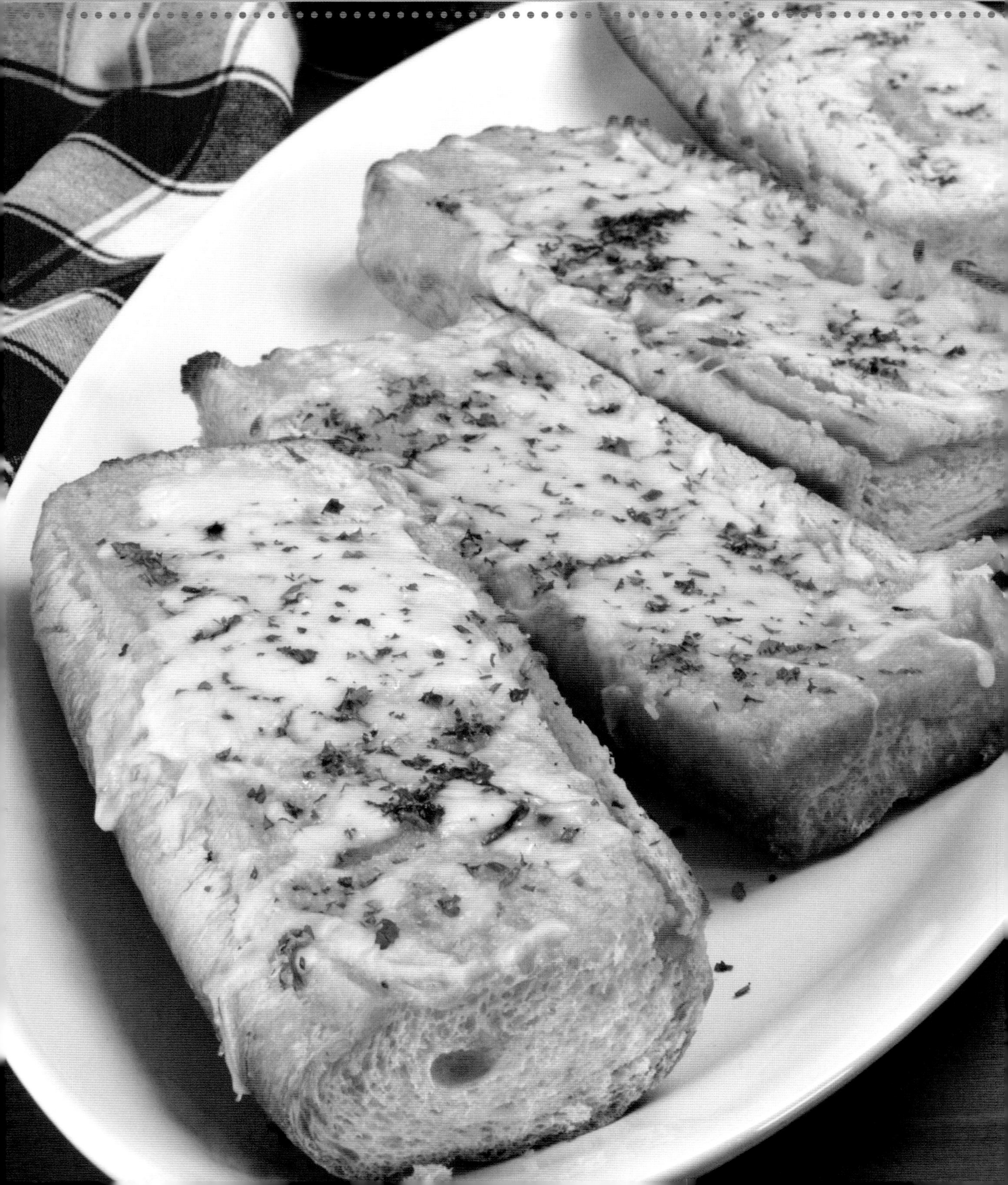

Nancy's Cheesy Garlic Bread

½ C. butter, softened

¾ C. mayonnaise

1 bunch green onions, chopped

3 cloves garlic, minced

1¼ C. Parmesan cheese, grated

1½ C. Monterey Jack cheese, shredded

1 loaf French bread, halved lengthwise

Preheat oven to 350. In a large bowl, combine butter, mayonnaise, green onions, garlic, Parmesan cheese, and Monterey Jack cheese. Cut each half of French bread into 4 pieces. Spread the cheese mixture evenly on the bread pieces, and arrange the pieces on a cookie sheet. Bake at 350 for 8 minutes. Set the oven to broil; broil until hot and bubbly, about 2 additional minutes. Makes 8 servings.

This is a secret recipe I got from a diner where I worked a long time ago. Only the owner knew the recipe, and he never gave it out—not even to me. So how did I get it? I watched him make this cheese bread every day for about a year. I went home after work and practiced making it until I had the recipe perfected. It is so delicious, I still go nuts over it!

Nancy Crabtree
Lake Shawnee Ward
Topeka Kansas Stake
Topeka, Kansas

Green Bread

½ C. butter

3–5 cloves garlic, peeled

1 tsp. garlic powder

¼ tsp. onion powder

2 tsp. Italian seasoning

1 pkg. baby spinach or 1 bunch spinach

2–3 Tbsp. Parmesan cheese, grated

Sprinkle of salt and pepper

1 loaf French bread

In a food processor, blend all ingredients except bread. Cut French bread in 2 long halves and spread mixture evenly across both halves. Bake at 350 for 10–15 minutes. Makes 8 servings.

JoLynn Packer
Glines 8th Ward
Vernal Utah Glines Stake
Vernal, Utah

This is my version of a recipe I saw on a TV cooking show several years ago. The secret is adding the spinach to the garlic spread. This makes it a healthier garlic bread and a way to get kids to eat spinach—it's hidden so well, they don't even know it's there. My family loves Green Bread and we don't usually have a lot left over. I often make this for holidays like Halloween and St. Patrick's Day. My two cute, crazy boys are good eaters but I still like to sneak in veggies and anything healthy where I can, especially on the holidays when they will be getting a lot of sweet treats too.

Buttermilk Biscuits

2 C. unbleached flour (White Lily if possible)
¼ tsp. baking soda
1 Tbsp. baking powder (use one without aluminum)

1 tsp. kosher salt or salt
6 Tbsp. unsalted butter, very cold
About ¾ C. buttermilk

Preheat oven to 450. In a bowl or a food processor, combine the dry ingredients. Cut the butter into chunks and cut it into the flour until it resembles coarse meal. (If using a food processor, just pulse a few times to get this consistency.) Add the buttermilk and mix JUST until combined. If it appears on the dry side, add a bit more buttermilk. Turn the dough out onto a floured board. Very gently PAT the dough out (do NOT roll with a rolling pin) until it's about ½ inch thick. Use a round cutter to cut into rounds. You can gently knead the scraps together and make a few more, but they will not be anywhere near as good as the first ones. Place the biscuits on a cookie sheet. If you like soft sides, put the biscuits touching each other; if you like crusty sides, put them about 1 inch apart (these will not rise as high as the biscuits that are touching each other). Bake for about 10–12 minutes or until the biscuits are a beautiful light golden brown on top and bottom. Do not overbake. You can make these biscuits, cut them, put them on cookie sheets, and freeze them for up to a month. When you want fresh biscuits, simply place them frozen on the cookie sheet and bake at 450 for about 20 minutes. Makes 12 biscuits.

Biscuits are not all that common here in Canada and seem to be a real treat; my girlfriend's husband couldn't get enough and demanded I submit my recipe to this book. These biscuits are authentic—this recipe came from my great-great-grandmother and was handed down to all the women in my family. I am the first one to commit the sin of using a food processor, but I find it works very well. The secret to great biscuits is not in the ingredients but in the handling of the dough. The dough must be handled as little as possible, or it creates tough biscuits. I have found that a food processor produces superior biscuits, because the ingredients stay colder and there's less chance of overmixing. You also must pat the dough out with your hands very gently—rolling with a rolling pin is a guaranteed way to overstimulate the gluten, resulting in a tougher biscuit.

Emma Goeller
Bridgewater Ward
Dartmouth Nova Scotia Stake
Dartmouth, Nova Scotia
Canada

Hawaiian Sweet Bread

3 eggs
2 C. pineapple juice
¾ C. sugar
½ tsp. ginger

1 tsp. vanilla
½ C. butter or margarine, melted
6½ C. flour, divided
2 .25-oz. envs. yeast

(recipe continued on next page)

(Hawaiian Sweet Bread, continued)

In a large bowl, beat the eggs. Add the pineapple juice, sugar, ginger, vanilla, and melted butter. Add 3 C. flour; stir until well combined. Sprinkle in the yeast, one envelope at a time, and mix well. Add another 3 C. flour and mix well. Blending with a spoon will be hard, so you may have to use your hands. Make sure all ingredients are thoroughly combined. Cover the bowl with a cloth and set in a warm place to rise for 1 hour. Remove from the bowl and knead in ½ C. flour; knead about 10 times. Divide into three equal parts. Place in greased and floured loaf pans or shape into rolls. Cover and place in a warm place to rise for 1 hour. Bake at 350 for 25–30 minutes or until golden brown. Makes 3 loaves or 18 rolls.

Markay Mekeska
Saint Stephen Ward
Saint John New Brunswick Stake
Whiting, Maine

My husband loves Hawaiian sweet bread, so I went on a quest to make the perfect recipe. After a lot of mistakes and failures along the way, I have come up with and mastered the perfect recipe. This is it! I am known for these special rolls, and would like to share this amazing bread with everyone. I like rolls better, but this can be made into either loaves or rolls. These are so addicting. I have used this recipe with cinnamon buns as well and they are also very good.

Phili's 1st Ward Mighty Rolls

1 tsp. sugar
1 .25-oz. env. dry active yeast
¼ C. warm water (105–110 degrees)
1 C. warm milk
¼ C. butter, melted

½ C. sugar
1 room-temperature egg, beaten
1 tsp. salt
4 C. flour

Combine sugar and yeast in tepid water. Let stand 5–10 minutes, until yeast begins to foam. In a large bowl, thoroughly mix milk, butter, sugar, egg, and salt. Stir in the yeast mixture and 3½ C. flour, adding a bit more if necessary to make a soft, pliable dough. Turn dough out onto a floured board and let rest while you clean and butter the bowl. Knead dough gently 4–5 minutes, adding flour, if necessary, until dough is smooth and silky. Return to bowl, cover with plastic wrap, and let rise in warm place until doubled in size (about 1½ hours). Butter a 12-cup muffin tin. Punch down dough. Pinch off pieces that are about 1½ inches in diameter (enough to fill half of a muffin cup), and roll into smooth spheres. Place two pieces of dough in each prepared muffin cup. It will be a tight fit. Cover dough loosely with plastic wrap and let rise for 45 minutes. Bake rolls at 350 for 20–25 minutes, or until light brown. Serve as soon as they are cool enough to throw. Makes 12 rolls.

Dallin Aimes
Philadelphia 1st Ward
Valley Forge Pennsylvania Stake
Philadelphia, Pennsylvania

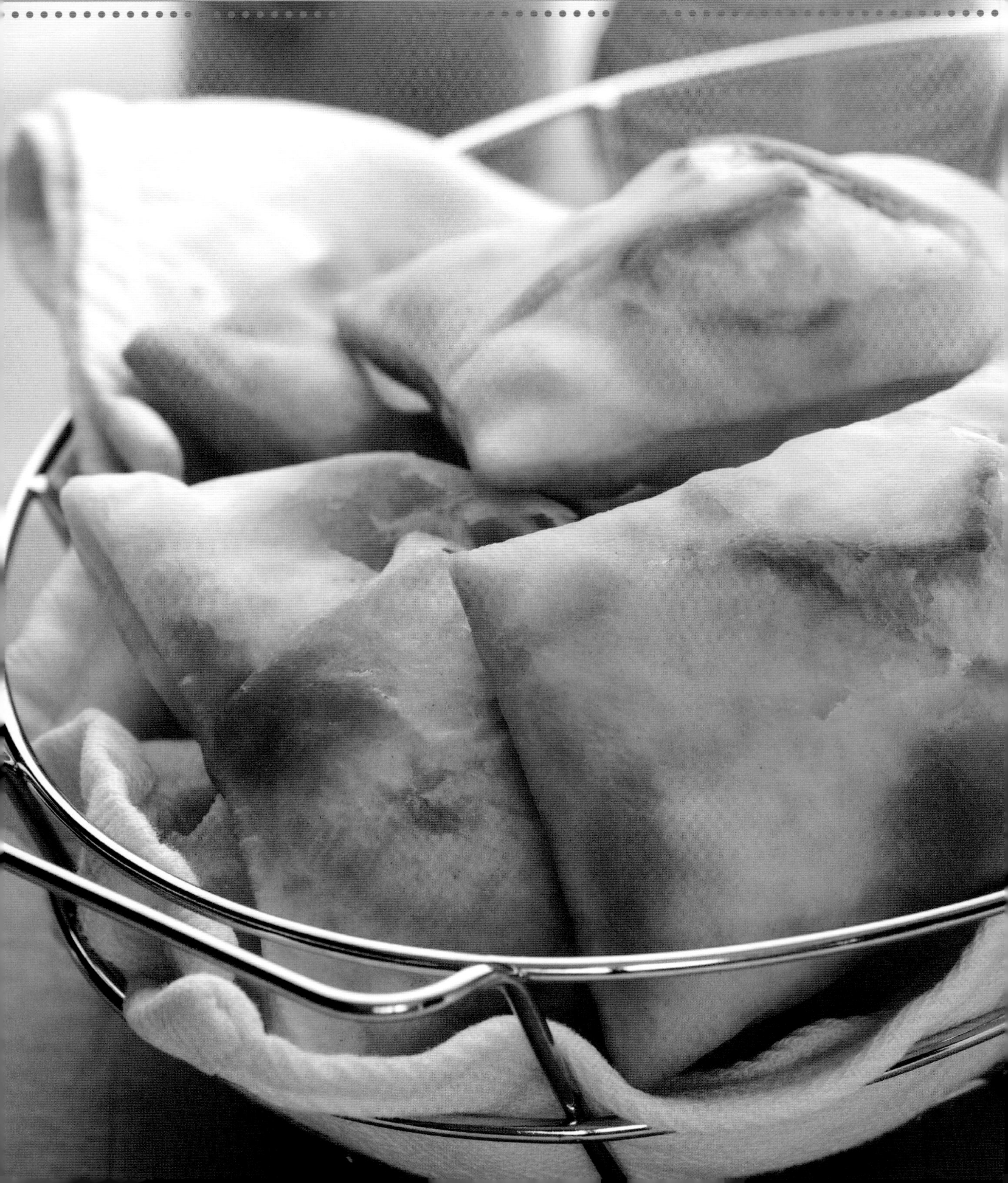

Sopapillas

1 env. active dry yeast

1 tsp. sugar

½ C. very warm water (around 110 degrees)

3 C. flour

1 Tbsp. melted butter, cooled

1 tsp. salt

1 egg

Oil for frying

In a large bowl, dissolve yeast and sugar in warm water. In a separate bowl, mix flour, butter, salt, and egg. Pour flour mixture into yeast mixture. Add enough water to create a consistency like bread dough. Knead for 15 minutes. Cover with a towel or plastic wrap. Place in a warm, draft-free area, and let rise for 30 minutes or until doubled in size. Punch down dough. Divide dough in half, since it is easier to work with half at a time. On a lightly floured surface, roll each half of the dough ¼ inch thick. Cut into 2-inch squares. Heat oil to 375. Stretch squares gently and drop into hot oil. Hold down in oil until dough begins to puff, then turn squares over. Fry only 3 or 4 sopapillas at a time, turning often until golden. Drain on absorbent paper. Serve hot with butter and lots of honey. Makes 3 dozen.

This is a family secret recipe from way back. We love these Sopapillas! Our favorite way to eat them is to sprinkle with cinnamon and sugar after buttering, then put the honey on top. DIVINE!

Alley Merris
Tom's River 1st Ward
East Brunswick New Jersey Stake
Seaside Park, New Jersey

Bunker Hill Brown Bread

1½ C. flour

1½ tsp. salt

2 tsp. baking soda

1 C. wheat germ

1 C. graham cracker crumbs

2 eggs

½ C. vegetable oil

1 C. molasses

2 C. buttermilk

Preheat oven to 350. Sift flour, salt, and baking soda into a large mixing bowl. Stir in wheat germ and graham cracker crumbs. In a separate bowl combine eggs, oil, molasses, and buttermilk. Add liquid ingredients to dry ingredients. Stir until blended. Pour batter into 2 tall, well-greased and floured 1-pound tin cans or a well-greased and floured bundt pan. Bake for 50–55 minutes or until done. Makes 2 loaves or 1 bundt pan.

This was my aunt's recipe. She used tin cans, but I use a bundt pan and then slice the bread into sections. Brown bread has been around for ages and it tastes so good. I probably would not have known what it was had it not been for my mom. She showed me the ropes around the kitchen and always made unique things for us while we were growing up. This was my parents' favorite bread, so they made it quite a bit. It's delicious served with honey butter.

Melodee Finch
Lake Norman Ward
Gastonia North Carolina Stake
Mooresville, North Carolina

Carrot Bread

¾ C. sugar

2 eggs, beaten

1 C. vegetable oil

1 tsp. vanilla

1½ C. carrot, grated

1 Tbsp. orange rind, grated

1 tsp. lemon juice

1½ C. flour, sifted

2 tsp. baking soda

½ tsp. salt

¼ tsp. cinnamon

Dash nutmeg

1 C. pecans or walnuts, finely chopped

In a medium bowl, combine sugar, eggs, oil, and vanilla. Stir in carrot, orange rind, and lemon juice. Into a separate bowl, sift flour, soda, salt, cinnamon, and nutmeg; stir dry ingredients into the wet mixture. Fold in nuts. Pour batter into a greased loaf pan and bake at 350 for 1 hour. Makes 1 loaf (8 servings).

My husband's grandmother was a nurse. She loved her job but secretly had always wanted go to culinary school. But back then they did not admit women into the program she desired, so she became a nurse. My father-in-law says he remembers his mom always baking for her patients, whom she quickly befriended. She tried many recipes and this was one of the most requested. To this day we still make many of her recipes.

Pemberlyn Knickerbocker
Portsmouth Ward
Exeter New Hampshire Stake
Portsmouth, New Hampshire

AWESOME, FABULOUS Pizza Crust

2¼ tsp. active dry yeast

½ tsp. brown sugar

1½ C. warm water (110 degrees)

1 tsp. salt

2 Tbsp. olive oil

3⅓ C. flour

In a large bowl, dissolve yeast and brown sugar in warm water. Let sit for 10 minutes. Stir salt and oil into the yeast solution. Mix in 2½ C. flour. Turn dough out onto a clean, well-floured surface, and knead in more flour until the dough is no longer sticky. Place the dough into a well-oiled bowl, and cover with a cloth. Let the dough rise until double; this should take about 1 hour. Punch down the dough and form it into a tight ball. Allow the dough to relax for a minute before rolling out. Use for your favorite pizza recipe. Preheat oven to 425. If you are baking the dough on a pizza stone, you may place your toppings on the dough and bake it immediately. If you are baking your pizza in a pan instead of on a stone, lightly oil the pan and let the dough rise for 15–20 minutes before topping and baking it. Bake pizza in preheated oven until the cheese and crust are golden brown, about 15–20 minutes. Brush crust with garlic powder and olive oil. Makes 1 pizza crust.

The secret to great pizza is making it yourself. What is better than homemade pizza? Don't be intimidated. This crust is very forgiving, and it's so easy. Our family is crazy over this crust.

Kierstyn Carr
High Desert Ward
Bend Oregon Stake
Bend, Oregon

Camp Mystic's Brown Bread

2 C. whole wheat flour
1 C. white flour
2 tsp. baking soda
1 tsp. salt

⅔ C. packed brown sugar
¼ C. molasses
2 C. buttermilk

Preheat oven to 350. Grease and flour a 9 x 5-inch loaf pan, knocking out excess flour.
In a large bowl, whisk the whole-wheat flour, white flour, baking soda, salt, and brown sugar. Mix in molasses and buttermilk until just combined. Pour batter into prepared pan. Bake for 40 minutes, or until done. Cool on a wire rack for 5 minutes, and then remove from pan. Cool completely before slicing. Makes 12 servings.

My parents own a summer camp, and this bread is a family recipe that always gets rave reviews from all the campers. It's sweet and delicious and was a secret until now . . . hope you enjoy!

Brie Suvalli
Seattle 5th Ward
Seattle Washington North Stake
Seattle, Washington

Spicy Molasses Bran Loaf

2 eggs, well beaten
⅔ C. dark molasses
3 Tbsp. butter, melted
1½ C. sour milk or buttermilk
1 tsp. vanilla
2 C. flour, sifted
2 tsp. baking powder
1 tsp. baking soda

1 tsp. salt
1 tsp. cinnamon
1 tsp. ginger
½ tsp. allspice
1 tsp. orange rind, grated
2 C. bran cereal (All Bran)
½ C. raisins
½ C. nuts, chopped

In a large bowl, combine eggs, molasses, melted butter, sour milk, and vanilla. Into a separate bowl, sift flour and spices; stir into wet mixture. Blend well. Add orange rind, bran cereal, raisins, and nuts. Pour into greased loaf pan. Bake at 350 for 1 hour. Makes 10 servings.

This is one of my favorite creations, because I made it up using a combination [of] things I love. My oldest is going off to college soon and has already [st]arted writing down some of my recipes to take with her. This was the very [fir]st recipe that she went searching for. It warms my heart to know my kids [wa]nt to carry my recipes away from home with them, and will hopefully pass [th]em down to their own children someday.

CeeCee Aiken
North Pole Ward
Fairbanks Alaska Stake
North Pole, Alaska

Kendrick Family's Zucchini Bread

3 C. flour

1 tsp. salt

1 tsp. baking soda

1 tsp. baking powder

3 tsp. ground cinnamon

3 eggs

1 C. vegetable oil

2¼ C. sugar

3 tsp. vanilla extract

2 C. zucchini, grated

1 C. walnuts, chopped

Crumb Topping (optional):

½ C. oats

½ C. packed brown sugar

¼ C. flour

¼ tsp. cinnamon

¼ C. butter

Grease and flour two 8 x 4-inch loaf pans. Preheat oven to 325. Into a large bowl sift flour, salt, baking soda, baking powder, and cinnamon. In a separate large bowl, beat eggs, oil, sugar, and vanilla. Add sifted ingredients to the creamed mixture; beat well. Stir in zucchini and nuts until well combined. Pour batter into prepared pans. Bake 15 minutes and then add crumb topping, if desired. To make crumb topping, combine oats, brown sugar, flour, cinnamon, and butter; sprinkle on top of bread. (You bake the bread for 15 minutes before adding the crumb topping so the topping won't slide off.) Continue baking for 25–45 minutes, or until a toothpick or knife inserted in the center comes out clean. Cool in pan on rack for 20 minutes. Remove bread from pan and cool completely. Makes 2 loaves.

Sage Kendrick
Lakeside Park Ward
Cincinnati Ohio Stake
Villa Hills, Kentucky

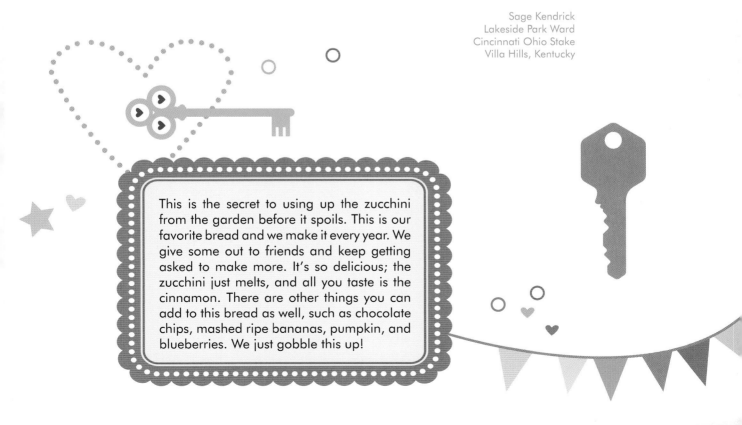

This is the secret to using up the zucchini from the garden before it spoils. This is our favorite bread and we make it every year. We give some out to friends and keep getting asked to make more. It's so delicious; the zucchini just melts, and all you taste is the cinnamon. There are other things you can add to this bread as well, such as chocolate chips, mashed ripe bananas, pumpkin, and blueberries. We just gobble this up!

Pan de Papa (Potato Bread)

1 large potato	2 Tbsp. sugar
1 C. milk	¾ C. warm water
¼ C. butter	1 large egg
1½ tsp. salt	2 C. flour
1½ tsp. dry instant yeast	2 C. bread flour

Peel potato and cut into 4 pieces. Boil until tender, then mash thoroughly. In a small saucepan, bring milk to a boil and remove from heat. Add butter and salt to hot milk. Let cool until just a little warmer than room temperature. In a separate bowl, dissolve yeast and sugar in warm water. Let stand for 5 minutes. In a mixer bowl, combine egg, mashed potato, cooled milk mixture, and dissolved yeast; knead with a dough hook on low speed. Gradually add flour and continue to knead for 5–10 minutes. The dough should remain fairly soft; if it seems to be getting stiff, don't add all the flour. The dough should be smooth, elastic, and slightly sticky after kneading. If the dough seems too wet, add a little more flour. Turn dough into an oiled bowl and let rise in a warm place until double in size. Punch down dough and cut into pieces the size of a small tangerine. Roll pieces into a ball shape on a floured surface and place on a greased cookie sheet, about an inch apart. Make a 1-inch slash in the tops of the rolls with a sharp knife. Preheat oven to 425. Let rolls rise until almost double in bulk. Bake at 425 for 5 minutes, then lower temperature to 350 and bake for an additional 10–15 minutes. Rolls should be a light golden brown color when ready. Makes 16 rolls or 2 loaves of bread.

Potatoes are the secret to really great bread. Potato rolls are so soft and have a buttery, sweet taste. Potatoes also cost less than wheat—so not only does my family love these rolls, but I can make them often.

Antonella Martinez
Mocha Ward
Trujillo La Libertad Stake
Trujillo, Peru

Golden Knots

2 .25-oz. envs. active dry yeast	1 C. sugar
2 Tbsp. sugar	2 eggs
1½ C. warm water (110 degrees)	2 tsp. salt
1 C. milk	8 C. flour, divided
½ C. butter	2 Tbsp. butter, melted

In a small bowl, dissolve yeast and 2 Tbsp. sugar in warm water. Let stand until creamy, about 10 minutes. In a small saucepan, warm the milk until it bubbles, then remove from heat. Mix in the butter and 1 C. sugar; stir until melted. Let cool until lukewarm. In a large bowl, combine the yeast mixture with the milk mixture;

(recipe continued on next page)

(Golden Knots, continued)

add eggs, salt, and 3 C. flour; stir well to combine. Stir in the remaining flour, ½ C. at a time, beating well after each addition. When the dough has pulled together, turn it out onto a lightly floured surface and knead until smooth and elastic, about 8 minutes. Place in a greased bowl, turning once to grease the top. Cover and let rise in a warm place until doubled, about 1 hour. Punch down dough and divide into thirds; roll each portion into a 14-inch roll; divide each roll into 14 pieces. Roll each piece into a 9-inch rope and tie into a knot. Place the rolls 2 inches apart on greased baking sheets. Cover and let rise in a warm place until doubled, about 45 minutes. Meanwhile, preheat oven to 350. Bake for 15 minutes or until lightly browned. Remove from oven and brush with melted butter. Makes 42 rolls.

These are the best sweet rolls. My mother makes these for all our big family dinners. They don't last long around our house. Once you get the hang of it they are not very hard to make. I have never met anyone who didn't go nuts over them.

Katya Yakushev
Nevsky Branch
St. Petersburg Russia Stake
St. Petersburg, Russia

Zeigler's Chocolate Chip Pumpkin Bread

3 C. flour
2 tsp. cinnamon
1 tsp. salt
1 tsp. baking soda
4 eggs

2 C. sugar
2 C. canned pumpkin
1½ C. canola oil
1½ C. (6 oz.) semisweet chocolate chips

In a large bowl, combine the flour, cinnamon, salt, and baking soda. In a separate bowl, beat the eggs, sugar, pumpkin, and oil. Stir the pumpkin mixture into the dry ingredients just until moistened. Fold in chocolate chips. Pour into two greased 8 x 4-inch loaf pans. Bake at 350 for 60–70 minutes or until a toothpick inserted near the center comes out clean. Cool for 10 minutes before removing from pans to wire racks. Makes 2 loaves.

Nina Zeigler
Brownsburg Ward
Indianapolis Indiana North Stake
Brownsburg, Indiana

This is our top-secret pumpkin bread that we make a lot during the fall months. We end up sending loaves to all our family and friends because, in their words, "This stuff is so good it should be illegal." I think the chocolate chips really set this apart from your average pumpkin bread.

Whole-Wheat Tomato Juice Bread

3 Tbsp. yeast
1 C. warm water
1 Tbsp. sugar
1½ qt. water
1 qt. tomato juice

4 Tbsp. salt
1 C. honey
½ C. molasses
½ C. shortening
20 C. whole-wheat flour

In a small bowl, combine yeast, warm water, and sugar. Let stand until foamy. In a separate bowl, combine water, tomato juice, salt, honey, molasses, and shortening. Mix thoroughly. Add yeast mixture, then beat in 10 C. flour. Knead in 8–10 more cups of flour. I usually substitute about 2 C. of white flour. Add a little more flour if needed. Let rise until double. Shape into 7 loaves and place in well-greased pans. Let rise again to the tops of the pans. Bake at 350 for 40–45 minutes. Butter tops of loaves and turn on side to cool. Makes 7 loaves.

Ardith Pearson
Legacy Retirement Branch
South Jordan Utah River Ridge Stake
South Jordan, Utah

The secret ingredient in this recipe is tomato juice! It may not sound appealing, but it really does taste good! Ardith's daughter, Marylou Rimmasch, remembers: "Mom made bread every week, and usually about six to eight loaves. When I was little, I don't recall eating out very often and Mom was a killer with her budget. That pretty much meant that she made my clothing, quilts, bottled everything in sight, and never gave in when I begged for anything."

Hawaiian Zucchini Bread

2 C. flour
1 C. whole-wheat flour
1 tsp. salt
1 tsp. baking soda
1½ tsp. baking powder
1 Tbsp. ground cinnamon
½ tsp. nutmeg
2 ripe bananas, mashed
3 eggs

½ C. vegetable oil
½ C. unsweetened applesauce
1 C. packed brown sugar
1 C. sugar
2 tsp. vanilla extract
2½ C. zucchini, grated
1 C. walnuts, chopped
½ C. shredded coconut

(recipe continued on next page)

(Hawaiian Zucchini Bread, continued)

Preheat oven to 325. Grease and flour two 9 x 5-inch loaf pans. In a large bowl, whisk flour, whole-wheat flour, salt, baking soda, baking powder, cinnamon, and nutmeg. In a separate large bowl, beat the bananas, eggs, vegetable oil, applesauce, brown sugar, sugar, and vanilla. Stir the flour mixture into the wet mixture. Fold the zucchini, walnuts, and coconut into the batter until evenly combined. Pour into the prepared pans. Bake until a toothpick inserted into the center comes out clean, 40–50 minutes. Cool in the pans for 25 minutes before removing to cool completely on a wire rack. Makes 2 loaves (18 servings).

Tylie Vick
Hanalei Branch
Kauai Hawaii Stake
Princeville, Hawaii

We make this a lot to give to friends. People always say this is the best zucchini bread they have ever tasted. Now I just go ahead and attach the recipe to each loaf I give out, because everyone ends up wanting the recipe. My grandmother created this recipe, and fifty years later it's still the best.

Lunch Lady Rolls

3 C. warm water

1 Tbsp. sugar

3 .25-oz. envs. active dry yeast

¼ C. milk

2 eggs

1 Tbsp. salt

10 C. flour

⅔ C. sugar

¼ C. shortening

¼ C. butter, melted

In a large bowl, mix warm water and 1 Tbsp. sugar. Sprinkle yeast over the top; let it stand for about 10 minutes, until the yeast is foamy. Mix the milk, eggs, and salt into the yeast mixture. Into a separate bowl, measure the flour; add ⅔ C. sugar, and crumble the shortening into the flour mixture using your fingers until it is barely noticeable. Gradually stir the flour mixture into the yeast mixture. Using a wooden spoon, mix until the dough pulls away from the sides of the bowl and starts to form a ball around the spoon. Cover with a hot wet towel that has been wrung out, and set in a warm place to rise until double in bulk. This should take about 45 minutes. When the dough has risen, pour the melted butter over it, and knead for about 2 minutes. Let the dough rest for a few minutes, then roll out on a lightly floured surface to 1 inch thick. Use a knife to cut into 2-inch squares. Roll squares into balls, and place into greased round pans, spacing about 1 inch apart. Let rise again until doubled in size. You could also refrigerate the dough, letting it rise overnight for baking the next day. Bake at 400 for about 12 minutes, until golden brown. Makes 30 rolls.

Patricia Cabrera
Cabudare Ward
Barquisimeto Venezuela Stake
Barquisimeto, Lara
Venezuela

My sister Sylvie and her family immigrated to Florida, and she works in the cafeteria at my nephew's school. My nephew raves about his school rolls, so I asked Sylvie for the recipe. She makes these every day for the kids and I think they are heavenly—so fluffy.

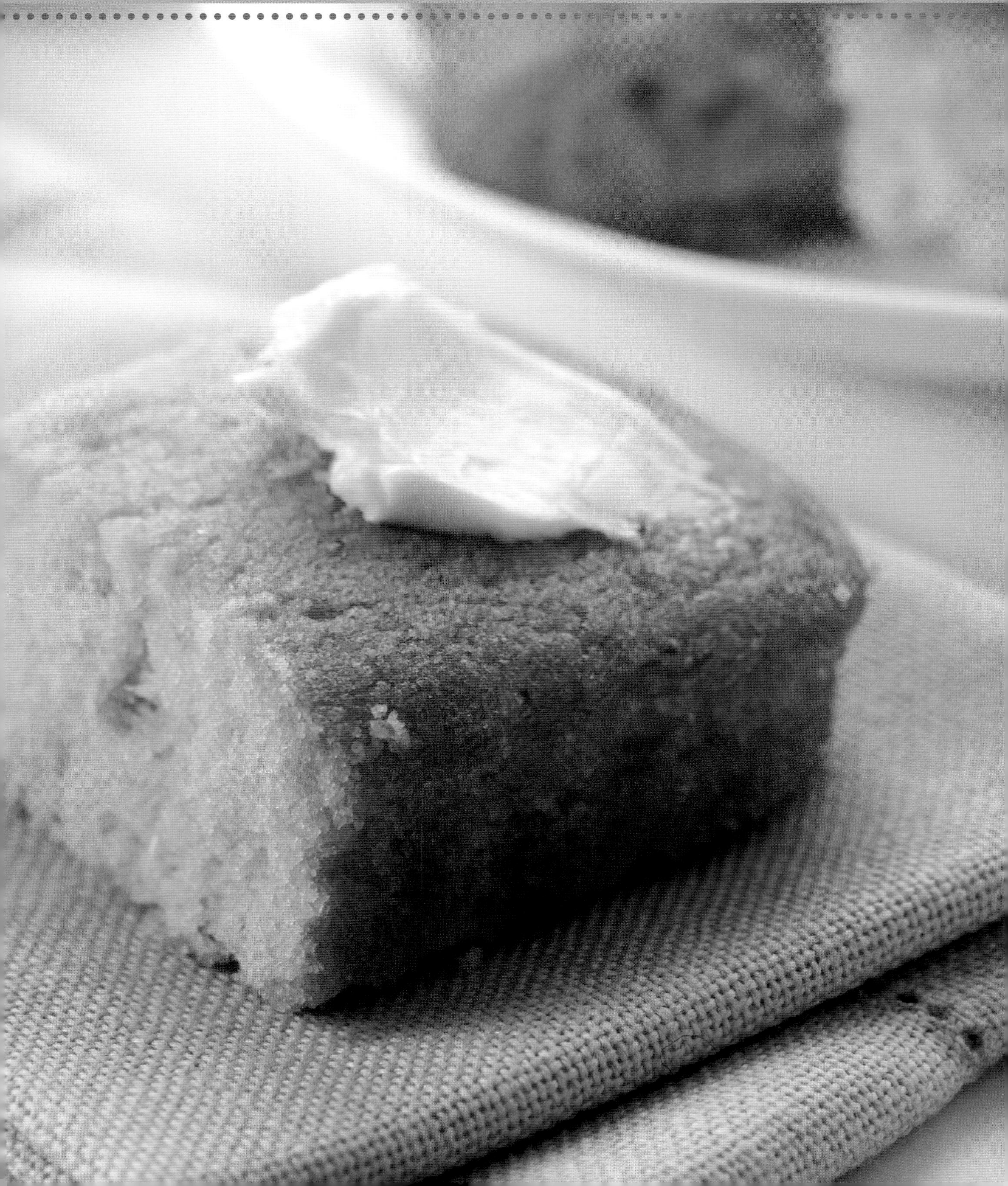

Cornbread with Honey Butter

Bread:

½ C. vegetable oil

1 C. sugar

2 eggs

2½ C. water, divided

2½ C. flour

1 C. pastry flour

½ C. powdered milk

2 Tbsp. baking powder

1 Tbsp. salt

1 Tbsp. vanilla

1 C. yellow cornmeal

Honey Butter:

⅓ C. honey

1 C. butter, softened

Bread: Preheat oven to 400. Grease a 9 x 13-inch baking pan. Set aside. In a large bowl, beat oil, sugar, and eggs for 2 minutes. Add 2 C. water and mix until blended. Add flours, powdered milk, baking powder, salt, and vanilla. Mix 10 minutes on low speed. Add remaining ½ C. water and cornmeal. Mix 5 additional minutes. Pour into prepared pan. Bake 40–50 minutes or until golden brown and toothpick inserted near center comes out clean. Serve with Honey Butter.

Honey Butter: Beat honey into softened butter until blended. Refrigerate in small molds or serve in bowls. Makes 12 servings.

Charles Wells
Terenure Ward
Dublin Ireland Stake
Dublin, Ireland

Bannoch

3 C. flour

1 Tbsp. baking powder

1 tsp. baking soda

1 Tbsp. sugar

1 tsp. salt

1½ C. buttermilk

½ C. sour cream or plain yogurt

Preheat oven to 350. Into a large bowl, sift flour, baking powder, baking soda, sugar, and salt. Sift the mixture two more times. Add buttermilk and sour cream; mix well. Form dough into a ball and transfer to a lightly floured surface (dough will be sticky). Roll dough into a 12 x 7 x 1-inch oval; score the top carefully and transfer to an ungreased baking sheet. Bake about 30 minutes or until loaf is brown. Serve warm. Makes 1 loaf.

This is definitely the most popular bread at our house. It is so easy and tastes out of this world. Most people think there is some secret ingredient, and are shocked when they find out that the recipe is full of nothing more than ordinary ingredients. It's amazing that combining those ingredients can make such delicious bread.

Clark Manning
Chevy Chase Ward
Washington DC Stake
Washington, DC

Super Moist Banana Bread

1 C. sugar

1 C. packed brown sugar

½ C. oil (I use olive oil, but any kind will do)

3 eggs

3 tsp. vanilla

1 12-oz. carton sour cream

4 ripe bananas

2½ C. flour

1 tsp. baking soda

1 tsp. baking powder

Pinch of salt

1 env. whipped topping mix (Dream Whip)

½–2 C. walnuts, coarsely chopped

Preheat oven to 350. Spray two loaf pans with nonstick spray or grease and flour them. Cream sugars, oil, and eggs. Add vanilla. Add sour cream and bananas; mix well with mixer. In a separate bowl, combine flour, baking soda, baking powder, salt, and powdered whipped topping. Add dry mixture to wet mixture and mix well. Stir in nuts. For an extra something, I'll sometimes add chocolate chips or flavored coffee creamers (Amaretto, hazelnut, etc). Just add whatever matches your mood or the season. Pour into prepared pans. Bake for approximately 40 minutes or until toothpick inserted near center comes out clean. Makes 2 loaves.

I got this recipe from a friend. The original was good, but I experimented with it and added some different ingredients. Everyone loves this bread and always asks for more. Some tell me this is their gift of choice. I have a housecleaning business and this is what I always give my customers for Christmas, their birthdays, or just to say thank you.

Jaelynne Nebeker
Stanley Lake Ward
Arvada Colorado Stake
Westminster, Colorado

Molly's Mom's Soft Biscuits

2 C. baking mix (Bisquick)

½ C. light sour cream

½ C. lemon-lime soda

Mix Bisquick and sour cream with pastry blender. Stir in soda. Pat lightly on a floured surface. This is a wet dough, so be sure to flour your surface well. Cut out biscuits and place 2 inches apart on ungreased cookie sheet. Bake at 400 for 10–12 minutes. Brush with melted butter and enjoy. Makes 10 servings.

Emma Goeller
Bridgewater Ward
Dartmouth Nova Scotia Stake
Dartmouth, Nova Scotia
Canada

This is a recipe my best friend's mother made for us when we were kids. I loved eating at their house. These biscuits are very soft and fluffy. These biscuits are truly secret because nobody ever guesses the unusual ingredient combination.

{ SIDE DISHES }

Secrets are things we give others to keep for us.

{ Elbert Hubbard }

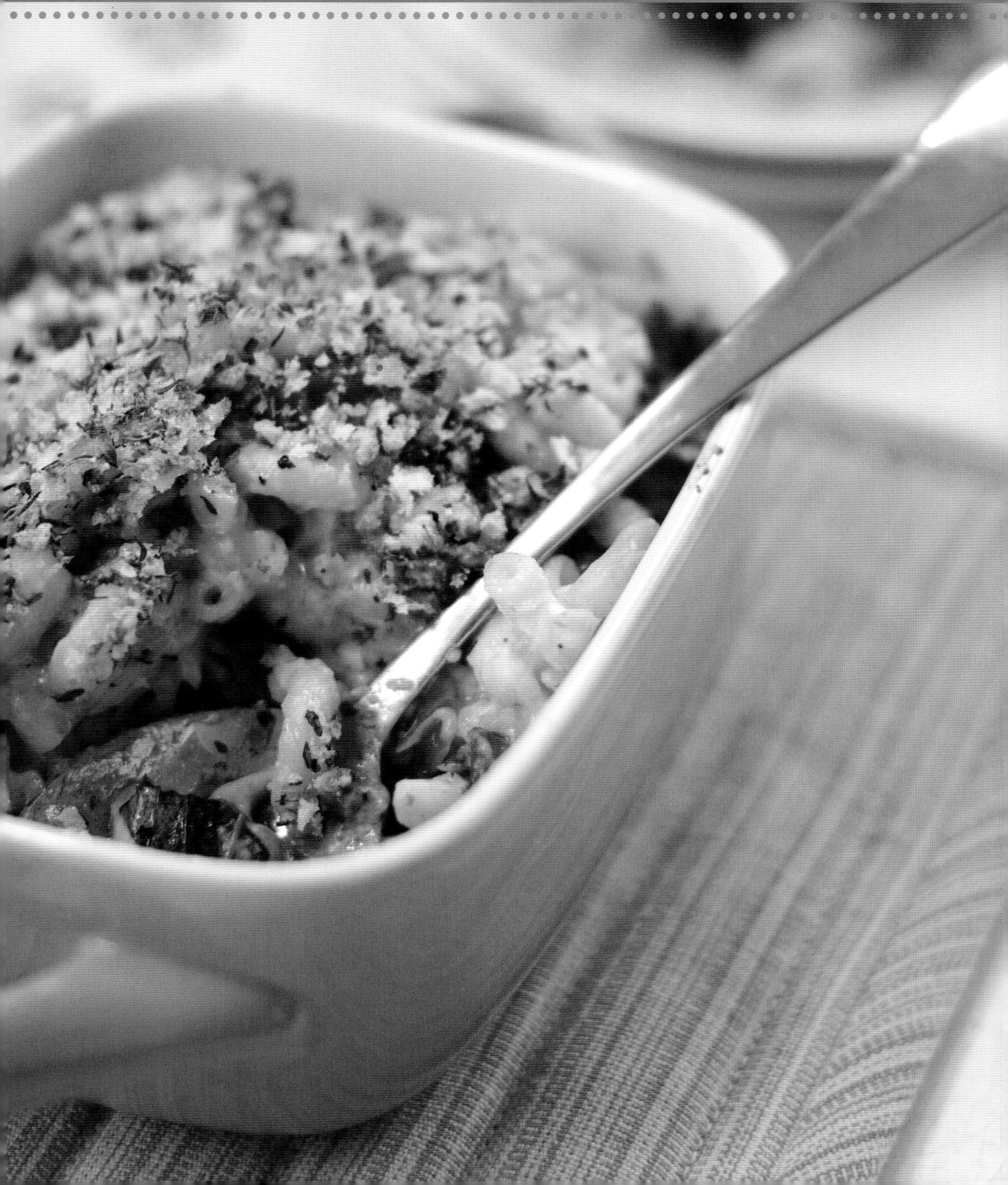

Cath's Mac

1 16-oz. pkg. macaroni
½ C. butter
2½ –3 Tbsp. flour
1½ C. heavy cream
1½ C. whole milk
Scant ½ tsp. granulated garlic
About 1 tsp. salt
About 1 tsp. fresh-ground black pepper

1½ C. Fontina cheese, shredded
1 C. Parmigiano Reggiano cheese, shredded
3 green onions, chopped (using both white and green parts)
3 or 4 whole pickled jalapeños, chopped
5 pieces good thick-cut bacon, fried and cut into pieces
½ C. Garlic Focciaca Croutons, smashed

Cook macaroni in salted water according to package directions; drain and return to pan. While pasta is cooking, chop and shred all ingredients and make sauce: Melt butter in sauté pan. Add flour; cook and stir. Add cream and milk; whisk into a loose roux. Whisk in granulated garlic, salt, and pepper. Cook over medium-high heat until it comes to a boil and thickens. Add cheeses and stir until melted. Stir in green onions, jalapeños, and bacon until well mixed. Pour sauce over pasta and stir well, thoroughly coating all the pasta. Place in baking dish and sprinkle crushed croutons on top. Place under broiler in oven until the topping is browned (it happens really quickly—I have burned many a topping, so watch carefully!). It is great as leftovers but different than when first made, because as it cools and sits the pasta absorbs the sauce. Makes 4–5 servings for people with a healthy appetite.

The secret to excellent mac and cheese is to not skimp on the ingredients. Start with good-quality pasta. Use real butter, whole milk, fresh cream, and excellent bacon. Perhaps the most important ingredient is the cheese. Get quality Fontina cheese. Sometimes I can find it shredded; other times I buy a wedge and shred it myself. Same with the Parmigiano Reggiano cheese; I use it over regular Parmesan because it melts the best. Cut fat and calories on other recipes but not when making great mac and cheese!

Cathy Croxton
South Mountain 7th Ward
South Mountain Utah Stake
Draper, Utah

Green Chile Rice

1 C. white rice
2 tsp. oil
¼ C. onion, diced

¼ C. green chiles, chopped
2 C. water
2 Tbsp. chicken bouillon or to taste

In a medium saucepan, combine rice, oil, and onion; stir over medium heat until the rice is slightly brown. Add green chiles, water, and chicken bouillon. Bring to a boil, then cover and simmer for 20 minutes until the water has evaporated. Makes 6 servings.

My mom made the best Spanish rice ever, and she always said the secret was tasting the chicken bouillon for just the right amount of flavor before adding it. She gave me this recipe to try, and I made it for my fellow cooks at girls' camp one year. They loved it! I love this recipe for its simplicity and ease.

Faith Altamirano
Safford 3rd Ward
Safford Arizona Stake
Safford, Arizona

Broccoli Rice Casserole

2 C. cooked white rice

2–3 10-oz. pkgs. frozen chopped broccoli, cooked and drained

1 10.75-oz. can cream of mushroom soup

1 8-oz. can sliced water chestnuts, drained

1 8-oz. can bamboo shoots

1 8-oz. jar processed American cheese (Cheez Whiz)

½ C. butter, melted

8-oz. cheddar cheese, shredded

1 2-oz. jar pimientos, drained

Preheat oven to 325. Mix all ingredients except for the shredded cheddar cheese and the pimientos. Pour into a greased 9 x 13-inch pan. Sprinkle cheese and pimientos over the top. Bake for 30–40 minutes. Makes 12 servings.

Vicki Tanner
Chapel Hill Ward
Lenexa Kansas Stake
Kansas City, Kansas

This is my own creation. I love broccoli cheesy rice casserole, so I made my own version by merging a few different recipes together. I always get asked for the recipe when I take this somewhere. It is one of the dishes my family looks forward to me making, and one of the first things to go at church gatherings.

Spinach Parmesan Rice Bake

1 12-oz. pkg. frozen spinach

2 C. cooked, cold white rice or brown rice

⅓ C. butter, melted

2 C. cheddar or Swiss cheese, shredded (or ¼–⅓ C. feta)

¾ C. Parmesan cheese, grated (or to taste)

⅓ C. onion, chopped (or 2 large green onions, chopped)

1–2 garlic cloves, minced (or ½–1 tsp. powder)

3 large eggs, beaten

¾ C. milk or half-n-half

Seasoning salt or salt to taste

½ tsp. fresh-ground black pepper (or to taste)

⅛ tsp. cayenne pepper, to taste (optional)

¼ C. Parmesan cheese, grated, for topping

Mozzarella cheese, grated (optional)

(recipe continued on next page)

(Spinach Parmesan Rice Bake, continued)

Preheat oven to 350. Generously grease an 11 x 7-inch baking dish. Cook spinach according to package directions; squeeze to remove all excess moisture. In a large bowl, combine spinach, cold rice, butter, cheeses, onion, garlic, eggs, and milk or half-n-half. Use a wooden spoon to mix well. Season with salt, pepper, and cayenne pepper to taste. Transfer the mixture to the prepared baking dish; sprinkle with ¼ C. Parmesan cheese. Bake, covered or uncovered, for 25 minutes or until set. Overbaking will cause a heavier, denser texture; if you prefer a lighter texture, bake just until set. If you like, top with mozzarella cheese the last 5 minutes of baking. Makes 10 servings.

I don't keep secrets too well when it comes to food, which is why I am sharing my mother-in-law's famous spinach rice bake. This recipe is a GRAND SLAM. This innovative and tasteful dish not only provides great food, but will make your family think you're a genius. It goes extremely well with chicken or steak. Trust me—you will enjoy it!

Josiah Brenner
Forest Lake Ward
Centennary Australia Stake
Brisbane, Australia

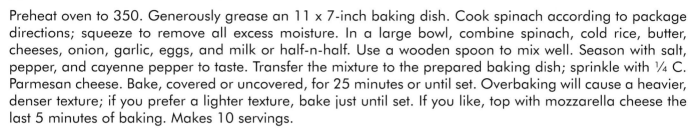

Aranitas

Aranitas:
1 green plantain
3 cloves garlic, minced
Salt and pepper to taste
Oil for frying

Garlic Dipping Sauce:
1 C. olive oil, warmed
1 head of garlic, peeled, crushed, and finely chopped
1 small onion, finely diced
3 Tbsp. cilantro, finely chopped
Juice of 1 lemon
Juice of 1 lime
Salt to taste

Aranitas: Peel the plantain and shred with a coarse grater. Place the grated plantain in salted water and let soak for about 10 minutes. Drain the grated plantain and dry with paper towels to soak up excess water. Mix the grated plantain with the garlic, salt, and pepper. Heat oil in a frying pan over medium-high heat. Fry the shredded mix by the spoonful in clumps until golden, about 5 minutes. Drain on paper towels and serve with Garlic Dipping Sauce. Makes 5 servings.

Garlic Dipping Sauce: Blend all ingredients in a glass or plastic bowl; it can also be processed in a blender, which makes it smoother.

Aranitas is a common dish. The secret that makes this recipe stand out is the Garlic Dipping Sauce—without it, these Aranitas are just like any other.

Walter Rivas
Palermo Ward
Buenos Aires Belgrano Stake
Buenos Aires, Argentina

FOR YOUR EYES ONLY

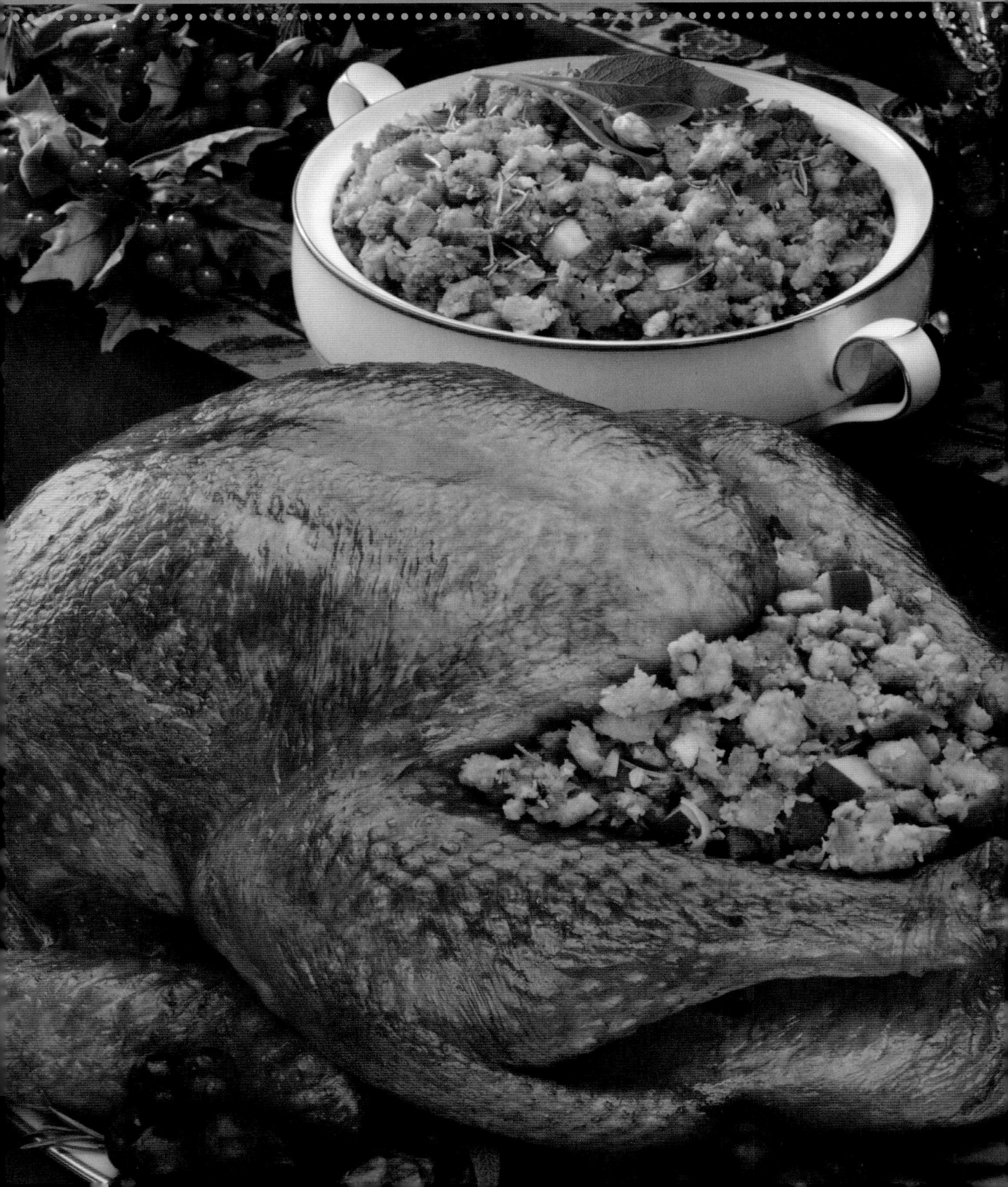

Mom's Awesome Secret Stuffing

1 loaf whole-wheat bread
1 loaf white bread
3 tsp. salt
1 tsp. pepper
3 tsp. sage
¾–1 C. raisins

¾ C. butter or margarine
1 C. onion, diced
¾ C. celery, diced
1 egg
½–¾ C. boiling water

Break bread into pieces into a very large bowl. Add salt, pepper, sage, and raisins. Add more sage if you like, but do NOT omit it or use any substitutions. Mix well with clean hands. In a saucepan, melt the butter; add diced onions and celery, and sauté just until soft (the onions and celery don't have to be completely tender, because they will cook inside the turkey). Pour the onion/celery mixture over the bread. In a small bowl, lightly beat the egg with a fork just until blended, then mix into bread mixture. Add boiling water to bread mixture: you want just enough water to moisten the mixture and hold it together; none of the bread should be dry. Start with ½ to ¾ C. and go from there, adding more if needed. Stuff the bird and stitch the end of the bird closed. Cook as directed for the bird. Will stuff up to a 15-lb. turkey.

My mom's stuffing has been a staple at every Thanksgiving since the day I was born. When I told my mom that I wanted to send in a recipe to this cookbook, she kept hinting at this recipe. She invented this stuffing when she first got married—she simply combined three different stuffing recipes that she liked, and this little beauty was born. Through the years, so many have requested it. I know Mom would be so flattered to see her "famous" stuffing here. Everyone needs a good stuffing recipe . . . packaged mixes just can't compare.

Elizabeth Henwood
Vicksburg Ward
Hattiesburg Mississippi Stake
Vicksburg, Mississippi

Lip-Smackin' Good Cinnamon Applesauce

4 apples, peeled, cored, and chopped (golden delicious)
¾ C. water

¼ C. sugar
½ tsp. ground cinnamon

In a saucepan, combine apples, water, sugar, and cinnamon. Cover and cook over medium heat for 15–20 minutes, or until apples are soft. Allow to cool, then mash using beaters or potato masher. Doesn't homemade applesauce make you think of home? Makes 6 servings.

Claire Mandrake
Bismarck Ward
Bismarck North Dakota Stake
Bismarck, North Dakota

Baked Zucchini

5 medium zucchini
1 large green pepper
1 large onion
2 C. bread crumbs
½ tsp. sweet basil

½ C. sharp cheese, grated
⅓ C. salad oil
2 eggs, beaten
Salt and pepper to taste

Grind zucchini, pepper, and onion together; my mom used a meat grinder, but a food processor would also work well. Mix with bread crumbs, basil, cheese, oil, eggs, salt, and pepper. Bake in buttered casserole dish at 350 for 45 minutes. Makes 10–12 servings.

Derlene Housley
Battlecreek 10th Ward
Pleasant Grove Utah East Stake
Pleasant Grove, Utah

In the 1950s this recipe won $100 in a *Los Angeles Times* recipe contest. My mom picked it up and served it every Thanksgiving and Christmas as our holiday vegetable. It was delicious to me even as a child. I am very grateful to this day that Mom fixed dinner every night and our family gathered to eat together. Her mother was raised on a farm in Illinois, always grew a big garden, and served chicken and dumplings every Sunday. I am grateful for my heritage of home-cooked meals with the family together at the table!

Waverly's Sweet Potatoes

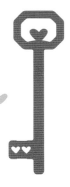

4 lbs. sweet potatoes, pared and sliced
1½ C. sugar
2 eggs
½ C. raisins
Grated rind and juice of 1 lemon
½ tsp. cinnamon
½ tsp. nutmeg

½ C. evaporated milk
½ C. pecans, chopped
½ C. butter or margarine, melted
½ C. shredded coconut
Miniature marshmallows

(recipe continued on next page)

(Waverly's Sweet Potatoes, continued)

Place the potatoes in a pot and add enough salted water to cover. Cook until tender. Drain. Preheat the oven to 350. Mash and whip the potatoes. Add the remaining ingredients (except marshmallows) and mix well. Pour into a greased casserole dish. Bake for 30 minutes. Remove from the oven and cover with marshmallows. Return to the oven and continue cooking until browned. Makes 8 servings.

I got this recipe from my sister, Waverly. My mom always made her sweet potatoes every Thanksgiving, then suddenly, out of nowhere, my sister insisted on making a new sweet potato dish. We all love it so much, and it's been a staple at our holiday meals for the last seven years. I love the addition of coconut and raisins. You won't find a gem like this anywhere—it's definitely a recipe our family will keep carrying down the line.

Emerson Jeter
Kihei 1st Ward
Kahului Hawaii Stake
Kihei, Hawaii

Kokonut Rice

2 Tbsp. canola or vegetable oil
½ tsp. garlic, minced
⅓ C. Spanish or red onion, diced
1 C. Basmati rice (may substitute with Jasmine or long-grain rice)
1 C. water
1 can unsweetened coconut milk (shake well)

1 tsp. kosher salt
Pinch white pepper (optional)
¼ C. carrots, grated
¼ C. shredded sweetened coconut
1 Tbsp. cilantro, finely chopped (may use parsley)

Place oil in saucepan over medium-high heat. Add garlic and onion and sauté for 1 minute. Add rice and stir until rice is coated with oil. Add water and stir well. Bring to a boil. Add coconut milk; stir and cover. Lower heat to a simmer. Let cook for 15 minutes undisturbed. Remove lid and add salt, pepper, carrots, and coconut. Fluff and mix with a fork quickly. If rice looks too dry, add a couple tablespoons of water. Replace lid and let simmer for five minutes. Remove from heat and let set for five minutes. Fluff rice gently, taste, and adjust seasoning if needed. Garnish with cilantro and serve. Makes 6 servings.

Monique David
Nancy Ward
Nancy France Stake
Nancy, France

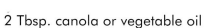

This is my family's secret rice recipe. We have eaten our rice this way for as long as I can remember. I love spices and seasonings and tons of flavor in my food. This is one of my favorite ways to prepare rice, and I hope you find it just as lovely as I do.

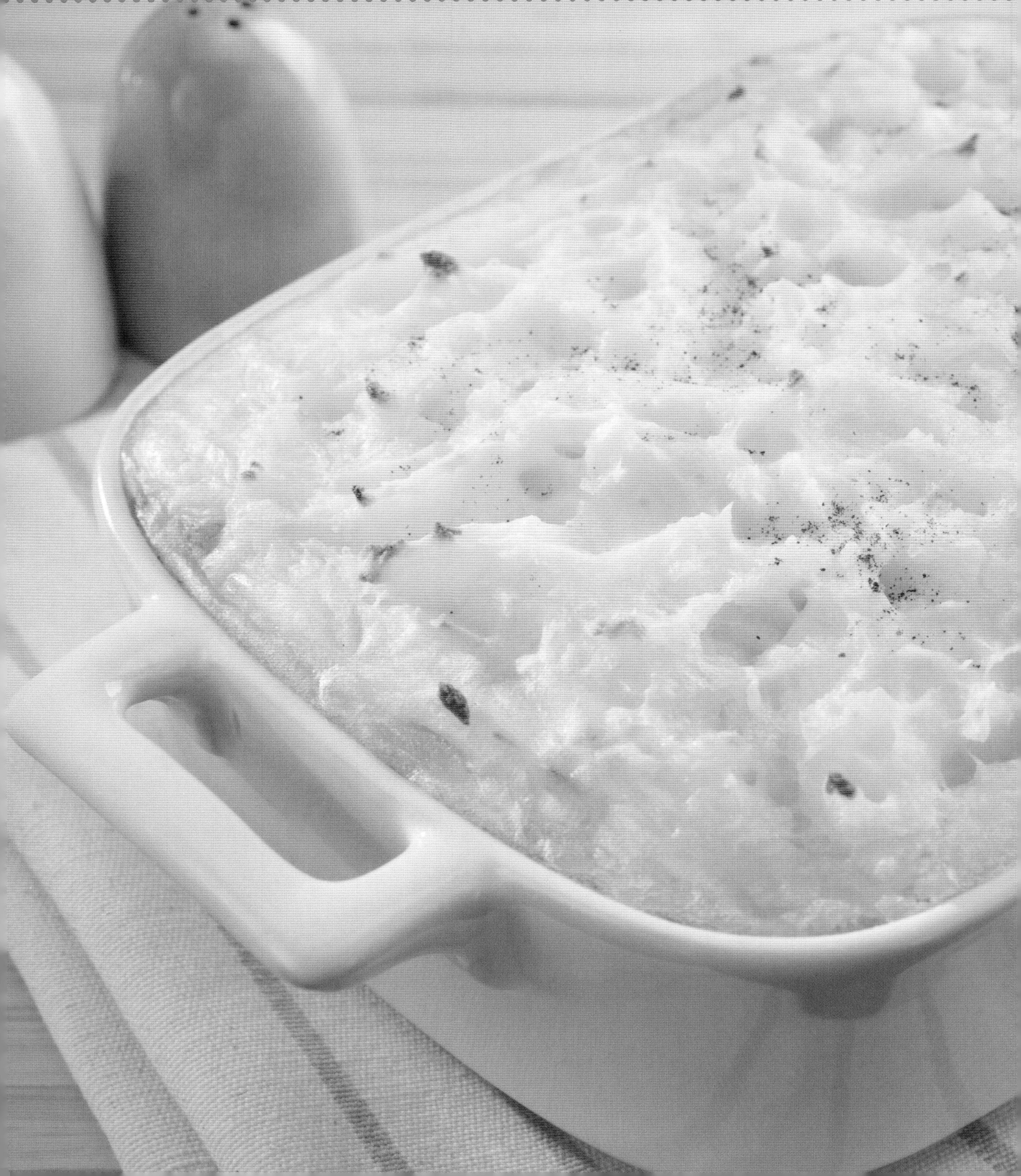

Slow-Cooker Mashed Potatoes

5 lb. red potatoes, cut into chunks
1 Tbsp. minced garlic, or to taste
3 cubes chicken bouillon
1 8-oz. container sour cream

1 8-oz. pkg. cream cheese, softened
¼ C. butter
Salt and pepper to taste

In a large pot of lightly salted boiling water, cook the potatoes, garlic, and bouillon until potatoes are tender but firm, about 15 minutes. Drain, reserving water. In a bowl, mash potatoes with sour cream and cream cheese, adding reserved water as needed to attain desired consistency. Transfer the potato mixture to a slow-cooker. Cover with a terrycloth towel (to soak up any water and keep moisture from seeping back into potatoes) and then cover with lid. Cook on low for 2–3 hours. Check and stir every so often. Just before serving, stir in butter and season with salt and pepper to taste. To make garlic mashed potatoes, use garlic and herb cream cheese, sprinkle some garlic salt in place of regular salt, and put in a couple of sprinkles of oregano at the beginning of cooking. Then stir in 1 C. Italian cheese blend near the end of cooking. Makes 12 servings.

This is the only way I make potatoes. I can do all the prep work a day or two ahead of time and store the crock in the cooler. Then the only step I have to do is cook them in the slow-cooker for a few hours. It makes everything easier, especially when trying to prepare a big dinner. My family really loves these potatoes. They would have a fit if they were not served at all the family gatherings.

Nancy Crabtree
Lake Shawnee Ward
Topeka Kansas Stake
Topeka, Kansas

Mom's Super Sneaky Broccoli

1 bunch broccoli, cut into bite-size pieces
1 tsp. kosher salt (more to taste if desired)

1 Tbsp. sesame seed oil

Steam broccoli in water to desired doneness. Drain and immediately toss with the kosher salt and sesame seed oil. We use the same recipe to make green beans, carrots, and brussels sprouts, and my children LOVE them. Makes 4 servings.

The secret is that kids will actually eat these healthy veggies when prepared this way! YOUR KIDS WILL EAT THIS. I cannot explain the magic, but my children would not touch broccoli until I prepared it this way. They never realize that they are eating wholesome veggies!

Sarah Coleman
Iowa City 1st Ward
Iowa City Iowa Stake
North Liberty, Iowa

Porches' Hot Pineapple Casserole

54-oz. can pineapple chunks
¾ C. sugar
¼ C. flour

1 C. sharp cheddar cheese, shredded
1 sleeve Ritz crackers, crushed
3 Tbsp. butter, melted

Preheat oven to 350. Pour pineapple into colander and drain for about 20 seconds. Combine pineapple, sugar, flour, and cheese. Mix well. Pour into greased baking dish. Spread crushed crackers over the top. Pour melted butter evenly over the crackers. Bake for 25 minutes or until golden brown and slightly bubbly. Makes 12 servings.

Rita Woolley Penix
Lindon 16th Ward
Lindon Utah West Stake
Lindon, Utah

This recipe comes from my cousin, Celia, and her husband, Al McSweyn. They own and operate a wonderful restaurant called Porches in Wesson, Mississippi. It is in an old Victorian home with the big front porch that was so popular in the old South, and all who come to visit are treated like family. It is always so much fun to visit every year when I return to my Mississippi roots. This pineapple casserole is one of my favorites. It is served at Porches as a side dish, but it is also a terrific dessert with a scoop of ice cream. Yum!

Grandma Givens' Mac and Cheese

2 C. dry elbow macaroni (8 oz.)
4 Tbsp. nonfat dry milk powder
2 Tbsp. flour
1 Tbsp. butter or margarine, melted

1¼ C. boiling water
3 C. American cheese, shredded, divided
   (12 oz.)
¼ tsp. salt

Cook macaroni according to package directions; drain well. Preheat oven to 350. In a large bowl, mix dry milk, flour, and butter. Gradually add boiling water, beating constantly. Add 1½ C. of the cheese and continue beating until smooth and creamy. Stir in cooked and drained macaroni, 1 C. of the remaining cheese, and salt. Transfer to lightly greased 2-qt. baking dish. Cover with foil. Bake 25 minutes. Remove foil. Sprinkle with remaining ½ C. cheese. Continue baking 1 minute or until cheese melts. Makes 6 servings.

Chezna Givens
Durban 1st Ward
Durban South Africa Stake
Durban, South Africa

Grandma Givens is known for this creamy mac, and she would probably throw a fit if she knew I was giving away her secret recipe for mac and cheese. It is my absolute favorite mac and cheese ever, so it would be tragic not to pass this gem on to others. I guess what Grandma Givens doesn't know can't hurt her, so enjoy!

Baked Corn

3 eggs, well beaten
1 tsp. salt
⅛ tsp. pepper
¼ C. green pepper, chopped
¼ C. onion, chopped
1 small jar pimiento, drained and chopped

4–6 soda crackers, crushed
1 16-oz. can cream-style corn
1 14.5-oz. can evaporated milk
2 Tbsp. butter
Paprika

In a medium bowl combine eggs, salt, pepper, green pepper, onion, pimiento, crackers, and corn. Set aside. In a small saucepan, heat milk and butter until butter melts. Stir milk into egg-corn mixture. Pour into a buttered 1½-quart casserole dish. Bake at 350 for 50 minutes. Sprinkle top with paprika. Makes 8 servings.

The secret to my corn is baking it. I love creamed corn, and even the creamed corn haters I have served this to enjoy this dish.

Pemberlyn Knickerbocker
Portsmouth Ward
Exeter New Hampshire Stake
Portsmouth, New Hampshire

Smokestack Cheesy Corn Bake

2 Tbsp. butter or margarine
4 tsp. flour
⅛ tsp. garlic powder
¾ C. milk

1½ C. sharp cheddar cheese, shredded
1 3-oz. pkg. cream cheese, cut up
3 10-oz. pkgs. frozen whole-kernel corn, thawed
3 oz. ham, diced

In a large saucepan, melt butter; stir in flour and garlic powder. Add milk; cook and stir over medium heat until thick and bubbly. Stir in cheeses; cook and stir over low heat until cheeses melt. Stir in corn and ham. Pour into a 2-qt. casserole. Bake at 350 for 45 minutes. Makes 10 servings.

This recipe has been carried down for generations. My grandparents were great cooks who passed the cooking gene down to me. This is on my top five list of favorite family recipes.

Gaines Jopplin
Lake Nokomis Ward
Minneapolis Minnesota Stake
Minneapolis, Minnesota

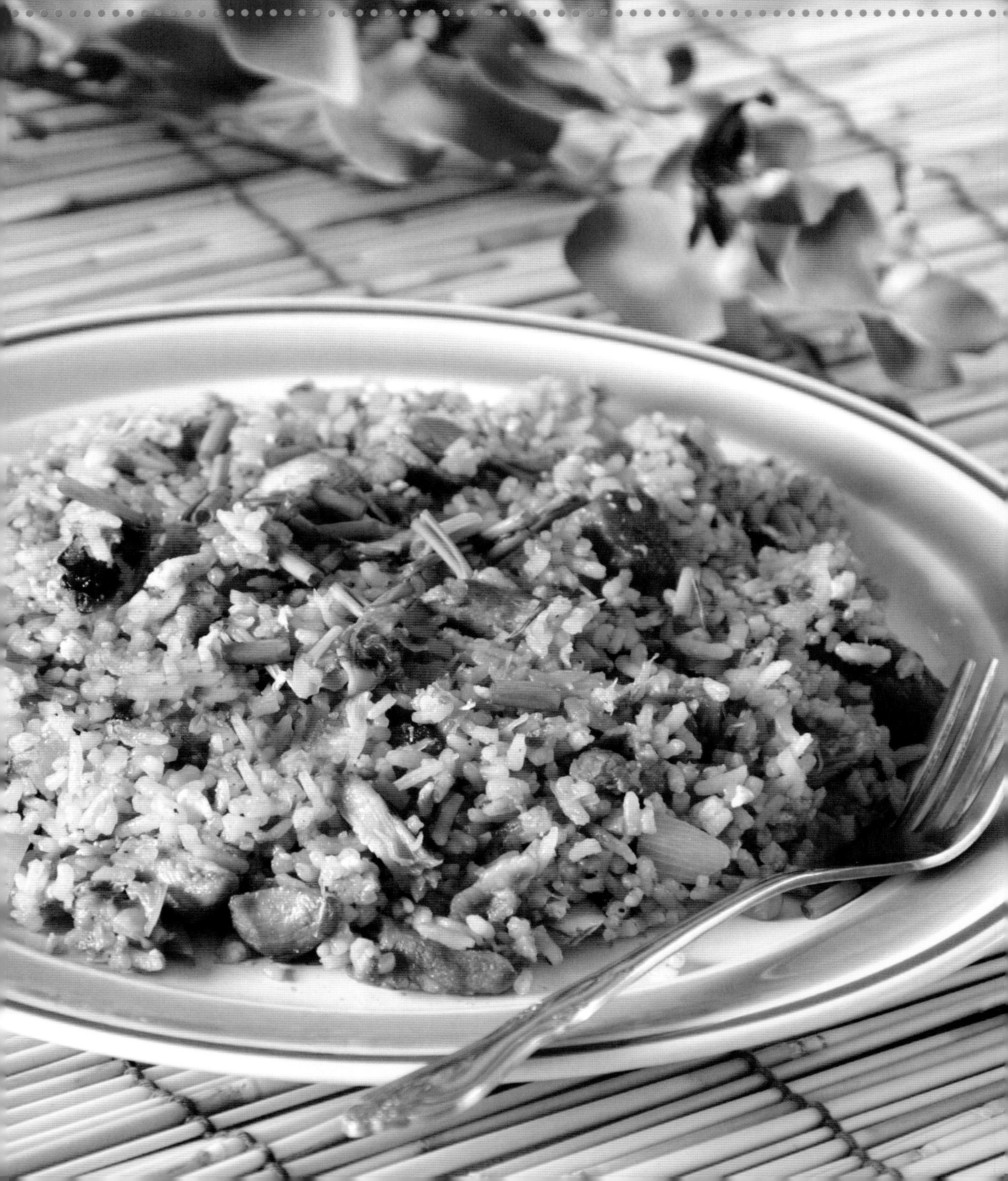

Taiwanese Fried Rice

5 C. cooked white rice

2 eggs

4 stalks spring onion, thinly sliced

Pinch salt

Pinch pepper

1 tsp. oil (for eggs)

1 Tbsp. oil (for rice)

4 cloves garlic, crushed

5 oz. lean pork, julienned (can use chicken or a can of tuna)

½ C. carrot, finely sliced

2 C. cabbage, sliced

⅓ C. chicken stock

3 Tbsp. soy sauce

Break the rice into individual grains with your hands and set aside. Beat eggs; stir in ¼ of the spring onions and the salt and pepper. Mix well. Heat a frying pan to a low heat and smear with 1 tsp. oil. Poor the egg mixture into the hot pan and spread to a thin layer. Cook just until done. Slice into small pieces and put aside. Heat 1 Tbsp. oil in wok at a very low heat. Add garlic and fry for a minute to flavor the oil, but don't let the garlic brown. Remove garlic, leaving as much oil in the wok as possible. Bring wok to full heat. Add pork, stirring rapidly for 30 seconds. One by one add the carrots, cabbage, and remaining spring onions while stirring. Add the stock and the soy sauce. Return the garlic to the wok if you like. Cook vegetables for no more than a few minutes. Add rice and stir everything together for a few minutes. If rice starts to stick to wok, reduce heat. Add the egg pieces and cook for a minute more before serving on a plate. Makes 4 servings.

Glen Brownlee
Xihu Ward
ZhongXing Taiwan Stake
Xihu, Taiwan

The secret to great fried rice is the rice—always use leftover rice. Fresh-cooked rice is too gooey to make good fried rice. If you don't have leftover rice, then make the rice, remove the lid, let it cool for a while, and then put it in the refrigerator for a couple of hours with the lid off. Stir it a few times so that it cools and dries before you use it.

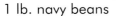

Cider Baked Beans

1 lb. navy beans
1 tsp. salt
3 Tbsp. brown sugar
1 tsp. dry mustard
¼ C. molasses

¼ C. ketchup
1 C. onion, chopped
2 C. cider
¼ lb. bacon

Soak beans overnight in a covered crock. Drain and place in a 2-qt. baking dish. Add remaining ingredients except bacon and stir to mix. Arrange bacon strips on top. Bake at 275 for 6 hours. Check occasionally and add more cider if needed. Makes 8 servings.

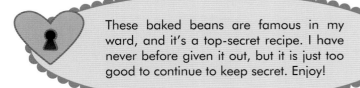

These baked beans are famous in my ward, and it's a top-secret recipe. I have never before given it out, but it is just too good to continue to keep secret. Enjoy!

Pemberlyn Knickerbocker
Portsmouth Ward
Exeter New Hampshire Stake
Portsmouth, New Hampshire

McCall Family Smashed Taters

5 large russet potatoes, quartered
½ C. butter (no substitute!)
2-4 Tbsp. sour cream
¼ C. heavy cream

Green onion, finely chopped (optional, use any amount desired)
Salt and pepper (lots of pepper!)

Cook the potatoes in boiling salted water for 13–15 minutes or until just fork-tender. Don't overcook the potatoes, or your smashed potato mixture will be very soft. Drain well and place in a large bowl. While the potatoes are still hot, add butter and mash lightly. Add sour cream and heavy cream; mash, but leave chunks in the potato mixture. Stir in the chopped green onions, if you like. Season with salt and lots of pepper to taste. Makes 8 servings.

Jerry McCall
Casper 6th Ward
Casper Wyoming Stake
Casper, Wyoming

Stuffed Spuds

4 medium sweet potatoes

¾ C. pecans, coarsely chopped

¼ C. butter

1 large apple, chopped

¼ C. golden raisins

½ C. firmly packed brown sugar

½ tsp. ground cinnamon

¼ tsp. ground nutmeg

Place potatoes on foil-lined baking sheet. Bake at 425 for 1 hour and 15 minutes, or until tender. In a skillet, heat pecans over medium-low heat, stirring often, for 5–7 minutes or until toasted. Set aside. In a medium saucepan, melt butter over medium-high heat. Add apples and raisins. Sauté 2–3 minutes or until apples are tender. Stir in brown sugar, cinnamon, and nutmeg. Remove from heat. Cut potatoes in half lengthwise; scoop out pulp into a large bowl, leaving shells (skins) intact. Add apple mixture to pulp in bowl. Stir until blended. Spoon mixture into shells. Place on baking sheet; bake at 350 for 15–20 minutes or until heated through. Top with additional nuts. Makes 8 servings.

This is a secret recipe my grandmother used to make for me on special occasions. It's a recipe that has been passed down for generations. We love making these feel-good treats. I was especially delighted to see these at a steak house in the United States when I visited a few years ago—although I have to say my recipe is better than the steakhouse version. Toasting the nuts and adding the apples make this recipe outstanding.

Nell McPhee
Invergordon Branch
Aberdeen Scotland Stake
Aberdeen, Scotland

Au Gratin Potatoes

3 lb. potatoes, peeled and sliced thin

1 onion, sliced thin

2 C. heavy cream

¼ tsp. thyme

2 Tbsp. garlic, minced

1¼ tsp. salt

1¼ tsp. pepper

1 Tbsp. butter

4 oz. Parmesan cheese, grated

Preheat oven to 350. Combine potatoes and onion and put into a baking dish. Mix cream, thyme, garlic, salt, and pepper; pour mixture over potatoes and onions and cover. Bake for about one hour. When potatoes are tender, remove from oven and sprinkle with Parmesan cheese. Put back in the oven uncovered and bake for 10 minutes more until cheese is browned. Makes 12 servings.

Charles Wells
Terenure Ward
Dublin Ireland Stake
Dublin, Ireland

Sheryl's Easy Potato Bake

8 potatoes, peeled and thinly sliced

Aromat (Knorr all-purpose seasoning)

2 C. heavy cream

2 C. cheese, grated

In a buttered dish, layer the thinly sliced potatoes and sprinkle very, very generously with Aromat. Pour cream over the potatoes, cover with tin foil, and bake at 350 for 30–40 minutes. Check to see if it is done by pricking potatoes with a fork; the cream should also have thickened. When done, remove the tin foil and sprinkle grated cheese over the potatoes; put back in the oven for 15 minutes. When the cheese has melted and is crispy, serve (preferably immediately) as a side dish with any meal. Especially good with a braai (barbecue). Makes 6–8 servings.

Sheryl Human
East London 1st Ward
East London South Africa Stake
East London, Eastern Cape
South Africa

The secret to this recipe is the Aromat; it's worth the search to find it. You can always buy it online if you can't find it in your stores. In South Africa, for as long as I can remember, we had a braai (barbecue) or two every weekend, and my mom always made this potato dish. Today, forty years later, we seldom braai with out having this potato dish as a side dish. When braaiing with friends, we often take it along instead of a salad.

St. Paul's Rice

1 lb. hot spicy breakfast sausage

4 C. water

½ C. rice

2 1.25-oz. envs. dry chicken noodle soup mix

1 green pepper, diced

1 onion, diced

1 C. celery, chopped (optional)

⅓ C. blanched almonds (for topping)

Crumble sausage and brown in skillet or microwave until no longer pink. Drain and break up with fork until crumbled. Bring water to a boil; add rice and chicken soup mix. Cook for 7 minutes. Mix in all remaining ingredients and spoon into a 9 x 13-inch dish. Sprinkle almonds on top. Cook uncovered at 350 for 1 hour. Makes 6 servings.

Lucia Delgado
Andres Bello Branch
Barquisimeto Venezuela Stake
Barquisimeto, Lara
Venezuela

FOR YOUR EYES ONLY

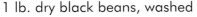

Cuban Black Beans

1 lb. dry black beans, washed
¼ C. olive oil
1 large onion, chopped
1 medium green bell pepper, chopped
6 cloves garlic, peeled and minced
5 C. water

1 6-oz. can tomato paste
1 4-oz. jar diced pimientos, drained
1 Tbsp. vinegar
2 tsp. salt
1 tsp. white sugar
1 tsp. black pepper

Place beans in a large saucepan with enough water to cover. Soak 8 hours, or overnight; drain. In a large saucepan, heat oil over medium heat; sauté onion, green bell pepper, and garlic until tender. Into the onion mixture, stir the drained beans, water, tomato paste, pimientos, and vinegar. Season with salt, sugar, and pepper. Bring to a boil. Cover, reduce heat, and simmer 1½ hours, stirring occasionally, until beans are tender. Makes 8 servings.

Growing up in Miami means lots of Cuban-style food. This is a secret black bean recipe from my grandmother. They are the only beans I make, and I have to say they are awesome! The vinegar and sugar make these beans so unique.

Melissa Stehling
Miami 4th Ward
Miami Florida South Stake
Miami, Florida

Sticky Rice with Mango

1 C. sticky rice
1 C. coconut milk
2 Tbsp. sugar

2 pinches salt
1 ripe mango

Cover the rice with water and let soak for at least an hour or as long as overnight. Put water in the bottom of a rice steamer and cover the steam section with cheesecloth or muslin. Pour the rice on the cheesecloth, cover with the lid, and put the steamer on the stove over medium to high heat. Steam for approximately 20 minutes; the rice will become translucent when done. In a medium saucepan, heat the coconut milk over medium heat, stirring constantly, until the milk simmers. Stir in the sugar and salt. Remove from heat. Pour ¾ of the hot coconut milk over the hot sticky rice. Let it sit for 5 minutes; the sticky rice will absorb all the coconut milk, and it should be a little mushy. Peel and slice the mango. Place the sticky rice on small plates, top with the mango, and spoon the remaining coconut milk over the mango and sticky rice. Makes 4 servings.

Summer Xia Chen
Bangkok International Ward
Bangkok Thailand Stake
Bangkok, Thailand

Sticky Rice with Mango is one of my favorite things. Mangoes are plentiful during the summer months of April and May. I crave this dish—not just because it is so delicious, but because eating it reminds me of the carefree days of summer when I was a child.

{ SOUPS }

Of course I can keep secrets. It's the people I tell them to that can't keep them.

{ Anthony Haden }

Beef Stew for Busy Bees

2 lb. beef stew meat, cut into 1-inch cubes
¼ C. flour
½ tsp. salt
½ tsp. pepper
1 clove garlic, minced
1 bay leaf
1 tsp. paprika

1 tsp. Worcestershire sauce
1 onion, chopped
1½ C. beef broth
3 potatoes, diced
4 carrots, sliced
1 stalk celery, chopped

Place meat in slow-cooker. In a small bowl, mix the flour, salt, and pepper; pour over meat, and stir to coat meat with flour mixture. Stir in the garlic, bay leaf, paprika, Worcestershire sauce, onion, beef broth, potatoes, carrots, and celery. Cover and cook on low for 10–12 hours or on high for 4–6 hours. Remove the bay leaf before serving. Makes 6 servings.

The secret to this stew is that you don't have to brown the beef and you can just throw all the ingredients into a slow-cooker at the same time. It is so easy and SO yummy. This is my favorite stew, especially on a cold night, and the kids gobble it up! This is definitely the perfect recipe for busy people who don't have time to slave over the stove yet want a good home-cooked meal.

Ada Bach
Pinneberg Ward
Neumünster Germany Stake
Pinneberg, Germany

Down-Home Cheddar Cheese Soup

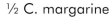 ½ C. margarine
½ C. each celery, green pepper, onion, carrot, and cauliflower, all finely chopped
1 Tbsp. granulated chicken bouillon or 2 cubes chicken bouillon
2 C. water

½ C. margarine
⅔ C. flour
4 C. whole milk
½ pound (2 C.) sharp cheddar cheese, shredded

In a soup pot, heat ½ C. margarine over medium heat. Add vegetables. Cook until tender, stirring often. Add chicken bouillon and water. Heat to boiling. Cover; cook over low heat for 10 minutes. Meanwhile, in a large saucepan, heat ½ C. margarine. Stir in flour and cook until bubbly. Remove from heat and gradually stir in milk. Cook over medium heat, stirring often until thickened, but do not boil. Stir in cheese until fully blended. Stir cheese mixture into vegetable/chicken broth mixture. Enjoy! Makes 8 servings.

This is my favorite soup. The secret is to use a high-quality cheese, and don't be afraid to add a little extra if you feel like it. I use smoked sharp cheddar, which I think gives this the best flavor, but plain cheddar is very nice too.

Melodee Finch
Lake Norman Ward
Gastonia North Carolina Stake
Mooresville, North Carolina

Vickie's Clam Chowder

8 slices bacon
1 C. onions, finely chopped
1 C. celery, finely diced
2 C. potatoes, diced
1 C. carrots, diced
1 6½-oz. can minced clams
1 6½-oz. can chopped clams

¾ C. butter
¾ C. flour
1 qt. half-n-half
1½ tsp. salt
Dash of pepper
1 Tbsp. sugar
1 tsp. thyme

Cook bacon (I do it in the oven), let cool, and crumble. Set aside. Place all veggies in a saucepan and drain clam juice from both cans over the top of the veggies. Add enough water to barely cover; cook the veggies until tender but not falling apart, about 20 minutes. Meanwhile, melt the butter in a large pot. Add flour, blending with a wire whisk, cooking for at least 2 minutes. Add half-n-half to the butter/flour mixture and stir until smooth. Drain veggies; stir veggies into the half-n-half mixture. Stir in the clams, seasonings, and the bacon! Heat through and serve immediately with bread bowls or lots of rolls. Makes 8–10 servings.

My mom died of pancreatic cancer in April 2009, but her smile, her love, and her love of cooking live on through her family. I remember making this recipe with her on a crisp autumn evening and begging her for the recipe that night. It was always her "Top Secret Clam Chowder," but I think that she would be very honored to know that so many other people can enjoy it as well. She loved to cook because it brought our family together every day no matter what our day was like. Her food brought out the best in all of us. I recently discovered that cooking is fun not because of the food, but because of what it does for people. It fulfills us and makes us stronger—and what more could a mother want to do for her family?

Krystal Webb
Sharon 8th Ward
Orem Utah Sharon Stake
Orem, Utah

REAL Tortilla Soup

1 C. carrot, diced
1 C. celery, sliced
1 C. onion, diced
2 Tbsp. corn oil
½ tsp. garlic powder or 1 garlic clove, minced
⅛ tsp. salt
¼ tsp. pepper
4 15-oz. cans chicken broth
1 15-oz. can tomatoes, diced (optional)

1 10-oz. can tomatoes & chiles, diced (Rotel)
1 env. taco seasoning
12 oz. chicken meat, poached and diced
1 pkg. (8–10) corn tortillas
12 oz. Monterey Jack cheese or Mexican blend cheese, shredded, divided
1 C. milk
Corn tortilla chips, broken into small pieces

(recipe continued on next page)

(REAL Tortilla Soup, continued)

Sauté carrots, celery, and onions in corn oil, garlic, salt, and pepper until tender. Add chicken broth and bring to boil. Add tomatoes, tomatoes/chiles, taco seasoning, and chicken. Cut tortillas into small pieces and add to broth mixture (use more tortillas for thicker soup). Let boil for 20 minutes or until tortillas are thoroughly incorporated into soup, stirring occasionally to keep from sticking. Reduce heat and add 8 oz. cheese. Simmer for additional 10 minutes. Add milk and simmer for additional 10 minutes. Garnish with remaining shredded cheese and broken tortilla chips. Substitutions: Use 1 C. masa harina (masa flour) instead of the corn tortillas. Gradually add masa flour, mixing thoroughly into broth. (Use more masa for thicker soup.) You can also use grilled chicken fajita meat instead of poached diced chicken. Makes 6 servings.

Emma Goeller
Bridgewater Ward
Dartmouth Nova Scotia Stake
Dartmouth, Nova Scotia
Canada

I spent a year on the border between Mexico and Texas and saw many versions of tortilla soup. Now that I've had great tortilla soup there, it's hard to adjust to tortilla soup anywhere else. Many so-called tortilla soup recipes are nothing but a glorified chicken soup with tortillas and tomatoes added. Here's the real McCoy. Hope you like it!

Ajiaco

2 Tbsp. butter

3 lb. chicken

1 C. onions, finely diced

2 cloves garlic, minced

1 tsp. cayenne pepper

2 tsp. sweet paprika

1 C. chicken stock

3 C. milk

2 large yucca

4 ears corn

Juice of 1 lime

Melt the butter in a pot over medium heat. Cut chicken into bite-size pieces and cook in the butter until no longer pink. Remove chicken and place in a bowl. Put onion, garlic, cayenne, and paprika in pot and cook, stirring, until onion is soft and colored with the paprika. Add chicken stock and milk to the pot. Peel the yucca and cut into 1-inch cubes. Shuck the corn and slice the ears into 2-inch wheels. Add the yucca, corn, and chicken to the pot. Bring almost to a boil, then reduce heat, cover, and simmer, stirring occasionally, for about 1 hour, or until yucca is tender. Remove from heat and stir in lime juice. Makes 6 servings.

Julieta Arturo Sandoval
Las Villas Ward
Soacha Colombia Stake
Bogotá, Colombia

The secret to this wonderful soup is the corn on the cob. You can put in frozen or fresh corn kernels instead, but I think it is the fresh corn cobs that add that perfect extra something to this soup. Don't be afraid to pick up the corn wheels with your fingers and nibble off the kernels. Mmmm!

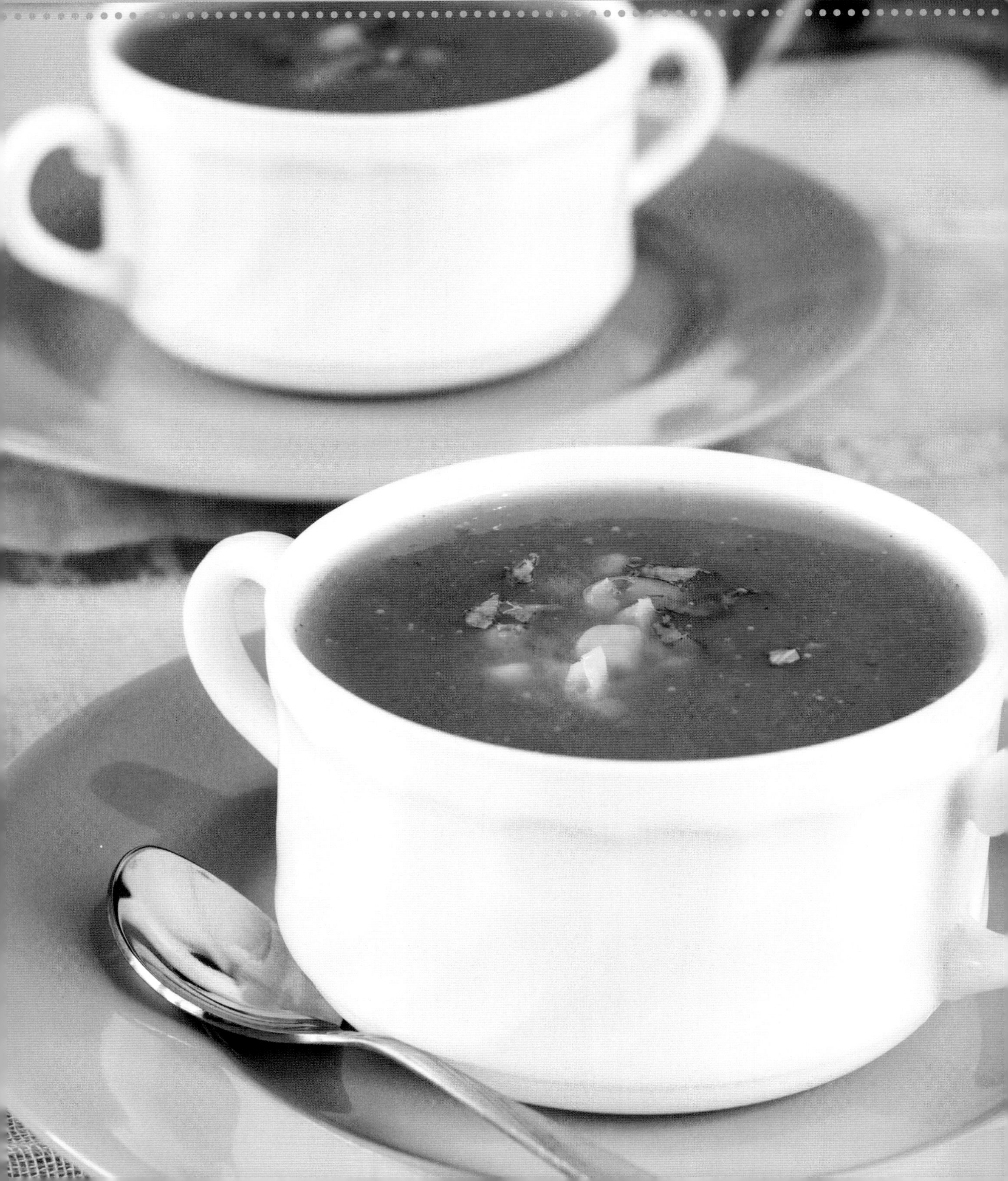

Chinese Chicken and Sweet Corn Soup

1 boneless, skinless chicken breast
4 C. chicken broth
2 green onions
3 Tbsp. cornstarch

1 egg
1 15-oz. tin creamed sweet corn
2 tsp. soy sauce

Trim the chicken and cut in slices. Place chicken and chicken broth in a pot. Bring to a boil, turn the heat down, and put the lid on the pot. Simmer for 15 minutes. Trim the bottom of the green onions and cut off about an inch from the tops. Cut the rest of the onions and tops into very thin slices. Set aside. In a small bowl, whisk just enough water into the cornstarch to dissolve it. In another bowl, beat the egg with a fork; add about a tablespoon of water and beat it into the egg until it is foamy. Set aside. After the chicken is cooked through, shred the slices with a fork. Add the creamed corn and the soy sauce. Turn up the heat and bring the soup to a boil. When it is boiling, stir in the cornstarch mixture. Cook and stir for about a minute, until the soup is slightly thickened. Turn off the heat and stir in the egg mixture—while stirring the soup, pour a very thin stream of the egg mixture into the pot. Spoon the soup into bowls and top each with green onion. Makes 4 servings.

We serve this delicious soup before our main meal. The secret to this soup is the egg: To get the egg into such thin bits, you have to thin the egg with water and mix it very well. Then remember to keep stirring the very hot soup as you pour in a tiny stream of egg. The tinier the stream, the more delicate the bits of egg. It takes only a little practice to do this properly. I hope you love this soup as much as I do.

Zhai Su Nuan
Suzhou Branch
International District
Changshu, China

Tamil Tomato Soup

2½ C. tomatoes, chopped
½ C. yellow moong dal (mung beans)
3–4 C. water
2 tsp. butter
1 onion, finely chopped
1 Tbsp. flour or cornstarch

1–2 tsp. sugar
½ C. warm milk
Salt and pepper to taste
Fresh cream
Bread croutons

In a large pan, boil the tomatoes, moong dal, and water until the beans are soft. Blend in a blender and strain. Melt butter; add the onion and fry for 3–4 minutes. Add the strained tomato and bean mixture. In a small bowl, mix the cornstarch with a little water until smooth, then pour into the soup. Boil for 2 minutes, stirring occasionally. Add sugar, milk, salt, and pepper. Serve with cream and bread croutons. Makes 4 servings.

Chandra Prassad
Chennai 1st Branch
India Bangalore Mission
Chennai, Tamil Nadu
India

Secret Yum Yum Soup

1 lb. sweet Italian sausage, casings removed
1 C. onion, chopped
2 cloves garlic, minced
5½ C. beef broth
½ C. red cooking wine
4 large tomatoes, peeled, seeded, and chopped
1 C. carrots, sliced

½ Tbsp. packed fresh basil leaves
½ tsp. dried oregano
1 8-oz. can tomato sauce
1½ C. zucchini, sliced
8 oz. fresh cheese-filled tortellini pasta
3 Tbsp. fresh parsley, chopped
Parmesan cheese for garnish

In a 5-quart Dutch oven, brown sausage. Remove sausage and drain, reserving 1 Tbsp. of the drippings. Sauté onions and garlic in drippings. Stir in beef broth, cooking wine, tomatoes, carrots, basil, oregano, tomato sauce, and sausage. Bring to a boil. Reduce heat; simmer uncovered for 30 minutes. Skim fat from the soup. Stir in zucchini and parsley. Simmer covered for 30 minutes. Add tortellini during the last 10 minutes. Sprinkle Parmesan cheese on top of each serving. Makes 8 servings.

Ohio winters are freezing! When it gets bitter cold, I love snuggling up with my mom's wonderful Secret Yum Yum Soup. This, along with some crusty bread, is my favorite food to get stuffed with. It truly warms the soul. Nothing compares to watching the snow fall outside while eating a bowl of warm soup. The name comes from my sister. It was called "Tortellini Soup," but when she was little she called it "Yum Yum Soup," and we've called it that ever since.

Kara Carpenter
Mayfield Ward
Kirtland Ohio Stake
Shaker Heights, Ohio

Sweet Soup

1 quart EACH pears, peaches, apricots, and cherries (do not drain)
1 C. raisins
½ C. rice
2 C. water

1 stick or 1 tsp. cinnamon
(½ C. lemon juice if using commercially canned fruit)
1 lemon, sliced thin

Combine all and simmer for 1–2 hours. Serve warm. Makes 8–10 servings.

This recipe has been handed down for generations! The most important part, if at all possible, is to use fruit that you canned yourself. And the secret part? Whoever gets a cherry pit in his or her soup has to clean up dinner! (It's inevitable that someone will get a cherry pit when you can the fruit yourself!)

Krystal Bockholt
Goshen Ward
Goshen Utah Stake
Goshen, Utah

Creamy Split Pea Soup

½ lb. sliced bacon, diced
1 large onion, chopped
2 celery ribs, sliced
1 lb. dried green split peas
2 qt. water
2 medium potatoes, peeled and diced

1–2 carrots, diced
2 C. fully cooked ham, diced
2 tsp. salt
1 bay leaf
¼ tsp. pepper
1 C. heavy cream

In a Dutch oven or soup kettle, cook bacon over medium heat until crisp. Using a slotted spoon, remove bacon to paper towels; reserve drippings. Add onion and celery to drippings. Sauté until vegetables are tender; drain. Stir in the split peas, water, potatoes, carrot, ham, salt, bay leaf, and pepper. Bring to a boil. Reduce heat; cover and simmer for 45 minutes or until peas are very tender, stirring occasionally. Discard bay leaf. Cool slightly. Process in small batches in a blender until smooth. Only process half if you want some chunks. Return to Dutch oven; stir in cream. Heat through but do not boil. Garnish with bacon. Makes 10 servings.

The secret to this soup is the heavy cream; it puts a little twist on regular split pea soup that I love. I got this recipe from a friend years ago. She always made the best soups. Every time I make this, I remember sitting at her kitchen table for hours having girl talk.

Karoline Bradley
Washington DC 3rd Ward
Washington DC Stake
Washington, DC

Old-Fashioned Cream of Tomato Soup

2 32-oz. cans diced tomatoes
1 9-oz. can chicken broth
2 Tbsp. unsalted butter
2 Tbsp. onion, chopped

Pinch of baking soda
2 Tbsp. sugar
2 C. heavy cream

Combine tomatoes, chicken broth, butter, onion, soda, and sugar in a large saucepan over medium-high heat. Heat until just boiling, then reduce heat and simmer for 1 hour. Heat the heavy cream in the top half of a double-boiler until warm. Add cream to hot tomato mixture and stir until well combined. For a spicy alternative, add a can of tomatoes with chiles (Rotel). Makes 2 quarts.

Nathaly Manchaca
Yonkers Ward
Westchester New York Stake
Yonkers, New York

This is an old-fashioned soup that is perfect, in my opinion. I can't identify what one ingredient makes this soup so amazing—I think it's the combination of a bunch of simple things.

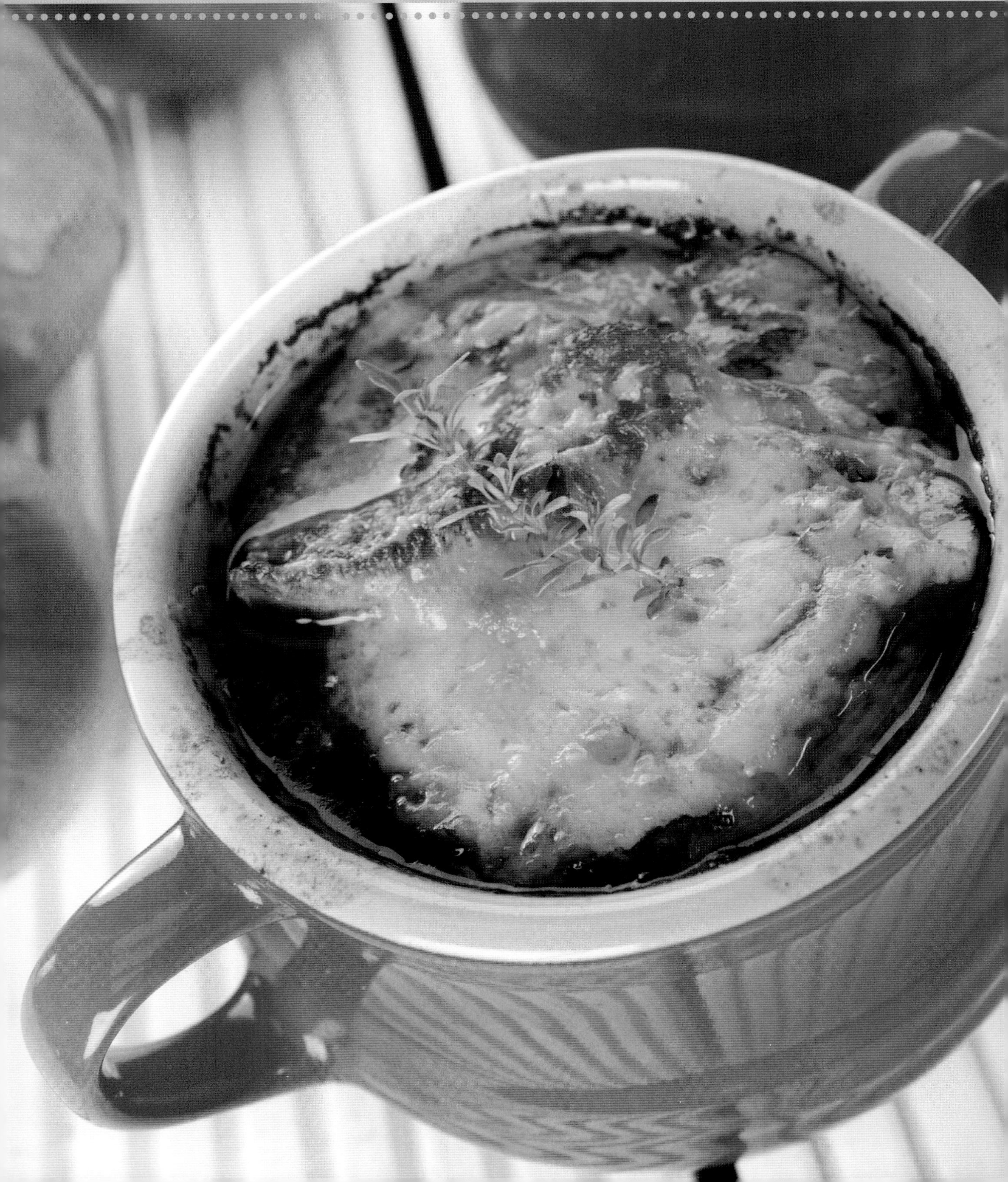

My Version of Walkabout Onion Soup

3 Tbsp. butter

2 C. yellow sweet onions, thinly sliced

1 15-oz. can chicken broth

2 chicken bouillon cubes

¼ tsp. salt

¼ tsp. fresh-ground pepper

3 Tbsp. butter

3 Tbsp. flour

1½ C. whole milk

¼ tsp. salt

¼ C. processed American cheese (Velveeta) cubed, compressed in measuring cup

Cheddar cheese, shredded (for garnish)

In a 2-quart saucepan, cook 3 Tbsp. butter and sliced onions over low to medium heat, stirring frequently until soft and clear but not brown. Add chicken broth, chicken bouillon cubes, salt, and pepper; stir until completely heated through. In a small saucepan, melt 3 Tbsp. butter. Stir in flour. Cook on medium heat until the flour turns thick and comes away from the sides of the saucepan. Pour in milk a little at a time, stirring constantly; add salt. Mixture should thicken and become like thick pudding; stir constantly, taking care not to let mixture lump. Remove from heat. Stir white sauce and American cheese into chicken soup. Simmer on medium-low heat until the cheese is melted and all ingredients are blended, stirring constantly. Turn temperature to warm and let simmer for additional 30–45 minutes. Garnish each serving with shredded cheddar cheese. Serve with warm dark Russian bread. Makes 4 servings.

Kristi Craft
Newport Ward
Providence Rhode Island Stake
Portsmouth, Rhode Island

My favorite soup on the planet is Outback Steakhouse's Walkabout Onion Soup! I follow this recipe precisely and it comes out perfect every time. I highly recommend this to anyone who loves the original from Outback, because this tastes so close to it—but is even more flavorful than the original. Trust me: your life is not complete without this recipe!

Pepper Pot Soup

4 chicken breasts, diced
1 gal. chicken stock or broth
2 C. soy sauce
2 Tbsp. garlic, minced
2 Tbsp. sugar
2 tsp. hot sauce
1 red bell pepper, diced
1 green bell pepper, diced

½ Poblano chili pepper, diced
1 onion, diced
1 C. mushrooms, diced
1 C. spinach or collard greens, roughly
    chopped
¼ C. lemon juice
2 tsp. sesame oil

Cook diced chicken until half done. Set aside. Heat chicken stock, soy sauce, garlic, sugar, and hot sauce. Add peppers, onion, mushrooms, and chicken. Cook until the vegetables are done. Add spinach and lemon juice when ready to serve. Drizzle with the sesame oil when serving. Makes 8 servings.

I got this fabulous recipe when I vacationed at Disney's Animal Kingdom Lodge in the United States. When I inquired about a cookbook with the recipe, the waitress told me she knew the recipe by heart and jotted it down for me. How nice was she? I am so excited to have this secret recipe. This soup is very tasty and borderline addictive. I've made it several times since then. It is absolutely perfect. This soup also freezes well for those who want to make a large portion and freeze the rest for later.

Monique David
Nancy Ward
Nancy France Stake
Nancy, France

Jamaican Seafood Chowder

1 6.5-oz. pkg. red beans and rice mix
    (Rice-a-Roni)
1 6-oz. can shrimp
1 6-oz. can minced clams
1 6-oz. can crab meat
2 C. light sour cream
3 C. milk

4 C. Pepper Jack cheese, shredded (use
    Monterey Jack for milder version)
2 Tbsp. Caribbean jerk seasoning
1 15-oz. can corn, drained
1 5-oz. can diced mild green chiles
1 Tbsp. lime juice
1 C. cheddar cheese, shredded (optional)

(recipe continued on next page)

(Jamaican Seafood Chowder, continued)

In a large kettle, prepare rice and beans according to package instructions. Over moderately low heat, add shrimp, clams, crab, sour cream, milk, Pepper Jack cheese, and jerk seasoning. Heat until cheese melts, but do not boil. Stir in corn, chiles, and lime juice. Serve hot, sprinkled with cheddar cheese if desired. Makes 6 servings.

This is an original recipe I created for one of the many cooking contests I enter as a hobby. This one was sponsored by Chicken of the Sea, and it won the Grand Prize—a cruise for four to the Caribbean. Our family loves seafood, but I've even served this to folks who claim they don't like fish, and they all gobble it up. Wait until you taste it—it's truly delicious. It's also fast and easy to make. Just add a salad and some crusty bread and you have a terrific dinner.

Joni Hilton
Rocklin 5th Ward
Rocklin California Stake
Rocklin, California

Royal Corn Chowder

2 large russet potatoes
¾ lb. bacon, chopped
½ small onion, diced
1 large celery rib, diced
1 large carrot, chopped
1 Anaheim chili or red bell pepper, diced

1–2 fresh Jalapeño peppers, diced
1 10-oz. box frozen corn
½ C. flour
2 14.5-oz. cans chicken broth or stock
1 qt. half-n-half
Salt and pepper

Peel and dice potatoes. Bring a pot of water to a boil. Parboil potatoes by placing in boiling water for 5 minutes. Pour off water and set potatoes aside. In a large pot, sauté bacon until well done. Add onion, celery, carrot, peppers, and corn to bacon and bacon fat. Sauté until tender. Add flour to bacon and vegetables to make a roux. Stir until smooth and thickening. Add potatoes. Gradually add chicken broth and stir until smooth. Bring to a boil. Add half-n-half and simmer for 5 minutes. The starch from the potatoes helps thicken the soup, and the parboiled potatoes will finish cooking in the soup. Salt and pepper to taste. Makes 8 servings.

This recipe—developed by one of the chefs in the royal palace—appeared in an old newspaper my grandmother kept. It tastes so creamy and is quite colorful. This is my favorite soup!

Amelia Jones
Guildford Ward
Staines England Stake
Guildford, Surrey
England

FOR YOUR EYES ONLY

Sunday's Broccoli Cheese Soup

½ C. butter

1 onion, chopped

2 16-oz. pkgs. frozen chopped broccoli

4 14.5-oz. cans chicken broth

2-lb. loaf processed cheese (Velveeta)

1 C. half-n-half

1 C. heavy cream

1 Tbsp. garlic powder

⅔ C. cornstarch

1 C. chicken broth

1 C. cheddar cheese, shredded

3 Roma tomatoes, chopped

In a stockpot, melt butter over medium heat. Cook onion in butter until softened. Stir in broccoli and cover with 4 cans chicken broth. Simmer until broccoli is tender, 10–15 minutes. Reduce heat. Cube cheese very finely or melt it before adding it to the soup so it doesn't stick to the broccoli. Stir in cheese until melted. Stir in half-n-half, cream, and garlic powder. In a small bowl, stir cornstarch into 1 C. broth until dissolved. Stir into soup; cook, stirring frequently, until thick. Sprinkle each serving with shredded cheese and tomatoes. Makes 8 servings.

We eat soup every Sunday—by tradition at our house, Sunday is soup night. Serve this with your favorite crusty bread, and you have a delicious, homey, comfort meal. Out of all the many soups we love, this is my favorite to make, and I think it tastes similar to my favorite restaurant's soup.

Tara Sanchez
Jamestown Branch
Fargo North Dakota Stake
Jamestown, North Dakota

Sunday Night Fireside Soup

4 cubes chicken bouillon

6 C. water

1 C. celery, chopped

1 C. onion, chopped

3 C. potatoes, peeled and cubed

1 10-oz. pkg. frozen mixed vegetables

1 10-oz. pkg. frozen chopped broccoli

2 10.75-oz. cans cream of chicken soup

1 lb. processed cheese, cubed

In a large soup pot, dissolve chicken bouillon cubes in 6 C. water. Add all the vegetables, fresh and frozen, to the pot. Simmer for 30 minutes. Stir in cream of chicken soup. Add cheese; mix until melted. Serve. For a spicy kick, throw in a can of tomatoes with green chiles (Rotel). Makes 8 servings.

When I was in high school, we made this thick, chunky soup before every evening fireside at church. About ten of us gathered at my parents' house, ate, and then carpooled to the chapel. Those are some great memories, and I still keep in touch with those girls from my childhood, who also make this soup. The secret to this soup isn't in the ingredients, but in the love and memories that were made while sitting around devouring every last drop.

Chrissy Vanderkamp
Batesville Ward
Cincinnati Ohio Stake
Greensburg, Indiana

Gail's Chili

1 lb. hamburger
¼ onion, diced well
1 env. chili seasoning

1 8-oz. can tomato sauce
2 14.5-oz. cans stewed tomatoes
1 15-oz. can red kidney beans

Brown hamburger and add onion. Allow onion to soften and become transparent. Add chili seasoning, tomato sauce, and stewed tomatoes. (I use a spatula to chop the hamburger and stewed tomatoes into smaller chunks while they cook.) Stir in the kidney beans. Cook on medium-low for 20 minutes or until kidney beans are heated through and soft. Stir often so chili won't burn. I love a little crushed pepper on this chili. Delicious! Makes 6 servings.

My mother made this chili for our family, and it was a favorite while we were growing up. The secret to making it truly fantastic is to serve it on mashed potatoes with a side of corn. My mother is no longer with us, but I have sweet memories of her making this dish. One time she came to visit while I was going to BYU, and all my siblings were here as well. She made a huge pot of this chili and asked me to watch it and stir it as it cooked. Thinking it would cook faster if I turned up the heat, I turned it from low to high—and, to my family's great disappointment, I scorched the chili. Today, my own family—five daughters and a wonderful husband—ask for this chili often.

Alicia Johnson
Mt. Mahogany 4th Ward
Mt. Mahogany Utah Stake
Pleasant Grove, Utah

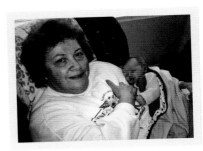

Cheezy Soup

4 potatoes
1 lb. carrots
½ C. celery
¼ C. minced dry onions
⅓ lb. butter
1 C. flour

3 qt. water
⅓ C. dry soup base or 2–3 bouillon cubes, dissolved
8–oz. jar processed American cheese (Cheez Whiz)
½ C. frozen peas (optional)

Peel, dice, and cook potatoes, carrots, celery, and dry onions in water until almost done. Drain. In a separate large soup pot, make roux: Melt butter; stir in flour until it thickens. Add 1 C. water and soup base or bouillon cubes dissolved in ½ C. water. Stir in Cheez Whiz; add water to desired thickness (we like it quite thick). Add all vegetables, bring to a boil, then simmer for 10–15 minutes. Makes 6 servings.

Most cheese soup recipes use Velveeta or cheddar cheese. The unique flavor of Cheez Whiz is the secret that makes this soup so good. I have been making this soup for my family for years. I got it from one of my good friends when we lived in a small town in southern Utah. I have added chicken and green chiles for variety, but the original recipe is the best.

Jan Lyman
Islands Ward
Gilbert Arizona Stapley Stake
Gilbert, Arizona

{ SALADS }

I'm not good at secrets, so don't tell me any.

{ AJ McLean }

#1 Creamy Coleslaw

8 C. cabbage, finely shredded (about 1 head)

¼ C. carrots, finely diced

2 Tbsp. onion, minced

⅓ C. sugar

½ tsp. salt

⅛ tsp. pepper

¼ C. whole or 2% milk (the lower the fat in the milk, the runnier the salad will be)

½ C. mayonnaise

¼ C. buttermilk

1 ½ Tbsp. white vinegar

2 ½ Tbsp. lemon juice

In a large bowl, combine cabbage, carrots, and onion; mix well. In a separate bowl, mix all other ingredients; pour over the veggie mixture and mix thoroughly. Cover bowl and refrigerate 5 hours. Makes 12 servings.

Amanda De Boise
Santa Fe Ward
Santa Fe New Mexico Stake
Santa Fe, New Mexico

This is the king of all coleslaws. I stumbled onto this recipe years ago when I was searching for something to bring to our annual 4th of July cookout. Everyone raves when I make this yummy slaw, which tastes so much like the "famous fried chicken's" slaw. Be prepared to share the recipe, because someone will ask for it—I promise!

Fitzgerald Family Lime Salad

20 regular-size marshmallows

2 C. boiling water

1 3-oz. pkg. lime gelatin

1 20-oz. can crushed pineapple

1 C. cheddar cheese, grated

1 C. pecans, chopped

1 C. heavy cream, whipped

Melt marshmallows in boiling water; add gelatin and stir until dissolved. Set in refrigerator until partially set. Stir in other ingredients, folding in whipped cream last. Pour into a lightly oiled mold and let set at least six hours, preferably overnight. Makes 8 servings.

May Fitzgerald
Taos Ward
Santa Fe New Mexico Stake
Angel Fire, New Mexico

This is a traditional "go-to," always-a-winner Jell-O salad. We eat this a lot! The secret ingredients are the cheese and the nuts—they seem strange in a salad, but don't skip them. The flavors all work amazingly well together.

Not Your Average Cranberry Salad

1 20-oz. can crushed pineapple with juice
2 3-oz. pkgs. cherry gelatin
2 C. hot water
1 16-oz. can whole cranberry sauce

1 8-oz. pkg. cream cheese
1 Tbsp. mayonnaise
1 C. pecans, chopped

Drain crushed pineapple, saving ¼ C. of the juice. Dissolve gelatin in hot water. Stir in cranberry sauce and crushed pineapple. Pour ½ of the mixture into a bowl and leave at room temperature; set the other ½ in the refrigerator until firm. In a separate bowl, mix the cream cheese, mayonnaise, reserved pineapple juice, and chopped pecans. Spread mixture over chilled gelatin. Place in refrigerator for 10 minutes. Pour the room-temperature gelatin over the top of the cream cheese layer and refrigerate until set. Makes 8 servings.

Landon Gooch
Lowell Ward
Cambridge Massachusetts Stake
Chelmsford, Massachusetts

We have many picky eaters in my family of fourteen, so you can imagine the holiday spread we have to put out to satisfy everyone. Cranberry sauce is one of those items that many people turn their nose up at, but we discovered the secret to pleasing everyone. Now there isn't a drop of it left at our table. It puts a great twist on the average cranberry sauce.

Orange Almond Salad

Salad:
¼ C. almonds, sliced
4 tsp. sugar
¼ head iceberg lettuce
¼ head Romaine lettuce
1 C. celery, chopped
2 green onions, thinly sliced
½ C. green olives
1 C. artichoke hearts
½ C. fresh mushrooms, sliced
1 can cocktail baby corn
1 8-oz. can mandarin oranges, drained

Dressing:
½ tsp. salt
Dash of pepper
2 Tbsp. sugar
2 Tbsp. red wine vinegar
¼ C. oil
1 Tbsp. parsley, chopped

(recipe continued on next page)

(Orange Almond Salad, continued)

Salad: In small saucepan, cook almonds and sugar on low heat; stir constantly until sugar is melted and almonds are coated, about 3 minutes. When sugar is liquid, pour onto waxed paper. Cool and break apart, as for brittle. (This can be done a day ahead; store at room temperature.) Tear lettuces into bite-size pieces. In a large bowl, combine lettuces, celery, green onions, green olives, artichoke hearts, mushrooms, and baby corn. Garnish with mandarin oranges and almonds. Serve with dressing. Makes 10 servings.

Dressing: Combine all ingredients in a blender; blend, then refrigerate. Shake well before serving.

This is a salad that will impress. This contains everything under the sun and tastes spectacular. I received this recipe from a little old lady in my hometown ward when I got married more than fifteen years ago. She told me this recipe had been around for generations. This is probably one of my most cherished recipes. I make this a lot and have not seen a recipe like it anywhere, which makes it that much more special.

Marta McPherson
Salisbury 1st Ward
Wilmington Delaware Stake
Selbyville, Delaware

Sister Carrington's Fruit Salad

1 egg
2 Tbsp. lemon juice
2 Tbsp. sugar
Pinch salt
½ C. heavy cream, whipped until peaks form
1 C. miniature marshmallows
1 C. pineapple tidbits, drained

1 C. seedless grapes, cut in half
1 C. bananas, sliced
1 C. orange sections, diced (or mandarin oranges)
8–10 maraschino cherries, quartered
½ C. nuts, toasted and chopped (pecans, walnuts, or slivered almonds)

In a double boiler, beat egg with fork; stir in lemon juice, sugar, and salt. Cook over hot water, stirring until mixture thickens, about 5 minutes. Remove from heat and cool. Fold in whipped cream, marshmallows, and fruits. Refrigerate overnight. Fold in nuts before serving. Makes 6 servings.

Alejandra Alvarez Cardoza
San Sebastian Ward
Retalhuleu Guatemala Las Palmas Stake
Antigua, Guatemala

An elder from the United States who was serving in Guatemala told me that his favorite meal was his mother's fruit salad. I was able to get that recipe, and I made it for Elder Carrington on his birthday. The joy in that homesick young man's face was worth all the effort in the world. The fruit salad was so good that even though Elder Carrington has long since returned home, we still make this for special occasions in our family.

Bleu Cheese Pear Salad

¼ C. sugar

½ C. pecans

⅓ C. olive oil

3 Tbsp. red wine vinegar

1½ tsp. sugar

1½ tsp. mustard

1 clove garlic, chopped

½ tsp. salt

Fresh-ground black pepper to taste

1 head leaf lettuce, torn into bite-size pieces

3 pears, peeled, cored, and chopped

5 oz. Roquefort cheese, crumbled

1 avocado, peeled, pitted, and diced

½ C. green onions, thinly sliced

In a skillet over medium heat, stir ¼ C. sugar and the pecans. Continue stirring gently until sugar has melted and caramelized the pecans. Carefully transfer nuts onto waxed paper that has been coated with nonstick spray. Allow to cool; break into pieces. For the dressing, blend oil, vinegar, 1½ tsp. sugar, mustard, garlic, salt, and pepper. In a large serving bowl, layer lettuce, pears, cheese, avocado, and green onions. Pour dressing over salad, sprinkle with pecans, and serve. Makes 6 servings.

This is a big hit in our family. We LOVE salad, and are always looking for different ways to include veggies in our meals. This is one of our favorites, and I am pretty sure once you try it, it will become a favorite of yours, too. The secret is the pears and bleu cheese—a perfect combination!

Lauren Langston
Lake Shawnee Ward
Topeka Kansas Stake
Shawnee, Kansas

Spinach Salad with Honey Bacon Dressing

8 C. fresh spinach, torn into bite-size pieces

1 C. fresh mushrooms, sliced

¼ C. green onion, sliced

1 medium tomato, seeded and chopped

2 hard-boiled eggs, chopped

½ C. Parmesan cheese, shredded on large
   holes of grater

7 slices bacon, cooked and crumbled

½ C. honey

½ C. vinegar

⅓ C. vegetable oil

1 tsp. yellow mustard or spicy brown mustard

1 tsp. lemon juice

⅓ C. almonds, toasted and sliced

In a large bowl, combine first 6 ingredients with 5 of the cooked, crumbled bacon strips. In a small bowl, whisk the honey, vinegar, oil, mustard, lemon juice, and remaining 2 strips of cooked, crumbled bacon. Pour over salad or serve on the side. Serve immediately. Makes 6 servings.

Wendi Moat
Brookings Ward
Sioux Falls South Dakota Stake
Brookings, South Dakota

Miracle Whip Potato Salad That Everyone Loves

5–6 large potatoes, cut into chunks
2 C. Miracle Whip
3 Tbsp. milk
1 Tbsp. sugar
1 Tbsp. mustard
1 tsp. Dijon mustard

½ tsp. white pepper
1 tsp. fresh-ground pepper
Salt to taste
1 bunch celery, cleaned and chopped
2 medium white onions, diced
6–8 hard-boiled eggs, diced

Boil potatoes until tender but not mushy. Set aside to cool. In a small bowl, combine Miracle Whip, milk, sugar, mustards, peppers, and salt. Adjust each of these ingredients to your taste; my dressing never turns out the same way twice, and depends on whether I'm in the mood for sweet, peppery, or salty. In a large bowl, mix potatoes, celery, onion, egg, and dressing; chill until ready to serve. Makes 10 servings.

My husband and I are currently serving a mission in Singapore. I absolutely love the people and culture here, but at times I long for home. One of the foods I miss making the most is my potato salad. The secret ingredient to great potato salad is Miracle Whip. I've had people who swear they hate Miracle Whip eat an ENTIRE PLATE of this potato salad. It's my mom's recipe, and you can try it with regular mayonnaise, but I won't stand by the results— it's so good with Miracle Whip that I've never tried it any other way!

Esther Lee
Bedok Ward
Singapore Stake
Bedok, Singapore

Beck Family Jell-O

1 6-oz. pkg. lime Jell-O
1 C. boiling water
1 8-oz. pkg. cream cheese, softened
½ tsp. vanilla
1 15-oz. can mandarin oranges, drained

1 8-oz. can crushed pineapple, drained
1 C. lemon-lime soda
½ C. pecans, chopped
1 8-oz. carton frozen whipped topping, thawed, divided

Dissolve gelatin in water. In a mixing bowl, beat cream cheese until fluffy. Stir in gelatin mixture and beat until smooth. Stir in vanilla, oranges, pineapple, soda, and pecans. Chill until the mixture mounds slightly when dropped from a spoon. Fold in three-fourths of the whipped topping. Pour into a 9 x 13-inch dish. Refrigerate for 3–4 hours or until firm. Cut into squares; garnish with the remaining whipped topping. Makes 12 servings.

Vicki Tanner
Chapel Hill Ward
Lenexa Kansas Stake
Kansas City, Kansas

I love this Jell-O salad. My grandmother made it, my mother made it, I make it, and now my own children make it—so four generations have tested and added here and there along the way. This is THE BEST Jell-O ever. For those who make Jell-O salad for holidays or pot lucks, I highly suggest trying this one. Happy cooking!

Cherry Compote

2 3-oz. pkgs. cherry gelatin
2 C. boiling water
1 10-oz. pkg. frozen sweetened sliced strawberries
1 21-oz. can cherry pie filling
1 20-oz. can pineapple chunks, drained
1 15-oz. can pear halves, drained and cut into chunks

3 medium firm bananas, sliced
2 medium navel oranges, peeled, sectioned, and chopped (or 1 medium can mandarin oranges, drained)
2 medium tart apples, peeled and chopped
1 C. fresh or frozen blackberries, thawed

In a large bowl, dissolve the gelatin in the boiling water. Stir in the strawberries until thawed. Stir in the remaining ingredients. Transfer to a 4-qt. serving bowl. Cover and refrigerate for 3–4 hours before serving. Makes 24 servings.

My next-door neighbors, oddly enough, were the ones who got me hooked on this. I was house-sitting while they were away, and came across it while looking through their refrigerator. When they got home I asked my neighbor everything she put in her Jell-O so I could make it exactly like she did. This is now my favorite Jell-O because it has more fruit than your average Jell-O dish. You know the lady in the ward who always brings the Jell-O? Well, that's now me because everyone requests my "fruity Jell-O" and loves it so much. My hubby, who hates Jell-O, dives into this stuff, so that alone should speak volumes.

Natalie Buchanan
Harbor Hills Ward
Newport Beach California Stake
Newport Coast, California

Orange Cream Jell-O Mold

2 6-oz. pkgs. orange gelatin
2 C. boiling water
2 C. orange soda

2 envs. whipped topping mix (Dream Whip), whipped
2 11-oz. cans mandarin oranges, drained
1 20-oz. can crushed pineapple, undrained

In a large bowl, mix gelatin, boiling water, and orange soda. Cool in the refrigerator for 20–30 minutes. Prepare Dream Whip according to package directions. Once gelatin is cooled, but not firm, whisk in the whipped topping, mandarin oranges, and crushed pineapple. Pour into a bundt pan and refrigerate until firm. Turn out onto a serving plate. Makes 8 servings.

Melissa Stehling
Miami 4th Ward
Miami Florida South Stake
Miami, Florida

This is one of my childrens' favorite things to eat during the holidays. We make this a lot just for them, and I also bring this to church a lot. It tastes like a creamsicle, which means it's a definite kid-pleaser, even though we adults secretly love it just as much. It's a five-star Jell-O mold in my book.

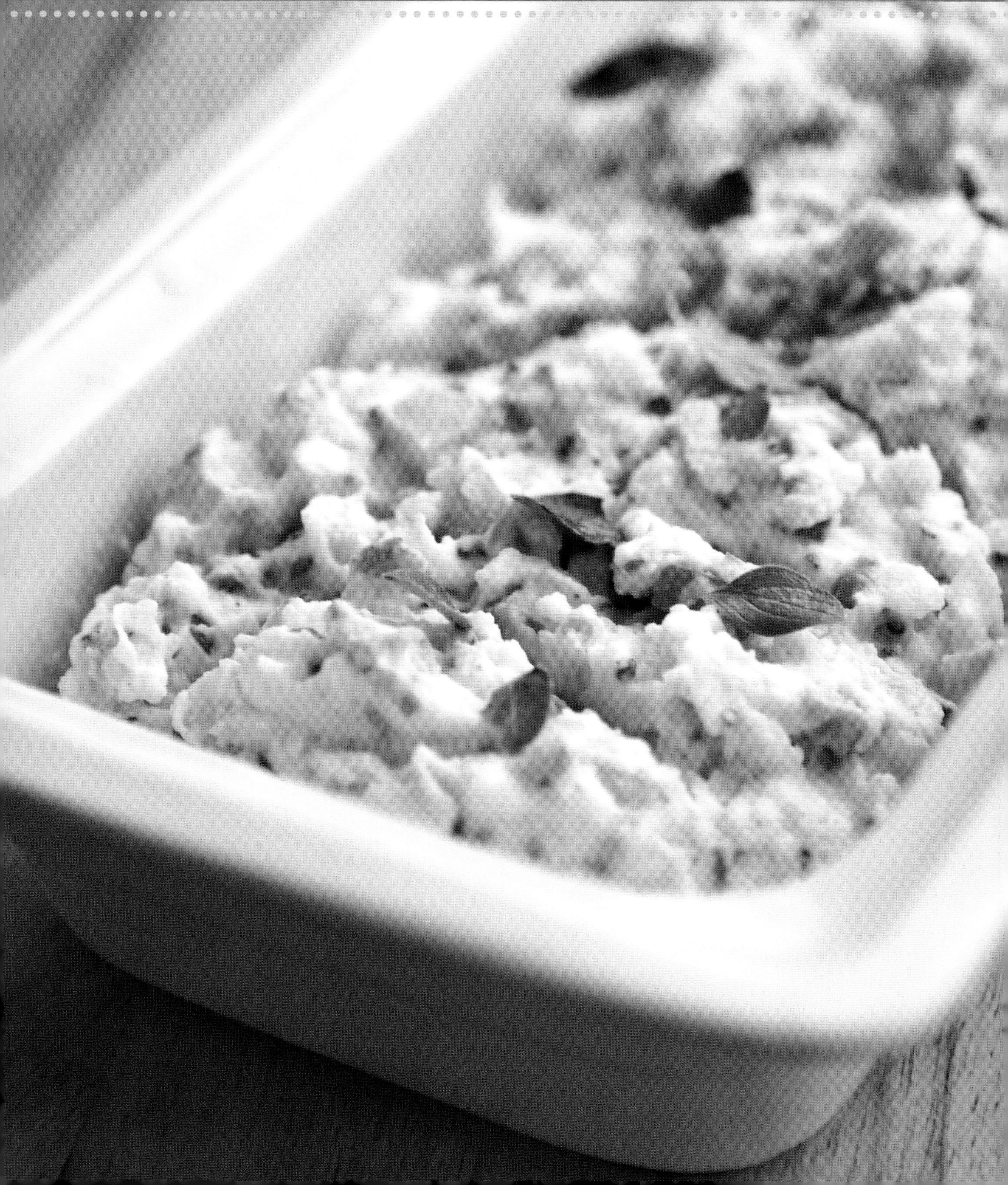

Cindy's Jalapeno Potato Salad

5 lbs. potatoes, peeled, cubed, and boiled

8 hard-boiled eggs, coarsely chopped

8 ribs celery, diced (cut off all white parts of the stalk)

10 green onion stems, chopped

1 large yellow onion, diced

3–4 C. good-quality mayonnaise

½ C. pickled jalapeños, chopped

2 Tbsp. juice from jalapeños

¼ C. parsley, chopped

2 tsp. cumin

1 Tbsp. black pepper

1 Tbsp. salt

In a large bowl combine potatoes, eggs, celery, green onion, and yellow onion. In a separate bowl, combine remaining ingredients; add to potatoes. Mix well and chill at least 4 hours or overnight. Makes 12 servings.

Cindy is my mother, and this is her version of potato salad. She is Latin, so she loves spicy food, and she is an amazing cook. The jalapeños are the secret ingredient that makes this by far the tastiest potato salad. I have never come across another jalapeño potato salad anywhere other than my mom's kitchen.

Natalia Stegall
Harvest Hills Ward
Rexburg Idaho East Stake
Rexburg, Idaho

Crab Pasta Salad

Salad:

2 C. uncooked medium garden shell pasta

1½ C. imitation crab, chopped

1 C. broccoli florets

½ C. cooked peas (use frozen, not canned)

½ C. cherry tomatoes, quartered

¼ C. green onion chives, chopped

Dressing:

½ C. mayonnaise

¼ C. creamy Italian salad dressing

¼ C. Parmesan cheese, grated

Cayenne pepper to taste

Cook pasta according to package directions; drain and rinse in cold water. Place in a large bowl. Stir in crab, broccoli, peas, tomatoes, and chives. In a separate bowl, combine first 3 dressing ingredients; pour over salad and toss gently to coat. Sprinkle top lightly with cayenne pepper for a little kick. Cover and refrigerate for 2–4 hours before serving. Makes 6 servings.

This wonderful salad always goes great with any dinner. A secret to making this salad even better is to use lime mayonnaise in the dressing; find this in the ethnic aisle of the grocery store, and it's fantastic.

Elizabeth Mortonsen
Charleston 1st Ward
Charleston South Carolina Stake
Folly Beach, South Carolina

Red Potato Salad

24 medium red potatoes

12 eggs

½ C. green onions, diced

1 carrot, finely grated

2 tsp. salt (more if you desire)

1–2 tsp. paprika

1 C. mayonnaise

1½ C. salad dressing (Miracle Whip)

2 Tbsp. mustard

1 pt. heavy cream, whipped, or 1 pt. cold canned milk

Parsley (for garnish)

In a large pan, cover whole potatoes with water; bring to a boil and turn heat down to medium. Cook until potatoes are tender, about 20 minutes. In a separate saucepan, cover eggs with water, bring to a boil, and turn heat down to medium. Cook eggs for about 15 minutes to hard-boil the eggs. Drain cooking water and run cold water over the eggs. (I like to cook the eggs and potatoes the night before.) Peel the potatoes and cut in bite-size cubes. Peel and dice 9 of the eggs; use an egg slicer to slice the remaining 3 eggs for the top of the salad when it is prepared. In a large bowl, toss cubed potatoes, onions, carrots, and diced eggs until they are mixed well. Add salt and paprika. In a separate bowl, mix mayonnaise, salad dressing, mustard, and cream (or canned milk) until smooth. Fold into the potato mixture; and mix well. Put salad into a large serving bowl; top with sliced eggs, a bit of parsley, and a sprinkle of paprika for color. Chill until you are ready to serve. Makes 24 servings.

Sue Heaton
Sunset Heights 3rd Ward
Sunset Heights Orem Stake
Orem, Utah

My mother was the cook for girls' camp in Provo Canyon for the four years I was there. Each year, the girls were asked what they wanted most to eat. They always requested her potato salad and oven-fried chicken. Mom's secret to this recipe is the shredded carrots, which make it so moist. The girls gave her the pet name Fancy because she always garnished each tray with parsley. She is greatly loved for her wonderful food and the way she always presented it. She is ninety-two now and no longer cooks, but we have wonderful memories that we continue to share.

Sweetwater Macaroni Salad

16 oz. uncooked elbow macaroni

4 carrots, shredded

1 large red onion, chopped

½ green bell pepper, seeded and chopped

½ red bell pepper, seeded and chopped

1 C. celery, chopped

2 C. mayonnaise

1 14-oz. can sweetened condensed milk

⅛ C. sugar

½ C. white vinegar

Salt and pepper to taste

½ C. bread and butter pickles, chopped (optional)

(recipe continued on next page)

(Sweetwater Macaroni Salad, continued)

Bring a large pot of lightly salted water to a boil. Add macaroni and cook until tender, about 8 minutes. Rinse under cold water and drain. In a large bowl, stir the carrots, red onion, green pepper, red pepper, and celery. Mix in the mayonnaise, condensed milk, sugar, vinegar, salt, pepper, and pickles (if desired). Add the macaroni, toss gently, cover, and refrigerate for at least 8 hours. I usually make this a day ahead of time and stir it occasionally to blend the flavors. The macaroni will absorb some of the liquid. Makes 16 servings.

We love those tubs of macaroni salads you can buy at the grocery store, the ones that have a little sweetness to them. My sisters and I are huge macaroni salad lovers, and this has become our go-to mac salad because we love the sweetness and it really tastes like the creamy kind you get at the store. My older sister even makes this when she caters barbecue dinners and sporting events. Everyone gobbles it up.

Katie Sweetwater
Glenville Ward
Albany New York Stake
Niskayuna, New York

Tossed Broccoli Salad

Salad:

2 lbs. fresh broccoli, trimmed and cut into
   1-inch pieces

½ lb. sliced bacon, cooked and crumbled

2 C. mozzarella cheese (8 oz.), cubed

½ medium red onion, chopped

1½ C. frozen peas

Dressing:

1 C. mayonnaise

½ C. sugar

1 Tbsp. cider vinegar

In a large salad bowl, combine broccoli, bacon, cheese, and onion. In a separate bowl, combine dressing ingredients. Add to salad. Toss and chill. Makes 8 servings.

Sandra Muir
Battlecreek 10th Ward
Pleasant Grove Utah East Stake
Pleasant Grove, Utah

This salad is the secret to the success of my book group potluck. Twice a year we have a potluck dinner before discussing the book for the month. The ladies lovingly tell me I can attend that month only if I bring this salad! It is also a favorite at family gatherings and Relief Society events. I found this recipe years ago and one day decided to add the peas. I have tried leaving them out or adding other things, but to me the peas are the secret ingredient that makes it so yummy.

Foxy Lady's Chopped Salad

Vinaigrette:

1 egg yolk

1 Tbsp. water

1 Tbsp. Dijon mustard

2 Tbsp. garlic, minced

½ tsp. salt

1 tsp. coarse fresh-ground black pepper

½ tsp. dry mustard

2 tsp. dried oregano

½ tsp. sugar

⅓ C. red wine vinegar

2 Tbsp. lemon juice

⅓ C. Parmesan cheese, grated (optional)

1 C. olive oil

Chopped Salad:

4 oz. cooked chickpeas, lightly chopped

1 head iceberg lettuce, chopped into ¼- to
    ½-inch pieces

1 C. fresh basil leaf, chopped

1 C. mozzarella cheese, coarsely grated

12 oz. chicken breasts, poached and diced

8 oz. dry wine salami, diced

8 oz. plum tomatoes, diced and divided

½ C. provolone cheese, grated and divided

3 thin green onions, thinly sliced and divided

8 lettuce leaves

Vinaigrette: In a small bowl, combine egg yolk and water; whisk well. Cover the bowl with a small plate and microwave on high for 10 seconds or until the mixture starts to expand. Continue to cook 5 seconds longer. Whisk with a clean whisk. Cover, then cook on high for 5 seconds. Remove from the microwave, whisk with a clean whisk, cover, and let sit 1 minute. (This process heats the egg enough to kill any harmful bacteria.) In a food processor, combine egg mixture, Dijon mustard, garlic, salt, pepper, dry mustard, oregano, sugar, vinegar, and lemon juice; process to blend. Blend in grated Parmesan. Slowly add olive oil, processing until emulsified. Set aside.

Chopped Salad: Combine chickpeas, lettuce, basil, mozzarella, chicken, salami, half of the tomatoes, half of the provolone, and half of the green onions. Toss with dressing. (You may not need all of the dressing; refrigerate any that remains.) Divide evenly among 8 lettuce-lined plates. Garnish with remaining tomatoes, provolone, and green onions. Makes 8 servings.

Amelia Jones
Guildford Ward
Staines England Stake
Guildford, Surrey
England

There is a pub in England called The Foxy Lady, and they have the BEST salad ever. This is the recipe. The dressing is so good I could drink it. The secret to this recipe is the fresh chopped basil. I wouldn't recommend leaving out any of the ingredients! (It is the best chopped salad you will ever have—I promise!)

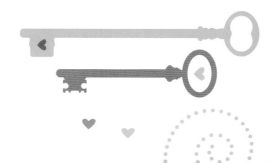

Hometown Potato Salad

5 lbs. unpeeled red potatoes, cubed
1 tsp. salt
Pepper to taste
8 hard-boiled eggs, chopped
1 lb. sliced bacon, cooked very well and
    crumbled

8 oz. cheddar cheese
1 small yellow onion, chopped
¾ C. dill pickles, chopped
1½ C. sour cream
1 C. mayonnaise
2–3 tsp. mustard

Place cubed potatoes in a large greased baking pan; sprinkle with salt and pepper. Bake uncovered at 425 for 40–45 minutes or until tender. Let cool. In a large bowl, combine potatoes, eggs, bacon, cheese, onion, and pickles. In a small bowl, combine sour cream, mayonnaise, and mustard. Pour over potatoes and toss to coat. Makes 10 servings.

This is my favorite potato salad and goes well with ribs or any type of barbecue. Of course, I am biased, because this is the potato salad I grew up on as a kid. My fondest memories were having family camping trips every summer by the lake, and my mom always made this salad. I didn't realize how good it was until I tried potato salad made by someone else. That's when I knew my mom had a secret recipe. I gave my wife the recipe and even she thinks it's the best potato salad she has ever had. It's awesome!

Ryan Murphy
West Hills Ward
Knoxville Tennessee Stake
Knoxville, Tennessee

Maw-Maw's Famous Slaw

Slaw:
1 head green cabbage (8–10 C.)
1 large carrot, peeled
2–4 green onions (or to taste), finely chopped
2 tsp. celery seeds (optional, or to taste)

Dressing:
1 C. mayonnaise (do not use salad dressing)
⅓ C. milk (light cream is even better)
⅓ C. buttermilk

2–3 Tbsp. white vinegar
3 Tbsp. fresh lemon juice (do not use bottled)
⅓ C. + 2 Tbsp. granulated sugar
2 Tbsp. white sugar
½–1 tsp. garlic powder
1 tsp. seasoning salt (or to taste) or 1 tsp. white
    salt (or to taste)
½ tsp. fresh-ground black pepper (or to taste)

(recipe continued on next page)

(Maw-Maw's Famous Slaw, continued)

In a food processor, chop the cabbage into small pieces (to about the size of confetti) or shred the cabbage. Transfer to a large mixing bowl. With a fine shredder, shred the peeled carrot; hand-squeeze out any excess moisture completely. Add carrots to the cabbage in the bowl. (In place of the cabbage and carrot, you could use 2 16-oz. bags of coleslaw mix.) Add the green onion and celery seed to the cabbage/carrot mixture; mix well with a wooden spoon. To make the dressing: In a medium glass bowl, whisk all the dressing ingredients; start with the lower amounts, then adjust to suit taste—but use the full ⅓ C. plus 2 Tbsp. sugar. Pour over the veggies in the bowl and mix well to combine. Store covered in the refrigerator for at least 8 hours or preferably overnight to blend flavors. Makes 10 servings.

This is the only coleslaw I will touch. It is so good that when I make it I can usually count on my husband eating half of it right out of the bowl with a big spoon, as if it were ice cream. Every year I am asked to bring this to our ward's 4th of July celebration. People who don't even like coleslaw love this one. It's a favorite recipe from my talented grandmother.

Lorna Walsh
Tickle Creek Ward
Mount Hood Oregon Stake
Parkdale, Oregon

Caesar Salad

6 cloves garlic, peeled and divided

¾ C. mayonnaise

4 anchovy fillets, minced (I know you are going to want to leave these out, but don't)

6 Tbsp. Parmesan cheese, grated and divided

1 tsp. Worcestershire sauce

1 tsp. Dijon mustard

1 Tbsp. lemon juice

Salt to taste

Fresh-ground black pepper to taste

¼ C. olive oil

4 C. day-old bread, cubed

1 head Romaine lettuce, torn into bite-size pieces

Mince 3 cloves of garlic; in a small bowl, combine garlic with mayonnaise, anchovies, 2 Tbsp. Parmesan cheese, Worcestershire sauce, mustard, and lemon juice. Season to taste with salt and black pepper. Refrigerate until ready to use. In a large skillet, heat oil over medium heat. Cut the remaining 3 cloves garlic into quarters and add to hot oil. Cook and stir until brown; remove garlic from pan. Add bread cubes to the hot oil. Cook, turning frequently, until lightly browned. Remove bread cubes from oil; season with salt and pepper. In a large bowl, toss lettuce with dressing, remaining Parmesan cheese, and seasoned bread cubes. Makes 8 servings.

I never knew anchovies were a key ingredient in Caesar salad until I made it. Resist the temptation to skip the anchovies! They are in all good Caesar dressings. Anchovies really are the secret ingredient, and the dressing won't turn out without them. I process my dressing in a food processor to make sure everything is nice and smooth. I tried making this salad for the first time a few years ago when I was preparing a birthday dinner for my husband. It turned out very well and now I have no need to buy Caesar dressing. This is way better! Even my children love it.

Elizabeth Mortonsen
Charleston 1st Ward
Charleston South Carolina Stake
Folly Beach, South Carolina

Cheese Tortellini Pesto Pasta Salad

8 oz. rotini pasta, cooked al dente, drained

1 20-oz. pkg. cheese-filled tortellini, cooked al dente, drained (fresh or frozen)

1 14-oz. can artichoke hearts, drained, quartered

1 10-oz. pkg. grape tomatoes, halved lengthwise

1 6-oz. can medium black olives, drained, sliced in half lengthwise

1 green bell pepper, diced

⅓ C. olive oil (more if needed)

¼ C. Parmesan cheese, grated (the kind in the can)

1 8-oz. jar basil pesto

½ tsp. salt (more if needed)

2 tsp. garlic, minced

12 oz. mozzarella cheese, cubed

Cook pastas in boiling water; set aside to drain and cool a bit. In a large bowl or punch bowl, combine all remaining ingredients, folding gently until well mixed. Gently fold in pastas. Adjust seasoning to taste. This can be served immediately or refrigerated. If you make this a day ahead of time, you'll need to add a bit more olive oil, salt, and Parmesan before serving. This salad is best at room temperature or even slightly warm. Makes 12 servings.

This is most definitely my favorite pasta salad in the world! I have been making it for years. I first tasted this at a bridal shower for one of my missionary companions. I have loved it ever since, and I think I have been asked for this recipe at least a dozen times since I have been back home.

Katya Yakushev
Nevsky Branch
St. Petersburg Russia Stake
St. Petersburg, Russia

Cherry Coke Salad

1 20-oz. can crushed pineapple

½ C. water

2 3-oz. pkgs. cherry gelatin

1 21-oz. can cherry pie filling

¾ C. cola-flavored soda

Drain pineapple, reserving juice; set fruit aside. In a saucepan or microwave, bring pineapple juice and water to a boil. Add gelatin; stir until dissolved. Stir in pie filling and soda. Pour into a serving bowl. Refrigerate until slightly thickened. Fold in reserved pineapple. Refrigerate until firm. Sounds strange, but this is really great. We make this anytime we want Jell-O. The secret is the soda: we love the zing it provides! Makes 8–10 servings.

Johana Keough
Harpers Ferry Ward
Winchester Virginia Stake
Charlestown, West Virginia

All Your Favorite Things Salad

½ C. walnuts, chopped

1 bunch spinach, rinsed and torn into bite-size
   pieces

½ C. dried cranberries

½ C. bleu cheese, crumbled

2 tomatoes, chopped

1 avocado, peeled, pitted, and diced

½ red onion, thinly sliced

2 Tbsp. red raspberry jam (with seeds)

2 Tbsp. red wine vinegar

⅓ C. walnut oil or olive oil

Fresh-ground black pepper to taste

Salt to taste

Preheat oven to 375. Arrange walnuts in a single layer on a baking sheet; toast in oven for 5 minutes, or until nuts begin to brown. In a large bowl, toss walnuts, spinach, cranberries, bleu cheese, tomatoes, avocado, and red onion. In a small bowl, whisk jam, vinegar, oil, pepper, and salt. Pour over the salad just before serving and toss to coat. Makes 6 servings.

Tara Sanchez
Jamestown Branch
Fargo North Dakota Stake
Jamestown, North Dakota

The secret to this recipe is all the yummy things my family loves in salads mixed together. Avocados, walnuts, cranberries, and bleu cheese make this the best salad ever!

Janelle's Fruit Salad

1 29-oz. can peach slices, undrained

1 20-oz. can pineapple chunks, undrained

1 3-oz. box vanilla instant pudding mix

1 lb. strawberries, stemmed and quartered

1 banana, sliced

½ pt. blueberries

1 bunch red grapes

1–2 Tbsp. sugar (optional)

In a large bowl, combine peaches and pineapple (including the juice from each). Stir in instant vanilla pudding. Mix well until pudding is dissolved. Stir in strawberries, banana, blueberries, grapes, and sugar, if desired. Chill. Makes 12 servings.

Janelle Snow
Peoria Ward
Peoria Illinois Stake
Peoria, Illinois

I get compliments on this fruit salad wherever I take it. It is super easy to make and a great dish to bring to a potluck or family party. Kids love it too. Everyone asks, "What's in the sauce?" The secret ingredient is the vanilla pudding mix.

MAIN DISHES }

Whoever wishes to keep a secret must hide the fact that he possesses one.

{ Johann Wolfgang Von Goethe }

Tandoori Chicken

1 2-lb. whole fresh roasting chicken

3 Tbsp. Tandoori curry paste

½ C. plain yogurt

2 Tbsp. lemon juice

2 Tbsp. butter, melted

Onion, tomato, and lemon for serving

Prepare a roasting rack and a baking dish; set aside. Rinse chicken inside and out; pat dry with paper towels. Make deep gashes in thighs and on each side of breast. Pin back the wings. Place chicken in a nonreactive bowl. Set aside. In a small bowl, combine Tandoori curry paste, yogurt, lemon juice, and melted butter. Stir to blend. Spread mixture all over the chicken, rubbing well into the gashes. Cover and refrigerate for 6 or more hours. Place chicken in a baking dish, and place the dish on the prepared roasting rack in the center of the oven. Spoon any remaining marinade over chicken. Bake at 375 for an hour and a half. Baste with pan juices every 15 minutes during baking. Transfer chicken to a cutting board and cut into serving portions. Arrange on a platter and garnish with onion, tomato, and lemon wedges.

Dhadha Zulueta
University Ward
Manila Philippines Stake
Manila, Philippines

Mexican Deelish

1 lb. lean ground beef or chicken

1 15-oz. can low-sodium black beans

2 10-oz. bags frozen white rice OR enough
    instant rice to make 4 servings

1 1-oz. env. low-sodium taco seasoning mix

2 C. frozen corn

1 14.5-oz. can all-natural Mexican tomatoes,
    chopped

In a medium to large stockpot, brown ground beef or chicken. Drain and rinse meat and return to pot. Drain and rinse black beans. Add to meat in stockpot. Cook frozen rice in microwave according to directions OR cook instant rice in separate saucepan according to directions on the box. Add cooked rice and taco seasoning to meat and beans in stockpot. Add frozen corn to stockpot. Slightly drain the tomatoes and add to mixture in stockpot. Serve warm, topped with broken tortillas, for gluten-free and dairy-free dietary needs. Or scoop mixture into warm tortilla shells and add cheese, sour cream, and taco sauce to taste. Serve with fresh fruit for a great meal. Makes 8 servings.

Rachel Anderson
Cedar Rapids 2nd Ward
Cedar Rapids Iowa Stake
Vinton, Iowa

I created this recipe in my quest to find something my six-year-old-son could eat. He can't have gluten or dairy. I have to be creative when it comes to dinnertime so it doesn't seem like he's eating the same thing all the time. This recipe originated one evening when I was standing in the kitchen with the cupboards and the fridge and freezer open. I just started pulling things out I knew he could eat and mixing them together. I've even browned the ground beef in the microwave, so I only used the pot on the stove to mix everything together and keep it warm. My son devours this and says it's his favorite dinner ever. My two-year-old eats it as is, and my husband and I like to put it in tortillas and make it more like a burrito.

Xiang Cheng Zhi Ma Chao Rou Pian (Orange Sesame Pork)

1 orange
1 lb. pork
2 Tbsp. soy sauce
1 Tbsp. sugar
2 Tbsp. orange juice
¼ tsp. pepper

½ C. cornstarch
2 C. oil
2 Tbsp. soy sauce
½ C. orange juice
2 Tbsp. orange rind jam (marmalade)
1 Tbsp. white sesame seeds

Peel and slice the orange onto a dish. Slice pork into thin pieces. In a shallow dish, combine 2 Tbsp. soy sauce, sugar, 2 Tbsp. orange juice, and pepper. Add pork slices and turn to coat. Allow to marinate for 15 minutes. Put cornstarch in a small bowl. Coat each slice of pork with cornstarch. Heat oil in a wok. Add pork and deep fry until cooked through and golden. Drain pork slices. Remove nearly all the oil from the wok. Add 2 Tbsp. soy sauce, ½ C. orange juice, and orange rind jam. Heat and stir until bubbly. Stir in deep-fried pork. Stir to coat. Spoon onto orange slices. Sprinkle with sesame seeds. Serve with rice. Makes 4 servings.

Zhou Yusheng
Sham Shui Po Ward
Kowloon Tong Hong Kong Stake
Kowloon Tong, Hong Kong

Maybe you don't like orange rind jam; that's okay—I don't really like it much, either. But don't skip it in this recipe! Orange rind jam is the secret to making this wonderful Xiang Cheng Zhi Ma Chao Rou Pian.

Grandma Hasek's Goulash

1 lb. ground beef
1 onion, chopped
1 green pepper, chopped
1 clove garlic, chopped
3 C. elbow macaroni
1 6-oz. can tomato paste

1 15-oz. can stewed tomatoes
1 10.75-oz. can tomato soup
Salt and pepper to taste
½ tsp. basil
1 C. cheddar cheese, shredded

(recipe continued on next page)

(Grandma Hasek's Goulash, continued)

In a large frying pan, brown ground beef with onion and green pepper. Stir in garlic. In a large saucepan, cook macaroni in boiling water. Drain. Add cooked macaroni to meat mixture. Stir in tomato paste, stewed tomatoes, tomato soup, salt, pepper, and basil. Cook and stir until hot and bubbly. Sprinkle the top with cheddar cheese. Makes 6 servings.

As a missionary mom, it is the highlight of my day to receive that long-awaited email each week from my son, John, who is serving in the Provo Utah Mission. One of his letters said, "I love the people in Utah and I wouldn't want to be anywhere else." Thank you to all those who have welcomed him, fed him, and strengthened his testimony. It is such a blessing when we hear from someone who has met or interacted with our missionary and who gives us a glimpse of how he is doing. This happened this week as I received a letter from Deanna Buxton. She visited with John and he wanted me to share a family recipe. This recipe is one of John's favorites. This was one of the first meals I had with my husband's family when we came home to visit right after John was born. The Hasek family secret is to eat the goulash with bread and peanut butter. The part I cherish the most about this meal is the times when my husband and I would come home from a hard day and my kids would have it made for us. Thanks to my mother-in-law who shared her recipes with me and who has always loved me like a daughter; and thank you to my husband, Eric, and our four kids, John, Greg, Katelyn, and Stephanie, who have made my life a dream come true. I love being a mom—especially a mom of a missionary!

Sonia Hasek
Lafayette Indiana 2nd Ward
Lafayette Indiana Stake
Lafayette, Indiana

Trash-Bag Taco Salad

3 lb. ground beef

3 envs. taco seasoning

3 heads lettuce, shredded

3 C. cheddar cheese, shredded

3 C. tomatoes, chopped

2 C. onions, chopped

3 4.25-oz. cans sliced black olives, drained

2 15-oz. cans beans, drained (ranch or chili)

1 16-oz. pkg. corn chips

1 16-oz. bottle Catalina dressing

1 12-oz. jar salsa

Brown ground beef; drain. Add taco seasoning and prepare according to package directions. Cool. Toss with remaining ingredients in a large plastic trash bag. Makes 30 servings.

A friend made this for us years ago and just called it "Trash." I have been making it for years and my kids LOVE it. They love saying that they had trash for dinner. Go figure! It is also great for potlucks. It is always the first to go.

Kristi Craft
Newport Ward
Providence Rhode Island Stake
Portsmouth, Rhode Island

Frikadeller (Danish Meatballs)

½ lb. ground veal
½ lb. ground pork
2 Tbsp. flour or 1 C. bread crumbs
2 C. milk

1 egg
1 lg. onion, minced
Salt and pepper to taste

In a large bowl, combine ground veal and ground pork very well. Add flour or bread crumbs, milk, egg, onion, salt, and pepper. Mix thoroughly. Forming balls with a large tablespoon, drop meatballs into a frying pan and fry over low heat. Makes 4 servings.

Mille Norgaard
Randers Branch
Aarhus Denmark Stake
Randers, Denmark

Chicken-Fried Steak

4½-lb. cubed beef steaks
2 C. flour
2 tsp. baking powder
1 tsp. baking soda
1 tsp. black pepper
¾ tsp. salt
1½ C. buttermilk
1 egg

1 Tbsp. hot pepper sauce (Tabasco)
2 cloves garlic, minced
3 C. vegetable shortening for deep frying
¼ C. flour
4 C. milk
Kosher salt to taste
Ground black pepper to taste

Pound the steaks to about ¼-inch thickness. Place 2 C. flour in a shallow bowl. In a separate larger shallow bowl, stir the baking powder, baking soda, pepper, and salt; mix well. Stir in the buttermilk, egg, hot pepper sauce, and garlic. Dredge each steak first in the flour, then in the batter, and again in the flour. Pat the flour onto the surface of each steak so it is completely coated with dry flour. In a deep cast-iron skillet, heat the shortening to 325 degrees. Fry the steaks until evenly golden brown, 3–5 minutes per side. Place fried steaks on a plate with paper towels to drain. Drain the fat from the skillet, reserving ¼ C. of the liquid and as much of the solid remnants as possible. Return the skillet to medium-low heat with the reserved oil. Whisk ¼ C. flour into the oil. Scrape the bottom of the pan with a spatula to release solids into the gravy. Stir in the milk, raise the heat to medium, and bring the gravy to a simmer. Cook until thick, 6–7 minutes. Season with kosher salt and pepper. Spoon the gravy over the steaks to serve. Makes 4 servings.

I grew up in the South, where chicken-fried steak is a staple food at every restaurant. When I moved to North Dakota, I decided to figure out a way to make my own. This is my secret recipe for chicken-fried steak. It is down-home cooking at its finest, and it gets amazing reviews every time.

Tara Sanchez
Jamestown Branch
Fargo North Dakota Stake
Jamestown, North Dakota

Out of Thin Air Chicken Enchiladas

3 large chicken breasts, cut into bite-size pieces
½ C. onion, chopped
1 env. taco seasoning
1 10.5-oz. can cream of chicken soup
1 10.5-oz. can cream of mushroom soup

½ C. sour cream
½ C. olives, chopped
12–14 corn tortillas
1 10.5-oz. can enchilada sauce
3 C. cheddar cheese, shredded

In a frying pan, cook chicken and onion with taco seasoning. In a large bowl combine soups, sour cream, and olives. Add cooked chicken and onion. Dip tortillas in enchilada sauce and layer lasagna-style in a 9 x 13-inch pan with chicken mixture and grated cheese. Cook at 350 for about 30 minutes, or until cheese is bubbly! Makes 8–10 servings.

We never had much growing up, but Mom was sure creative in the kitchen. No matter what, we always sat down to a good meal! I remember walking into the kitchen one day and seeing Mom putting together something I had never seen her make before. She told me it was time to go grocery shopping, but we were on a tight budget. So Mom was making enchiladas with whatever she could find in the pantry! I was a little hesitant to try them . . . I had never heard of enchiladas made with mushroom soup! I couldn't believe how tasty they turned out! These enchiladas became a family favorite. They were also the missionaries' favorite, and Mom made them almost every time the missionaries came over. I make them for my family and friends now, and every time they ask where I got the recipe I tell them it is our family's secret recipe!

Cami Adams
Hillcrest 3rd Ward
Orem Utah Hillcrest Stake
Orem, Utah

Fancy Shrimp Ravioli

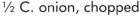

½ C. onion, chopped
2 Tbsp. butter
2 Tbsp. flour
1 14.5-oz. can Italian stewed tomatoes
1 Tbsp. brown sugar
1 bay leaf
1 whole clove
½ tsp. dried basil

½ tsp. salt
⅛–¼ tsp. pepper
18 oz. fresh or frozen cheese ravioli
1½ C. heavy cream
½ lb. cooked medium shrimp, peeled and deveined
1 Tbsp. Parmesan cheese, grated
1 Tbsp. chives, minced

In a large skillet, sauté onion in butter until tender. Stir in flour until blended. Bring to a boil; cook and stir until thickened. Place tomatoes in a blender; cover and process until pureed. Add tomatoes to onion mixture. Stir in brown sugar, bay leaf, clove, basil, salt, and pepper. Bring to a boil. Reduce heat; cover

(recipe continued on next page)

(Fancy Shrimp Ravioli, continued)

and simmer for 10 minutes. Meanwhile, cook ravioli according to package directions. Remove and discard bay leaf and clove from the sauce. Reduce heat; gradually stir in cream. Add shrimp; heat through. Drain ravioli; top with sauce, Parmesan cheese, and chives. Makes 5 servings.

This recipe is amazing. It tastes just like something you would pay $20 for at a nice Italian restaurant, so we call it "Fancy Shrimp Ravioli." This dish is a lot easier than it seems. The creaminess of the sauce is what makes this dish so incredible. We got this recipe from the caterers at my wedding reception. My little brother liked it so much he had the caterers make it and serve it at his wedding reception three years later. It has become a favorite in our family for sure. It's rich, but perfect for those special occasions.

Alexia Hinkley
Palmyra Ward
Palmyra New York Stake
Palmyra, New York

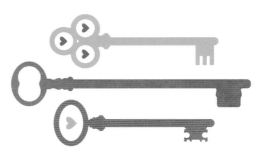

Grandma's Barbecued Hamburgers

1 lb. ground beef
½ large onion, diced
1½ Tbsp. mustard
1 Tbsp. vinegar
2 Tbsp. flour

2 Tbsp. brown sugar
½ Tbsp. Worcestershire sauce
½ C. tomato sauce
¼ C. ketchup
Salt and pepper to taste.

In a skillet, brown ground beef and onion. Put into a slow-cooker and add all the other ingredients. Stir until well combined. Cook on low for 3–4 hours. You can also add all the remaining ingredients to the skillet and simmer on the stovetop for 1 hour. Serve on hamburger buns. Makes 5 servings.

Susan Tea
Pilgrims Landing 4th Ward
Lehi Utah Gateway Stake
Lehi, Utah

When I was a child, Grandma's Barbecued Hamburgers were the secret ingredient of our Labor Day festivities. It just wouldn't be Labor Day without them. We always went to the local Labor Day parade, then to Grandma's for her barbecued hamburgers. Once our tummies were full we went to the car show and fair. When Grandma passed away, the only thing I asked for was this recipe so I could keep the tradition alive with my kids. While I was growing up, I could never figure out why they were called barbecued hamburgers. Now I know it was because of Grandma's secret (not so secret anymore!) homemade barbecue sauce!

Root Beer Pot Roast

1 5-lb. Black Angus organic pot roast

Salt and pepper to taste

10 organic carrots, peeled and cut into chunks

Olive oil

36 oz. root beer, room temperature

1–2 onions, optional

Season roast on all sides with salt and pepper and set aside for 15 minutes while you peel and cut the carrots. Heat a frying pan and add just a touch of olive oil. Brown roast on all sides, just until you get that nice caramelized crispiness to the meat. Pour ⅓ of the room-temperature root beer into a slow-cooker. Add the meat carefully. Add the carrots and onions. Pour the remaining root beer over the roast and cook on low for 8–10 hours. Makes 10 servings.

The root beer seems unusual, but actually adds a sweet buttery flavor to the roast. Believe me, this will melt in your mouth. Don't knock it until you try it, because this makes the perfect roast.

Britt Beakley
Madison 1st Ward
Madison Wisconsin Stake
Madison, Wisconsin

Dynamites

2 lb. lean ground beef

1 large yellow onion, diced

2 medium to large green peppers, diced

1 29-oz. can crushed tomatoes

3 Tbsp. tomato paste

1 tsp. Italian seasoning

1 Tbsp. (or more) crushed red pepper

1 bay leaf

Brown ground beef, making it crumbly. Drain well. Place in either a slow-cooker (our preferred way) or a heavy-duty pot. Stir in remaining ingredients. Mix well. If cooking in slow-cooker, cook on high for 4 hours or on low for 6–8 hours. If cooking on stovetop, cook over low heat for 4 hours. It can also be baked in the oven in an oven-proof pot at 250–275 for 4 hours. Pile onto torpedo-shaped rolls. Makes 6 servings.

This recipe has been handed down from my *memere* (grandma in French), who gave the recipe to my mom; now that I am married and going to be starting a family, my mother gave it to me. I believe that Dynamites are something you can only find in Rhode Island, where I was raised. The Travel Channel did a special on Autumn Fest in Woonsocket, Rhode Island, and the commentator said that Dynamites are a one-of-a-kind food that can't be found anywhere else. They are so yummy! My family has always eaten them at big family gatherings with chips and soda, with milkshakes for dessert. I remember as a child coming home from school on cold days and walking into the house to the smell of Dynamites. That aroma made me so excited because I knew that it meant the family would soon be here and that good times and TONS of laughs were about to happen.

Mary Graef
Kennebecasis Ward
Saint John New Brunswick Stake
Rothesay, Canada

Kitten's Marinara Pasta Sauce

3–4 Tbsp. olive oil (enough to lightly coat the bottom of the pot)

1 large onion, chopped

4–6 garlic cloves, minced, or to taste—the more the better (I use 6 extra-large cloves)

1 Tbsp. dried basil (rubbed between fingers to release flavor)

2 tsp. dried oregano (rubbed between fingers to release flavor)

½ tsp. crushed red pepper flakes (optional or adjust to taste)

1 6-oz. can tomato paste (can use two cans for a thicker, richer sauce if desired)

1 28-oz. can whole Roma tomatoes, undrained (break up with a fork before cooking; go ahead and use two cans if desired!)

⅓–½ C. dry red cooking wine (optional)

2 tsp. sugar (optional or to taste)

1 tsp. salt (or to taste; a good tomato sauce needs lots, so don't be shy with the salt)

Fresh-ground black pepper (to taste)

In a heavy-bottomed stockpot or Dutch oven, heat oil over medium-high heat. Add onion, garlic, basil, oregano, and red pepper flakes; sauté for about 3–4 minutes. Add tomato paste and stir for 2–3 minutes. Add roma tomatoes with juice and cooking wine; simmer uncovered over low heat, stirring occasionally, for 1–2 hours (I usually cook it for at least a couple of hours). Season with sugar, salt, and pepper. Add a little water if you prefer a thinner sauce.

This sauce is not just the perfect marinara sauce for Spinach and Four-Cheese Manicotti (below), it is the secret to the success of the recipe!

Katya Yakushev
Nevsky Branch
St. Petersburg Russia Stake
St. Petersburg, Russia

Spinach and Four-Cheese Manicotti

¼ C. onion, finely chopped

3 Tbsp. oil

2 tsp. fresh garlic

1½ C. ricotta cheese

1½ C. mozzarella cheese, shredded and divided

4 oz. cream cheese, softened

⅓ C. Parmesan cheese, grated

1 tsp. Italian seasoning

Salt or seasoned salt, to taste

½–1 tsp. fresh-ground black pepper

1 10-oz. pkg. frozen, chopped spinach (cooked according to pkg. directions, then hand-squeezed dry to remove excess moisture)

8–10 manicotti, cooked and drained

4–6 C. marinara sauce (see Kitten's Marinara Pasta Sauce, above)

¼ C. Parmesan cheese (or to taste)

Mozzarella cheese, for topping (any amount desired)

(recipe continued on next page)

(Spinach and Four-Cheese Manicotti, continued)

Preheat oven to 350. Butter a 9 x 13-inch baking dish. In a skillet, sauté onion in oil for about 4 minutes or until softened, adding garlic the last 2 minutes. Set aside. In a mixing bowl, combine the ricotta cheese, 1½ C. mozzarella cheese, cream cheese, ⅓ C. Parmesan cheese, and Italian seasoning; beat with a wooden spoon until smooth and well combined. Season with salt or seasoned salt and black pepper to taste. Stir in onion mixture and cooked spinach; mix well to combine. Spoon into cooked and cooled manicotti shells. Pour half of the pasta sauce into the prepared baking dish. Arrange shells over sauce (at this point you may cover and refrigerate for up to 24 hours, or continue with the recipe as follows). Top with the remaining sauce, using a spoon to spread the sauce over the shells (the sauce does not have to cover the shells completely). Sprinkle about ¼ C. Parmesan cheese (or to taste) over the sauce. Cover and bake for 25 minutes. Uncover and top with mozzarella cheese (any amount desired). Bake 5 minutes longer, or until cheese is melted. Let stand 10 minutes before serving. Makes 8 servings.

I have been making this recipe for years. It is the best manicotti recipe hands down! The secret to this amazing recipe is actually another recipe— my recipe for the marinara sauce. You could make it with any marinara sauce, but try it with Kitten's Marinara Pasta Sauce (p. 132) and you'll never want to make it any other way! I have made this many times for dinner parties and have made it for socials and large gatherings. To save time I always mix up the filling a day ahead and refrigerate, which gives the flavors a chance to blend. Don't forget to cook the spinach first and squeeze all of the moisture out of it before using it for this recipe.

Katya Yakushev
Nevsky Branch
St. Petersburg Russia Stake
St. Petersburg, Russia

 # Chicken South of the Border

4 boneless, skinless chicken breasts
12 flour tortillas
1 can cream of mushroom soup
1 can cream of chicken soup

1 C. milk
¼ onion, finely chopped
3.5 oz. mild taco sauce
1 lb. medium cheddar cheese, shredded

Boil chicken and break into pieces. Grease a 9 x 13-inch pan. Cut tortillas into 1-inch strips and line bottom of the pan. Put broken chicken pieces over tortillas. Combine remaining ingredients except cheese. Pour the soup mixture over the chicken. Top with shredded cheese. Repeat for 3 layers. Refrigerate for 24 hours if possible. Bake at 300 for 1 to 1½ hours or until it bubbles. Makes 10–12 servings.

Deirdre Axelrod
Fredericksburg Ward
Fredericksburg Virginia Stake
Fredericksburg, Virginia

Oven-Baked Jambalaya

½ C. butter

1 large onion, diced

1 large green bell pepper, chopped

4 stalks celery, chopped

4 cloves garlic, minced

1 6-oz. can tomato paste

3 bay leaves

3 Tbsp. Creole seasoning blend

4 tsp. Worcestershire sauce

2 28-oz. cans whole peeled tomatoes

7 C. chicken stock

3 C. cooked ham, chopped

3 C. Andouille sausage, cooked and sliced (or beef little smokies)

3 C. raw chicken, cut into bite-size pieces

3 C. frozen cooked shrimp

4 C. uncooked, long-grain white rice

Preheat oven to 350. In a large stock pot, melt butter; sauté onion, green pepper, celery, and garlic until tender, being careful not to burn the garlic. Add tomato paste and cook to brown slightly, stirring constantly. Stir in bay leaves, Creole seasoning blend, and Worcestershire sauce. Pour into a large roasting pan. Squeeze tomatoes to break up into pieces, and add to mixture in pan. Stir in juice from tomatoes, chicken stock, ham, sausage, chicken, and shrimp. Mix well. Cover tightly with aluminum foil. Bake for 1½–2 hours, stirring once halfway through baking time. Remove bay leaves before serving. Cook rice separately and either mix in when jambalaya is done baking, or serve jambalaya over rice. Makes 16 servings.

This is a family recipe passed down for as long as I can even remember. It is really easy and a very forgiving recipe—just play with it. We make it different all the time. Sometimes we add king crab legs. Seriously, jambalaya really doesn't get easier than this. I hope this inspires you to try jambalaya from the South.

Paige Buckley
Petal Ward
Hattiesburg Mississippi Stake
Hattiesburg, Mississippi

Spicy Shrimp

4 Tbsp. water

2 Tbsp. ketchup

1 Tbsp. soy sauce

2 tsp. cornstarch

1 tsp. honey

½ tsp. crushed red pepper

¼ tsp. ground ginger

1 Tbsp. vegetable oil

¼ C. green onions, sliced

4 cloves garlic, minced

12 oz. cooked shrimp, tails removed

In a bowl, stir water, ketchup, soy sauce, cornstarch, honey, crushed red pepper, and ginger. Set aside. In a large skillet, heat oil over medium-high heat. Stir in green onions and garlic; cook 30 seconds. Stir in shrimp; toss to coat with oil. Stir in sauce. Cook and stir until sauce is bubbly and thickened. Serve over rice. Simply wonderful! Makes 4 servings.

Nancy Crabtree
Lake Shawnee Ward
Topeka Kansas Stake
Topeka, Kansas

Pancit Palabok (Filipino Shrimp and Noodles)

Palabok sauce mix (found in Asian markets)
8 oz. thin rice noodles
½ lb. shrimp, cooked and peeled
¼ lb. pork, cooked and diced
¼ C. tinapa flakes (dried fish found in Asian markets)

2 hard-boiled eggs, sliced
1 C. pork rinds, crushed
2 stalks of green onions, chopped
2 Tbsp. fish sauce
Salt and pepper to taste

Prepare Palabok sauce mix according to package instructions. Cook noodles according to package instructions and drain. Pour the Palabok sauce over the noodles. Garnish the noodles with the shrimp, pork, tinapa flakes, eggs, pork rinds, green onions, fish sauce, and salt and pepper. Makes 4 servings.

Grace Buxton
Cheyenne Ridge Ward
Lone Mountain Nevada Stake
Las Vegas, Nevada

The secret of this recipe is that the final product looks like it took a lot of work, but it is very simple. My mom and I both joined the Church within the past six years, but church has always been a part of our lives. Before we were members, we used to walk to a church in the Philippines every Sunday and afterward go out for lunch at a market place where they served a nice plate of these noodles. My mom makes this only on special occasions, but when I was pregnant with twins she made me a whole container full!

St. Francis School's Baked Spaghetti

8 oz. uncooked spaghetti, cooked and drained
½ C. milk
1 egg
1 lb. ground beef
1 medium onion, chopped
1 medium green bell pepper, chopped
2 garlic cloves, minced
1 tsp. chili powder

½ tsp. cumin
½ tsp. oregano
½ tsp. salt
¼ tsp. pepper
2 8-oz. cans tomato sauce
½ C. cheddar cheese, shredded
½ C. Monterey Jack cheese, shredded

(recipe continued on next page)

(St. Francis School's Baked Spaghetti, continued)

In a large bowl, combine hot spaghetti, milk, and egg; mix well. Pour spaghetti mixture into a buttered 9 x 13-inch casserole dish. In a large skillet, brown ground beef with onion, bell pepper, and garlic; drain. Return drained meat to the skillet and add chili powder, cumin, oregano, salt, and pepper. Cook for 2 minutes. Stir in tomato sauce and cook for 2 more minutes. Spread meat mixture over spaghetti. Sprinkle with cheese. Bake at 425 for 10 minutes or until cheese melts and is bubbly. Remove from oven and let stand for 10 minutes. Makes 10 servings.

Tasha Cooley
Cambridge Branch
Silver Spring Maryland Stake
Easton, Maryland

In my mom's effort to recreate my elementary school's spaghetti, she came up with this recipe. I am pretty sure she got it right because it tastes identical. It's the only spaghetti we ate growing up and it is still my favorite meal. Many people are baffled at the idea of baking spaghetti, but it really infuses flavor into the noodles and it is just delicious.

Cottage Meatloaf

1 egg
1 lb. cottage cheese
½ medium onion, minced
½ C. cracker crumbs
¼ C. celery, minced
¼ C. green pepper, minced
2 Tbsp. sesame seeds, toasted
½ clove garlic, crushed

1 Tbsp. Worcestershire sauce
½ tsp. salt
¼ tsp. basil
⅛ tsp. pepper
1 lb. lean ground beef
¼ C. ketchup
2 tsp. brown sugar
2 tsp. mustard

Preheat oven to 350. In a large bowl, beat egg lightly; add cottage cheese, onion, cracker crumbs, celery, green pepper, sesame seeds, garlic, Worcestershire sauce, salt, basil, and pepper. Mix well. Mix in ground beef. Place in a loaf pan or shape into a loaf and place on a baking pan. In a small bowl, combine ketchup, brown sugar, and mustard. Spread over loaf. Bake 1 hour or until done. Let stand for 10 minutes before slicing. Makes 4–6 servings.

Teri Rodeman
Benton City Ward
Kennewick Washington Stake
Benton City, Washington

I found this recipe in a *Reader's Digest* Knudsen Cottage Cheese ad years ago, and it is the best meatloaf I've ever tasted. I think the cottage cheese is the secret to such moist meatloaf.

School Meatloaf

Meat:

1½ lb. ground beef

1 slice bread, finely chopped

1 egg

1 small sweet onion (Vidalia), finely chopped

1 tsp. salt

¼ tsp. pepper

4 Tbsp. ketchup

½ C. whole milk or half-n-half

Sauce:

4 Tbsp. apple cider vinegar

2–4 Tbsp. packed dark brown sugar

½ C. ketchup

(I suggest doubling the sauce to serve on the side)

In a large bowl, combine ground beef, bread, egg, onion, salt, pepper, ketchup, and milk or half-n-half. Place into a loaf baking dish. In a separate bowl, combine vinegar, brown sugar, and ketchup. Pour over top and sides of meatloaf. Bake at 350 for 60–75 minutes, or until done. I always heat a second batch of the sauce to serve with the meatloaf. Makes 12 servings.

I know meatloaf has a bad reputation, but this is the only meatloaf I have ever enjoyed. It's so good. My sister moved to the United States and this is a recipe she makes for the kids at the school cafeteria where she works. The sauce is the secret that makes it so good that even the kids love it.

Patricia Cabrera
Cabudare Ward
Barquisimeto Venezuela Stake
Barquisimeto, Lara
Venezuela

Secret Alfredo Sauce . . . Shhh!

½ C. sweet butter

2 garlic cloves, minced

2 C. heavy cream

¼ tsp. white pepper

½ C. Parmesan cheese, grated

¾ C. mozzarella cheese

1 12-oz. box angel hair pasta or whatever pasta you like

In a medium saucepan, melt butter over medium-low heat. Add garlic, cream, and white pepper, and bring mixture to a simmer, stirring frequently. Add Parmesan cheese and simmer sauce for 8–10 minutes or until sauce has thickened and is smooth. When sauce has thickened, add mozzarella cheese and stir until smooth. STIR FREQUENTLY. While the sauce cooks, boil noodles for 3–5 minutes. Place pasta on serving plates and spoon sauce over top. Makes 5 servings.

This is the best Alfredo sauce. Sometimes I can't believe it's homemade. Add your choice of chicken, shrimp, or crab, if desired. I like it with angel hair pasta, but any pasta will do. This stuff seriously rocks!

Charles Whitney
Old Hickory Ward
Nashville Tennessee Stake
Nashville, Tennessee

Chicken Biryani

½ C. tomato puree

1 C. plain yogurt

1 tsp. ginger paste

½ tsp. garlic paste

1 tsp. green chile paste

2 tsp. red chili powder

1 tsp. turmeric powder

1 tsp. cumin powder

2 tsp. Garam Masala powder

1 tsp. coriander powder

Salt to taste

1½ lb. chicken pieces

7 Tbsp. oil

3 large onions, sliced

2 C. Basmati rice

3½ C. water

½ C. milk

Pinch of saffron

½ tsp. cardamom powder

2 Tbsp. green coriander leaves, chopped

In a small bowl, combine tomato puree, yogurt, ginger paste, garlic paste, green chile paste, red chili powder, turmeric, cumin, Garam Masala, coriander, and salt. Coat chicken on all sides with this mixture and allow to marinate for 3–4 hours. In a skillet, heat oil in a pan and fry the onions until they turn golden brown. Add the chicken with marinade to the onions and simmer for 10 minutes. In a pressure cooker, combine rice and water. Combine milk and saffron and stir into the rice. Add the chicken with marinade and the cardamom powder. Stir everything in the pressure cooker gently, cover with cooker lid, and pressure cook for 1 whistle. Garnish with green coriander leaves and serve hot. The coriander leaves not only add to the taste, but make the dish very pretty. Serve with the sauce if you like to eat spicy foods.

I served this recipe for Christmas dinner to the missionaries and the CES couple. I assured them that I had put only a little spice in the meal, but to them it must have still been quite spicy. Their skin and cheeks started turning red! The ginger, garlic, and green chili paste are products you can buy in an Indian grocery store, but you can also make them with fresh ginger, garlic, and green chiles by using a blender and a little water. The secret to this recipe is Garam Masala; just in case you can't find an Indian grocery store in your city that has a packet of the powder, I am also giving you my recipe for Garam Masala (below).

Mary Ganjayee
Madinaguda 2nd Branch
Hyderabad District
Hyderabad, Andhra Pradesh
India

Garam Masala

4 Tbsp. coriander seeds

1 Tbsp. cumin seeds

1 Tbsp. black peppercorns

1½ tsp. black cumin seeds

¾ tsp. black cardamom (3–4 large pods)

¾ tsp. cloves

¾ tsp. cinnamon (2 1-inch pieces)

¾ tsp. bay leaves, crushed

1½ tsp. dry ginger

(recipe continued on next page)

(Garam Masala, continued)

In a heavy skillet, combine all ingredients except the dry ginger; leave the cardamom in its pods until later. Gently roast over medium heat until the spices turn a few shades darker. Stir occasionally. Do not be tempted to turn up the heat to speed the process—the spices will burn on the outside and remain raw on the inside. When the spices are roasted, remove from heat and allow to cool. Remove the cardamom seeds from the pods and mix them back into the roasted spices. Grind the entire mixture to a fine powder. Store in an airtight container in a cool, dark place. Now you have the perfect secret ingredient to make delicious Chicken Biryani (p. 140). Makes about 6 Tbsp., so you'll have enough to make it about nine times!

Mary Ganjayee
Madinaguda 2nd Branch
Hyderabad District
Hyderabad, Andhra Pradesh
India

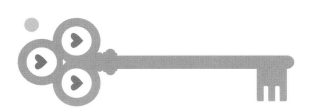

Swiss Enchiladas

2 C. chicken, cooked and chopped
1 4-oz. can diced Anaheim chiles
1 8-oz. can green chile salsa
½ tsp. salt

2 C. heavy cream
12 corn tortillas (or flour tortillas)
Oil for frying the tortillas
2 C. Monterey Jack cheese, shredded

Preheat the oven to 350. In a small bowl, mix the chicken, chiles, and salsa. In a large shallow dish, mix the salt and cream. In a frying pan, heat the oil over medium-high heat. Fry the tortillas one at a time for a few seconds until they start to blister and turn soft. Immediately dip each one in the cream mixture. Put a large dollop of the chicken mixture on each tortilla and roll it up. Place in an ungreased baking pan, seam side down. When all of the tortillas are done, pour the remaining cream over them and sprinkle the cheese over the top. Bake uncovered for 20 minutes or so, until they are thoroughly heated. Makes 8 servings.

Alejandra Walsh
Los Gatos Ward
Saratoga California Stake
Los Gatos, California

This is a recipe I got out of an old cookbook. I make this regularly, and it always gets rave reviews. I grew up in Mexico and this is not the traditional way of making enchiladas there, but who cares when they taste this good!

RAVE Cheese Enchiladas with Chili Sauce

1½ lb. lean ground beef
½ C. onion, chopped
2 tsp. garlic powder
½ tsp. salt
½ tsp. pepper
8 C. beef broth
2 14.5-oz. cans whole tomatoes
3 Tbsp. chili powder
4½ tsp. paprika

1 Tbsp. ground cumin
⅓ C. cornstarch
⅓ C. water
15–20 corn tortillas
Vegetable oil, enough to cover bottom of skillet
6 C. cheddar cheese, shredded
1 C. onion, chopped
1 C. American cheese, shredded

In a large saucepan or Dutch oven, brown ground beef with ½ C. onion, garlic powder, salt, and pepper. Drain meat on paper towels. Return meat to saucepan and add broth, tomatoes, chili powder, paprika, and cumin. Mix well, breaking up tomatoes with a spoon. Bring to a boil. Reduce heat and simmer uncovered for 1 hour. In a small bowl, mix cornstarch and water until cornstarch is completely dissolved. Gradually add the cornstarch mixture to the chili sauce, stirring constantly. Continue cooking sauce for 5 more minutes. Preheat oven to 350. In a small skillet, heat about ½ inch vegetable oil until hot but not smoking. Quickly fry each tortilla in hot oil to soften, about 2–4 seconds on each side; drain on paper towels. In a large bowl, combine cheddar cheese and 1 C. onion. Mix well. Spoon ⅓ C. cheese mixture down the center of each warm tortilla. Roll up and place seam side down in two 11 x 7-inch baking dishes. Top enchiladas with chili sauce. Cover each dish with foil. Bake for 10 minutes or until hot. Remove foil. Sprinkle with American cheese and continue baking 2 minutes or until cheese melts. Makes 6 servings.

Chezna Givens
Durban 1st Ward
Durban South Africa Stake
Durban, South Africa

This recipe is my specialty. Even though I am in South Africa, I can still make these enchiladas because all the ingredients are available. When I miss home, these enchiladas do the trick. I love this recipe! The secret is the chili sauce. I love the chunky, meaty sauce and of course the oooey, goooey cheese—they are amazing, I promise.

Snow on the Mountain

1 C. fresh mushrooms, sliced
½ C. green pepper, chopped
½ C. butter
½ C. flour
1 tsp. salt
¼ tsp. pepper
2 C. half-n-half
2 C. chicken broth
2 C. chicken, cooked and diced or shredded
Cooked rice

Toppings:
Celery, finely diced
Tomatoes, diced
Cheese, shredded
Green onion, chopped
Chinese noodles
Pineapple chunks
Almonds, blanched and sliced
Coconut, shredded

In a large skillet, sauté mushrooms and green peppers in butter. Blend in flour, salt, and pepper. Stirring constantly, add half-n-half and chicken broth until mixture boils. Add chicken and heat through. To serve, cover plate with cooked rice and top with chicken cream mixture. Add desired toppings to your individual serving, ending with coconut. Makes 6 servings.

While I was growing up, my parents had a rice farm, so we ate a lot of meals that included rice. I could go my whole life without eating any more rice, but I would never give up this family favorite. It's the only meal I love with rice. When you try it you will see why. It's so creamy and wonderful. I never grow tired of this wonderful mountain of deliciousness topped with coconut snow.

Chrissy Vanderkamp
Batesville Ward
Cincinnati Ohio Stake
Greensburg, Indiana

Chicken Supreme

1 large chicken
1 10.75-oz. can cream of chicken soup

2 C. sour cream
1 box stuffing mix

Cook and debone chicken. Cut into bite-size pieces. In a 9 x 13-inch pan, spread chicken evenly on the bottom. Cover chicken with cream of chicken soup. Spread sour cream on top of soup. Prepare stuffing mix as directed on box. Spread on top of sour cream. Cover with aluminum foil. Bake at 350 for 40 minutes and then uncovered for an additional 15 minutes. Makes 6 servings.

This is my signature recipe. When I was young, my mom was the Young Women president. This was our dinner on activity nights, since it is such an easy meal. We also made it after many holidays, using the leftover turkey or ham instead of chicken. Now that I am married, my husband also loves this dish.

Kathryn Donahue Bartholomew
Georgetown Ward
Exeter New Hampshire Stake
Georgetown, Massachusetts

Spaghetti 'n Meatballs

2 eggs
1 C. dry bread crumbs
½ C. Parmesan cheese, grated
½ C. tomato juice, milk, or beef broth
¼ C. green pepper, finely chopped
¼ C. onion, finely chopped
1 tsp. Italian seasoning
½ tsp. salt
½ tsp. poultry seasoning
½ tsp. garlic powder
2 lb. bulk pork sausage
4 C. water

2 11.5-oz. cans tomato juice
3 6-oz. cans tomato paste
1 .5-oz. jar dried celery flakes
1 bay leaf
1 tsp. Italian seasoning
1 tsp. salt
½ tsp. pepper
½ C. green pepper, finely chopped
½ C. onion, finely chopped
2 garlic cloves, minced
Hot cooked spaghetti

In a large bowl, combine eggs, bread crumbs, Parmesan cheese, tomato juice, ¼ C. green pepper, ¼ C. onion, 1 tsp. Italian seasoning, ½ tsp. salt, poultry seasoning, and garlic powder. Crumble sausage over mixture and mix well. Shape into 1-inch balls. In a skillet, brown meatballs over medium heat; drain. In a large saucepan, combine water, tomato juice, tomato paste, celery flakes, bay leaf, 1 tsp. Italian seasoning, 1 tsp. salt, and pepper. Add ½ C. green pepper, ½ C. onion, and garlic. Bring to a boil. Reduce heat; simmer, uncovered, for 30–45 minutes or until thickened, stirring occasionally. Discard bay leaf. Add meatballs to sauce; simmer for 1 hour or until meat is no longer pink. Serve over spaghetti. Makes 12 servings.

This is an old family recipe. The secret is using pork for the meatballs (which makes them tender) and using a whole jar of celery flakes. Use the whole jar, and trust the recipe. This recipe won the spaghetti cook-off in Woodstock, Vermont, when my dad entered in 2003. It's great spaghetti. Add a little brown sugar if you like a little sweetness.

Tim Channing
South Royalton Ward
Montpelier Vermont Stake
Woodstock, Vermont

Suzanne's Roast Beef

1 4-lb. beef roast
2 10.75-oz. cans cream of mushroom soup

½ can water
1 env. onion soup mix (Lipton)

Throw everything in a slow-cooker and cook on low for 8–10 hours. Makes 8 servings.

This is my mother's recipe; she got it from her mom, and it has been a family favorite longer than I can remember. It was my dad's favorite meal.

Audra Behling
Dutch Flat Ward
Ferron Utah Stake
Ferron, Utah

Halushki

1 16-oz. box bow tie pasta

1 head cabbage, chopped

1 large onion, finely diced

1 C. butter

1 kielbasa sausage

Salt

Pepper

Lemon pepper

Cook pasta according to package directions. Drain and set aside. Cook cabbage and onion in butter over medium-high heat for 20–25 minutes. Grill kielbasa and then dice, or dice first and cook in a pan on stovetop. Add the pasta and the sausage to the cabbage/onion mixture. Salt and pepper to taste. Add a little lemon pepper too! It's SO good! Makes 6 servings.

This recipe was given to me while I was working in my second television job in Springfield, Missouri. It is a Polish recipe that has been handed down in the family of my friend, Kelly, for years. I started making it for my husband when we were married and he wanted it every week! Now my two boys go nuts over it as well. It is a family pleaser! It also serves plenty of guests. I consider it my family recipe now!

Reagan Leadbetter
"Good Things Utah"
ABC Channel 4
Salt Lake City, Utah

Quick, Cheap 'n Yummy Spaghetti Sauce

½ lb. ground beef

1 45-oz. can tomato juice

1 7-oz. can sliced mushrooms

1 tsp. onion salt

1 tsp. Italian seasoning

¼ C. Parmesan cheese, grated

1–2 C. potato flakes

Brown ground beef and drain. In a large saucepan, combine browned ground beef, tomato juice, mushrooms, onion salt, Italian seasoning, and grated Parmesan cheese. Simmer over medium heat, stirring occasionally. SLOWLY add potato flakes, stirring until desired thickness is achieved. Do not add too many potato flakes, or you will have "tomatoed potatoes." Serve over cooked spaghetti noodles. Makes 12 servings.

Shanna Hugie
Hyrum 1st Ward
Hyrum Utah North Stake
Hyrum, Utah

The secret to this great spaghetti sauce is the potato flakes. My late husband had a particular dislike for onions, garlic, and peppers, but seemed to think he loved spaghetti. His mother made it from scratch and cooked it all day long. I read the packet of seasoning mix for spaghetti sauce, used tomato juice, and brainstormed for how to thicken it. This recipe has won awards in contests and is often asked for when I cook up a batch for someone else. It is economical, makes a ton, and is EASY.

Fruity Tunawiches

½ C. apple, chopped

1 8-oz. can crushed pineapple, well drained

1 6-oz. can solid white tuna, packed in water, drained

2 oz. cheddar cheese, shredded

2 Tbsp. sliced almonds

2 Tbsp. mayonnaise

Salt and pepper

½ tsp. garlic powder (optional)

4 French rolls, split

4 lettuce leaves

In a medium bowl, combine all ingredients except rolls and lettuce leaves; mix lightly. To assemble each sandwich, line bottom half of each roll with lettuce leaf. Spread each with ¼ tuna mixture; top with bun top. You will never make a tuna sandwich the same way again! Makes 4 servings.

Amelia Jones
Guildford Ward
Staines England Stake
Guildford, Surrey
England

Bull's Eye Meatloaf

1 lb. ground beef

½ lb. ground turkey

½ lb. sausage

1–2 slices of whole-wheat bread, broken into small pieces

1 egg

Splash of milk

1 env. meatloaf seasoning

⅓ C. onion, chopped

¼ C. raisins (optional)

¼ C. walnuts (optional)

½ C. barbecue sauce (I prefer Bull's Eye)

In a large bowl, hand mix all ingredients except barbecue sauce. Form into a loaf shape and place in an 8.5 x 8-inch glass dish. Bake at 375 for 1 hour. Remove from oven and spread barbecue sauce on top of meatloaf with brush. Return to oven and bake for an additional 10 minutes until glazed. Remove meatloaf from oven and allow to sit for 10 minutes before slicing into thick pieces. Makes 8 servings.

Deborah Seraydarian
Chesterfield 1st Ward
Chesterfield Richmond Virginia Stake
Chesterfield, Virginia

The secret to this meatloaf is the sausage, nuts, and raisins. My husband made this meatloaf for me and I fell in love with it. It wasn't until we were married for five years that he decided to show me how to make it. I love the crunchy nuts and the sweetness of the raisins and barbecue sauce. It is also very hearty. People always ask for more slices of this meatloaf.

Bar-B-Que Spareribs

5–6 lbs. spareribs

Salt and pepper

1 onion, sliced

1 C. packed brown sugar

2 10.75-oz. cans tomato soup

1 8-oz. can tomato sauce

¼ C. vinegar

1 Tbsp. Worcestershire sauce

¾ C. water

2 tsp. cinnamon

1 tsp. chili powder

Place meat in 9 x 13-inch pan; sprinkle with salt and pepper. Place onion slices on top and sprinkle brown sugar over the onion. In a large saucepan, combine soup, tomato sauce, vinegar, Worcestershire sauce, water, cinnamon, and chili powder; heat just until warm. Pour over meat and bake at 350 for 3–4 hours. Makes 6 servings.

Back when Primary was after school during the week, my mother would put these ribs, potatoes, and squash in the oven to bake while we were all at Primary and Dad was at work. By the time we all got home, dinner was ready and we could sit right down and eat. The secret to this recipe is the cinnamon and chili powder. I was surprised to find them in the recipe when I got it from my mother so I could serve it to my family of eight boys.

Lynne Fisher
Redlands 2nd Ward
Redlands California Stake
Redlands, California

Bierochs

1 small head cabbage, chopped

¼ tsp. garlic

1 onion, chopped

1 lb. ground beef

2 C. cheese, shredded, divided

Pepper

Beau Monde seasoning (McCormick)

Bread dough or frozen roll dough, thawed

In a large saucepan, cook cabbage, garlic, and onion until soft and transparent. In a skillet, brown ground beef. In a large bowl, combine cabbage mixture, browned ground beef, and 1 C. cheese. Season with pepper and Beau Monde seasoning to taste. Pinch dough into pieces about the size of very small roll. Flatten dough with your hand. Place about 1–1½ Tbsp. cabbage and beef filling onto dough. Place more shredded cheese on top. Fold dough up around filling, forming a stuffed roll. Place on greased baking sheet. Bake at 350 for 20 minutes or until light brown. Makes 18–24 rolls.

Emily and Linda Hess
Cedarcrest Ward
Marysville Washington Stake
Marysville, Washington

Kung Pao Chicken

1 lb. boneless, skinless chicken breast, cut into 1-inch pieces

1 Tbsp. cornstarch

2 tsp. light sesame oil or vegetable oil

3 Tbsp. green onions, chopped with tops

2 garlic cloves, minced

¼–1½ tsp. crushed red pepper flakes (to your own taste)

½ tsp. powdered ginger (can use fresh-grated if preferred)

2 Tbsp. rice wine vinegar

2 Tbsp. soy sauce

2 tsp. sugar

⅓ C. dry roasted peanuts

4 C. cooked rice, hot

Combine chicken and cornstarch in small bowl. Toss to coat chicken. Heat oil in large nonstick skillet or wok over medium heat. Add chicken. Stir-fry 5–7 minutes or until no longer pink in center. Remove from heat. Add onions, garlic, red pepper flakes, and ginger to skillet. Stir-fry 15 seconds. Remove from heat. In a small bowl, combine vinegar, soy sauce, and sugar; stir well. Add to skillet. Return chicken to skillet. Stir until chicken is well coated. Stir in peanuts. Heat thoroughly, stirring occasionally. Serve over hot rice. Makes 10 servings.

Esther Lee
Bedok Ward
Singapore Stake
Bedok, Singapore

This is my family recipe for Kung Pao Chicken. The flavor is very good and the ingredients are simple items you can find at any store. The secret sauce makes this the most popular dish in our home. Most people are amazed at how easy it really is, so don't let the long list of ingredients fool you. Once you start you will see Asian food is not as hard to prepare as you might think.

Mexican Chicken Manicotti

1 8-oz. pkg. manicotti shells

2 C. chicken, cubed and cooked

2 C. Monterey Jack cheese, shredded, divided

1½ C. cheddar cheese, shredded

1 C. sour cream

1 small onion, diced, divided

1 4-oz. can chopped green chiles, divided

1 10.75-oz. can cream of chicken soup

1 C. salsa

⅔ C. milk

(recipe continued on next page)

(Mexican Chicken Manicotti, continued)

Cook manicotti according to package directions. Meanwhile, in a large bowl, combine the chicken, 1½ C. Monterey Jack cheese, cheddar cheese, sour cream, ½ of the onion, and 6 Tbsp. green chiles. In a separate bowl, combine soup, salsa, milk, and remaining onion and chiles. Spread ½ C. soup/salsa mixture in a greased 9 x 13-inch baking dish. Drain manicotti and rinse in cold water. Stuff each manicotti with about ¼ C. of the chicken mixture. Arrange over sauce in baking dish. Pour remaining sauce over shells. Cover and bake at 350 for 30 minutes. Uncover; sprinkle with remaining Monterrey Jack cheese. Bake 10 minutes longer or until cheese is melted. Makes 8 servings.

Darcy Lind
Canyon Gate Ward
Las Vegas Nevada Sandstone Stake
Las Vegas, Nevada

For my bridal shower all the ladies in my ward brought a recipe and put it in a recipe keeper. This was one of my favorites. Twelve years later, I still love this as much as I did the first time I tried it. It's very easy and reminds me of all the wonderful ladies in my hometown.

Apple-Glazed BBQ Chicken

6 oz. frozen apple juice concentrate, thawed
¼ C. packed brown sugar
¼ C. ketchup
1 Tbsp. apple cider vinegar
1 tsp. dried thyme, crumbled

⅛ tsp. hot sauce (Tabasco)
3 lb. chicken pieces (wings, drumsticks, thighs)
Vegetable oil
Salt and pepper

In a heavy saucepan, combine apple juice concentrate, brown sugar, ketchup, vinegar, thyme, and hot sauce. Heat until sugar melts completely. Cool. In shallow baking dish, place chicken in a single layer. Pour half of the cooled sauce over chicken, turning once to coat both sides. Cover and marinate for up to 24 hours. Prepare the grill. Remove chicken from marinade. Brush each piece with oil. Season generously with salt and pepper. Grill until chicken is almost cooked through, turning occasionally, about 20 minutes. Brush with the reserved glaze. Continue grilling until chicken is cooked through, turning and brushing with glaze frequently, about 10 more minutes. Makes 4 servings.

Anastasia Upton
Falls Lake Ward
Raleigh North Carolina Stake
Raleigh, North Carolina

This is my favorite way to prepare chicken. The secret is the grilling. I can't vouch for how it would taste baked, although it would probably still taste awesome. I use this for chicken pieces and for boneless skinless breasts. This recipe will be a keeper once you try it.

Ginger-Glazed Salmon

¼ C. packed brown sugar

2 Tbsp. Dijon mustard

1 Tbsp. grated fresh or 1 tsp. ground ginger

4 6-oz. wild Pacific salmon fillets, about 1 inch thick, skinned

½ tsp. salt

½ tsp. freshly ground black pepper

Coat rack of broiler pan with nonstick cooking spray. Preheat broiler. In small bowl, whisk sugar, mustard, and ginger. Season both sides of fillets with salt and pepper. Place salmon on broiler rack and brush glaze on top. Broil 6 inches from heat for 8–10 minutes or until fish is lightly browned and opaque. Serve each fillet on top of a lightly dressed mixed green salad. Makes 4 servings.

The secret nature of this recipe is love. When my husband and I were dating, this meal was the first one he made for me. At the time, I had no idea I was going to fall for him, but I knew for a fact that I had fallen for his cooking. The first time he met my family they insisted he make the famous salmon they had heard all about. He did, and, of course, they loved it! Now, every time we get together with my family, we always make this scrumptious salmon dish together.

Stephanie Thompson
Holmes Lake Ward
Lincoln Nebraska Stake
Lincoln, Nebraska

Chicken Spaghetti

¼ C. butter

¼ C. flour

⅔ C. chicken broth

½ C. half-n-half or light cream

½ C. sour cream

1 C. Parmesan cheese, grated

¼ C. apple juice or white grape juice

1–2 garlic cloves, minced

1 tsp. lemon juice

½ tsp. dry mustard

Salt and pepper to taste

3 C. chicken breast, cubed and cooked

8 oz. cooked spaghetti

2 tsp. paprika

Extra Parmesan cheese

Fresh parsley, chopped

In a saucepan, melt butter; add flour, stirring constantly. When mixture thickens, add chicken broth, half-n-half, sour cream, Parmesan cheese, juice, garlic, lemon juice, dry mustard, salt, and pepper. Stir over medium heat until mixture again starts to thicken. Add chicken and spaghetti and stir well. Place in a baking dish and sprinkle with paprika and extra Parmesan cheese. Bake at 350 for 30 minutes. Sprinkle with parsley and serve. Makes 10 servings.

Wendi Moat
Brookings Ward
Sioux Falls South Dakota Stake
Brookings, South Dakota

Secretly Amazing Turkey and Swiss Sandwiches

6 Tbsp. butter, softened

8 slices country-style French bread

¾ C. red onion, chopped

1 Tbsp. dried thyme

½ C. mayonnaise

¼ C. coarse-grain brown mustard

1 lb. roast turkey, thinly sliced

8 slices tomato

8 slices Swiss cheese

Spread butter on one side of each slice of bread. In a small bowl, combine red onion, thyme, mayonnaise, and mustard. Spread mixture onto the other side of each slice of bread. Heat a large skillet over medium heat. Place 4 slices of the bread into the skillet with the butter side down. On each slice of bread, layer ¼ of the sliced turkey, then 2 slices of tomato, and top with 2 slices of Swiss cheese. Place remaining slices of bread over the top with the butter side up. When the bottoms of the sandwiches are golden brown, flip over, and cook until golden on the other side. Makes 4 sandwiches.

Dina Haines
Hoover Ward
Bessemer Alabama Stake
Pelham, Alabama

These sandwiches are incredible! We have been making these sandwiches for years. I first tasted them at my daughter's girls' camp fifteen years ago. My whole family has been addicted to these ever since. They are lifesavers when you just don't feel like cooking anything for dinner, because they are quick, easy, and taste like a million bucks!

Navajo Tacos and Indian Fry Bread

Tacos:

1½ lb. ground beef

1 16-oz. can refried beans

1 env. taco seasoning mix

1½ C. water

3 C. flour

1 Tbsp. baking powder

1 tsp. salt

1½ C. water

Vegetable oil (for frying)

Toppings:

Sour cream

Lettuce, shredded

Cheese, shredded

Tomato, diced

Onion, chopped

Salsa

(recipe continued on next page)

(Navajo Tacos and Indian Fry Bread, continued)

In a frying pan with a lid, thoroughly combine ground beef, refried beans, taco seasoning mix, and water. Bring mixture to a boil. Cover, reduce heat, and simmer for 1 hour. Uncover and continue to simmer until liquid is reduced and mixture is thick. This usually takes another 20 minutes or so—just enough time to make the Indian Fry Bread. In a large bowl, combine flour, baking powder, and salt; mix well. Add water gradually, forming a stiff dough. Pull off egg-sized balls of dough and quickly roll, pull, and, on a floured surface, pat them out into large, plate-sized rounds. They should be thin in the middle and about ¼ inch thick around the edges. Using a fork, poke holes in the dough to prevent bubbles from forming. In a skillet, heat ½ inch vegetable oil. Brown dough circles on each side until golden brown. Use a fork to poke any bubbles that may form. When golden brown, lift from oil, shake gently to remove bulk of oil, and place on paper towels to drain. Spread meat/bean mixture on Indian Fry Bread and top with your favorite toppings: sour cream, lettuce, cheese, tomato, onion, and/or salsa. Makes 10 servings.

This is one of my family's most-requested meals. It truly is awesome. I promise you will never eat tacos with the traditional shell after trying it this way. The Indian Fry Bread is the secret that makes these tacos so wonderful.

Celine Hawkins
Fishers 2nd Ward
Indianapolis Indiana North Stake
Cicero, Indiana

Pizza Casserole

1 12-oz. bag uncooked wide egg noodles (or any fun shape)

1 lb. sausage

1 8-oz. can sliced olives

1 8-oz. can sliced mushrooms

1 26-oz. jar meaty spaghetti sauce

1 lb. cheese, shredded (any kind)

Heat oven to 350. Cook pasta according to package directions and drain. While pasta is cooking, cook sausage in a pan over medium-high heat. Stir while cooking, and make sure it is broken down into small pieces and cooked through. In a large bowl, combine cooked pasta, browned sausage, olives, mushrooms, and spaghetti sauce. Set aside 1 C. of the cheese. Mix remaining cheese into bowl. Transfer to a large casserole dish. Sprinkle reserved cheese over top. Cover with tin foil and bake for 30 minutes or until hot and bubbly. Take off tin foil cover and bake uncovered for 10–15 additional minutes or until cheese has melted and is slightly crusted on top. Remove and let stand a few minutes so cheese can harden a little. Makes 8 servings.

Andrea Vogel-Cardon
Walnut Creek 2nd Ward
Oakland California Stake
Walnut Creek, California

Being a Marine Corps wife of ten years, I never know if my husband is going to be home for dinner or if I need to take dinner to him. This is a very easy dish that you can whip up in less than an hour. My secret is to double the recipe and make two. That way I can feed my family and put the other one in the freezer. Then, if I need a dinner fast, I can pop the frozen one in the oven for an hour, and voila! It's like magic happened!

Swiss Cheese Pie

1 unbaked pie crust

1 egg, separated

1½–2 C. Gruyère cheese, grated

1 Tbsp. flour

¼ C. onion, finely diced

½ C. milk

¾ C. plain yogurt

Salt to taste

Nutmeg to taste

Preheat oven to 400. Do not prick pie crust. Stiffly beat the egg white. In a bowl, combine cheese, flour, and onion. In a separate bowl, combine egg yolk, milk, yogurt, salt, and nutmeg. Add egg mixture to cheese mixture. Fold in beaten egg white. Pour into pie shell and bake 30–40 minutes, until browned and filling is just barely set.

Cheese is almost a national food in Switzerland. This is a yummy traditional Swiss treat that can be purchased in almost any Swiss pastry shop. It is usually made into small individual pies, about 5 inches in diameter. People buy it hot or cold and might eat it walking to work. I made and served the small version of this recipe as part of the buffet at my daughter's wedding reception.

Suzanne Ramseyer
Solothurn Ward
Bern Switzerland Stake
Bellach, Switzerland

Creamy Chicken Lasagna

3 boneless, skinless chicken breasts

6 uncooked lasagna noodles

1 cube chicken bouillon

¼ C. hot water

8 oz. cream cheese, softened

2 C. mozzarella cheese, shredded, divided

1 26-oz. jar spaghetti sauce

In a saucepan, place chicken with enough water to cover it and bring to a boil. Cook for 20 minutes or until no longer pink and juices run clear; shred. Bring a large pot of lightly salted water to a boil. Cook lasagna noodles for 8–10 minutes, rinse with cold water, and set aside. Preheat oven to 350. Dissolve bouillon cube in ¼ C. hot water. In a large bowl, mix chicken, bouillon, cream cheese, and 1 C. mozzarella cheese. Spread ⅓ of spaghetti sauce in bottom of a 9-inch square dish. Cover with half of chicken mixture; top with 3 noodles. Repeat layers. Top with remaining sauce and sprinkle with remaining mozzarella cheese. Bake for 45 minutes. Makes 9 servings.

My neighbor made this wonderful lasagna for me right after my daughter was born. My husband and I love this recipe and asked my neighbor for it. It has become one of our favorites. I was amazed when I read the recipe and found out that the secret ingredients are the cream cheese and a bouillon cube. I add more bouillon cubes to give it a little extra flavor!

Andrea Ingleby
Fort Herriman 3rd Ward
Fort Herriman Utah Stake
Riverton, Utah

Cuban Ropa Vieja

1 Tbsp. vegetable oil
2 lb. beef flank steak
1 C. beef broth
1 8-oz. can tomato sauce
1 small onion, sliced
1 green bell pepper, sliced
2 cloves garlic, chopped

1 6-oz. can tomato paste
1 tsp. ground cumin
1 tsp. fresh cilantro, chopped
1 Tbsp. olive oil
1 Tbsp. white vinegar

Heat vegetable oil in a large skillet over medium-high heat. Brown the flank steak on each side, about 4 minutes per side. Transfer beef to a slow-cooker. Pour in the beef broth and tomato sauce, then add onion, bell pepper, garlic, tomato paste, cumin, cilantro, olive oil, and vinegar. Stir until well blended. Cover and cook on high for 4 hours or on low for up to 10 hours. When ready to serve, shred meat and serve with tortillas or rice. Makes 8 servings.

I love Cuban food, and I especially love all the Cuban ladies in our ward who can make the most delicious meals. I got this recipe from Carla, a friend from Cuba, who I met a long time ago while in the singles' ward. I lost touch with Carla but I think of her each time I make this. This is a must-have according to the missionaries. Every time we ask them what they would like for dinner, this is almost always the meal of choice.

Karsyn Prevara
Boynton Beach Ward
Pompano Beach Florida Stake
Boynton Beach, Florida

Mrs. Geraldine's Ground Beef Casserole

1 lb. ground beef
¼ C. onion, chopped
¼ C. bell pepper, chopped
¼ C. celery, chopped
1 15-oz. can tomatoes
1 8-oz. can tomato sauce
1 8-oz. can mushrooms

2 Tbsp. brown sugar or sweet pickle juice
2 Tbsp. Worcestershire sauce
Salt and pepper
1 6-oz. pkg. angel hair pasta, cooked
1 10.75-oz. can cream of mushroom soup
¼ lb. sharp cheddar cheese, shredded

(recipe continued on next page)

(Mrs. Geraldine's Ground Beef Casserole, continued)

In a large skillet or Dutch oven, brown ground beef; add onions, bell pepper, and celery, and simmer for 15 minutes. Add tomatoes, tomato sauce, mushrooms, brown sugar, and Worcestershire sauce. Add salt and pepper to taste. Cook in skillet for 1 hour. Place cooked pasta in bottom of large casserole dish. Spoon cream of mushroom soup over pasta. Pour sauce over the soup, and top with cheese. Bake at 350 for 30–45 minutes. Makes 12 servings.

Emily Price
Laurel Ward
Annapolis Maryland Stake
Laurel, Maryland

This recipe came from a local church fundraising cookbook. Mrs. Geraldine is a good friend of the family. She reminds me so much of Mrs. Claus that I can't help but smile every time I think of her. This recipe freezes well—just put it together and freeze it without baking. Then thaw and bake on a busy day.

Chicken Chimichangas with Green Sauce

2 10.5-oz. cans cream of chicken soup

2 4-oz. cans diced green chiles

5 pitted green olives

1 jalapeño pepper, seeded and chopped

2 Tbsp. fresh lime juice

1 8-oz. pkg. cream cheese

1 8-oz. pkg. Monterey Jack cheese, shredded

½ env. taco seasoning

1 lb. chicken, cooked and shredded

8 10-inch flour tortillas

½ C. vegetable oil

1 8-oz. pkg. sharp cheddar cheese, shredded

1 C. green onion, chopped

1 C. sour cream

Pour the cream of chicken soup into a blender along with the green chiles, olives, jalapeño, and lime juice. Puree until smooth. Pour into a saucepan and warm over medium-low heat. In a large bowl, stir the cream cheese, Monterey Jack cheese, and taco seasoning until well blended. Fold in chicken. Evenly divide mixture among the 8 tortillas. Fold each tortilla into a rectangular packet around the filling. Heat the vegetable oil in a large skillet over medium-high heat. Fry 4 chimichangas at a time until golden brown. Drain on paper towels. Ladle warm sauce over each serving. Sprinkle with cheddar cheese and green onions. Finish with a dollop of sour cream. Makes 8 servings.

Bricelynn Jeeter
Savannah Ward
Savannah Georgia Stake
Tybee Island, Georgia

My family loves Mexican food—or Tex-Mex, I should say. I grew up in San Antonio, Texas, and I had never found any recipe even close to my favorite chimichangas until this one came along. These chimichangas are wonderful. You can bake them for a healthier version without altering the taste; just brush the tops with olive oil.

Millie's Meatballs

1 egg

1 env. dry onion soup mix

1 tsp. garlic from a jar or 1–2 cloves fresh garlic, peeled and chopped

½ tsp. black pepper

1½ lb. lean ground beef (at least 93% lean)

⅔ C. Italian seasoned bread crumbs

¾ C. evaporated milk

Preheat oven to 350. Spray a 9 x 13-inch glass baking dish with nonstick spray. In a large bowl, combine egg, soup mix, garlic, and pepper. With a fork, mix in ground beef and bread crumbs. Stir in evaporated milk. Mixture should not be too dry, but well moistened. Roll into about 24 golf-ball-size meatballs and place in sprayed baking dish so that meatballs do not touch each other. Cover with foil or glass lid. Bake for 28–35 minutes. These meatballs can be served drenched in your favorite sweet-and-sour sauce, but our family prefers to add them to a red sauce and serve them over cooked pasta. Enjoy! Makes 6–8 servings.

My mother's family came from Italy, and I grew up with the "dump-and-taste" method of cooking—in other words, very few written family recipes. If it looked good and tasted right, it was done. My mother died far too young in 2008. A few weeks after her death, a dear former BYU roommate sent me my mother's recipe for the meatballs I had grown up on. I was shocked, having completely forgotten that this recipe had ever been written down. Suffice it to say, no card or flowers could have comforted me as much as receiving this recipe. With delight, I share it with you.

Shannon McClary Smurthwaite
Tuscany Ward
Meridian Idaho South Stake
Meridian, Idaho

Skinny Alfredo

1 16-oz pkg. noodles (your choice)

6 Tbsp. butter

2 Tbsp. flour

¾ tsp. salt

½ tsp. garlic powder

¼ tsp. pepper

2½ C. milk

4 oz. cream cheese, cut in chunks

⅔ C. fresh Parmesan cheese, grated

Cook noodles according to package directions. Drain and set aside. In a heavy saucepan, melt the butter; remove from heat. Blend in the flour, salt, garlic powder, and pepper. Add the milk all at once. Return to heat. Cook over medium heat, stirring constantly, until mixture is thickened and bubbly. Cook for 1 more minute. Add cream cheese and stir with wire whisk. Add Parmesan cheese. Stir until both cream cheese and Parmesan cheese are melted. Add sauce to prepared noodles and serve. Makes 4 servings.

I love Alfredo sauce, and this is an easier, lower-fat recipe that still tastes amazing! It is the secret to being able to watch your waistline and still eat Alfredo.

Melinda Moss
Willard 3rd Ward
Willard Utah Stake
Willard, Utah

Delfina's AWESOME Enchiladas

2 lb. skinless, boneless chicken breast, cut into chunks

1 10.75-oz. can cream of chicken soup

1¼ C. sour cream

¼ tsp. chili powder

1 Tbsp. butter

1 small onion, chopped

1 4-oz. can chopped green chiles, drained

1 env. mild taco seasoning mix

1 bunch green onions, chopped, divided

1 C. water

1 tsp. lime juice

½ tsp. onion powder

½ tsp. garlic powder

5 12-inch flour tortillas

3 C. cheddar cheese, shredded, divided

1 10-oz. can enchilada sauce

1 6-oz. can sliced black olives

In a large pot, cover the chicken with water and bring to a boil over high heat; reduce the heat to medium-low, cover, and simmer until the chicken pieces are no longer pink, about 10 minutes. Shred chicken by placing two forks back to back and pulling meat apart. Set the shredded chicken aside. Meanwhile, in a saucepan, combine the cream of chicken soup, sour cream, and chili powder; bring to a simmer over low heat, stirring occasionally, until heated through. Turn off heat and cover to keep warm. In a skillet, heat butter over medium heat; stir in onion. Cook and stir until the onion has softened and turned translucent, about 5 minutes. Add shredded chicken, chopped green chiles, taco seasoning, half the chopped green onions, and water. Allow to simmer for 10 minutes. Stir in lime juice, onion powder, and garlic powder; simmer for an additional 10 minutes. Preheat oven to 350. Stir 1 C. soup mixture into the skillet with the chicken mixture. Spread the remaining soup mixture on the bottom of a 9 x 13-inch baking dish. Fill each tortilla with chicken mixture. Sprinkle cheddar cheese over the chicken filling and then roll up, reserving half of the shredded cheese for topping the enchiladas. Place enchiladas seam side down in the prepared pan. Pour enchilada sauce evenly over the enchiladas. Cover with the remaining half of the cheddar cheese. Sprinkle the reserved chopped green onions and the sliced olives on top of the cheese. Bake until filling is heated through and the cheese is melted and bubbling, about 25 minutes. Makes 8 servings.

While visiting the United States I came up with this enchilada recipe. I wanted to make my normal traditional Mexican dishes, but I never had all the ingredients on hand—so I threw this and that together. I used whatever I could find on hand in the pantry. I came up with these nontraditional Mexican enchiladas. The seasonings are my secret blend from the traditional recipe. My family loves this Tex-Mex version more than my traditional version.

Delfina Amate
Santo Domingo Ward
San Nicolás Mexico Stake
Ensenada, Mexico

Meat Pie

2 lb. round steak, diced

1 large onion, diced

7–8 potatoes, diced

Lots of salt and pepper

3½ C. flour

1½ tsp. salt

1¼ C. shortening

About ¾ C. water

(recipe continued on next page)

(Meat Pie, continued)

In a large pot, boil the meat and onion for about 2 hours. Add diced potatoes. Add salt and pepper liberally to taste. Boil for an additional 15 minutes, until potatoes are soft. In a large bowl, combine flour and salt. Cut in shortening until crumbs form. Add water a little at a time to form pastry dough. Divide dough in half. Roll out one half on a floured board to cover bottom and sides of a 9 x 13-inch baking pan. Spoon the meat mixture into the pan, reserving the broth. Sprinkle the meat mixture with salt and pepper. Roll out remaining dough and place over the top. Seal and crimp the edges. Vent the top crust and bake at 350 for about 45–55 minutes, until golden brown. Serve portions in a bowl and pour the reserved meat broth over the top. It usually needs more salt and pepper. If you have a meat-and-potatoes man, he will love it! Makes 10–12 servings.

WARNING: Meat Pie is extremely filling. It's tempting to have a second or third helping, but you'll be sorry. Once the meat pie settles a little in your tummy it has a tendency to swell. Newcomers to Meat Pie have been known to spend an hour or so rolling on the floor with very uncomfortable bloated stomachs! The secret to this recipe is the salt and pepper. Don't be tempted to add carrots, celery, or other ingredients, because they completely change the taste. In our family, Meat Pie is our favorite recipe and the ultimate family gathering meal. I even call my sisters long-distance just to taunt them that we are having Meat Pie and they're not. This recipe came out of the Depression when my grandmother had to feed a family of nine on pretty basic ingredients, and it has been handed down for four generations.

Jacqueline Price
Parkland Ward
Lakewood Washington Stake
Tacoma, Washington

Italian Chicken

4 boneless, skinless chicken breasts (slightly thawed works best for cutting raw)
½ C. margarine or butter
1 env. dry Italian salad dressing mix

1 10.75-oz. can cream of chicken soup
1 8-oz. pkg. cream cheese
½–1 C. water
Bow tie pasta or cooked rice

Cube raw chicken and put into a slow-cooker. Add butter or margarine and dressing mix. Cook on low for 6 hours, and then turn up to high and cook 1 additional hour. Stir in soup and cream cheese, and cook for an additional ½ hour. Stir in enough water to create a smooth consistency. Serve over rice or noodles. Makes 6–8 servings.

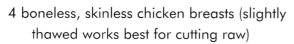

My first calling in Relief Society was as the enrichment counselor in the Relief Society presidency. We had to serve a dinner as part of my first assignment, and this main dish was a hit! The secret is that it's so easy! It's very rich and filling, and takes practically no work. We've served this dish for the missionaries, too, and they love it every time. Warning: this is not for the dieter—it's pure comfort food.

Katie Archer
Augusta Ranch 1st Ward
Desert Ridge Arizona Stake
Mesa, Arizona

Lemon Chicken

4 lb. chicken breasts, cut into large pieces

2 C. fresh lemon juice

2 C. flour

2 tsp. salt

2 tsp. paprika

1 tsp. pepper

½ C. corn oil

2 Tbsp. lemon zest

¼ C. brown sugar

¼ C. chicken stock

1 tsp. lemon extract

Combine chicken and lemon juice in bowl or zipper bag; marinate in refrigerator overnight. Drain chicken. In a plastic bag, combine flour, salt, paprika, and pepper; shake well to mix. Put a few pieces of chicken in bag at a time; shake to coat well. Preheat oven to 350. Heat corn oil in frying pan. Fry chicken pieces, a few at a time, for 5 minutes on each side until browned. Arrange chicken pieces in a single layer in a large, shallow baking dish. Sprinkle with lemon zest and brown sugar. Mix chicken stock and lemon extract; pour around chicken. Bake 35–40 minutes or until tender. Makes 6 servings.

Amanda Porter
North Ogden 15th Ward
Coldwater Utah Stake
North Ogden, Utah

Walking Taco

1½ lb. ground beef

1 small onion, chopped

1 tsp. garlic salt

Salt and pepper to taste

10 2.75-oz. bags corn chips (Fritos) or cheese tortilla chips (Doritos)

2 C. lettuce, shredded

1 C. tomatoes, chopped

1 C. cheddar cheese, shredded

1 C. sour cream

1 8-oz. can chopped black olives, drained

Taco sauce to taste

In a skillet, brown ground beef with onion, garlic salt, salt, and pepper. Cut ¼ inch off the top of chip bags. Crush chips slightly. Divide cooked hamburger mixture among the bags, and fill each one. Top with lettuce, tomatoes, cheese, sour cream, and olives. Add taco sauce on top. Stick fork in bag and serve. Makes 10 servings.

This a great, quick recipe that the kids love. We served these at our daughter's birthday party and at our son's Little League baseball party.

Marta McPherson
Salisbury Ward
Wilmington Delaware Stake
Selbyville, Delaware

Cajun Pasta

4 oz. linguine pasta

2 boneless, skinless chicken breast halves, sliced into thin strips, or 1 lb. shrimp, peeled and deveined

4 tsp. Cajun seasoning

2 Tbsp. butter

1 green bell pepper, chopped

½ red bell pepper, chopped

1 green onion, minced

1½ C. heavy cream

¼ tsp. dried basil

¼ tsp. lemon pepper

¼ tsp. salt

⅛ tsp. garlic powder

⅛ tsp. ground black pepper

2 Tbsp. Parmesan cheese, grated

Bring a large pot of lightly salted water to a boil. Add linguine pasta and cook for 8–10 minutes, or until al dente; drain. Meanwhile, place chicken or shrimp and Cajun seasoning in a bowl; toss to coat. In a large skillet over medium heat, sauté chicken or shrimp in butter until chicken is no longer pink and juices run clear, or until shrimp is pink—about 5–7 minutes. Add green and red bell peppers and green onions; cook for 2–3 minutes. Reduce heat and stir in heavy cream. Season the sauce with basil, lemon pepper, salt, garlic powder, and ground black pepper; heat through. In a large bowl, toss linguine with sauce. Sprinkle with grated Parmesan cheese. Makes 12 servings.

In Louisiana everyone likes crawfish. I don't like them, so I figured I'd better learn how to make something else that involves Cajun seasoning. This is really delicious. I make this when trying to impress a crowd. Works like a charm every time. It is one of our family's most cherished dishes. It can be made with shrimp or chicken. Also, don't hesitate to use a bag of frozen mixed bell peppers instead of fresh. It saves on chopping and prep time. Consider doubling the sauce—you won't regret it.

Danielle Martinez
Covington Ward
New Orleans Louisiana Stake
Abita Springs, Louisiana

Armenian Meat Pies

70 frozen dinner rolls (frozen unbaked dough)

Filling:

3 green peppers, ground or finely chopped

½ sweet onion, ground or finely chopped

1 big bunch parsley, chopped

4 C. canned, diced tomatoes

½ tsp. allspice

1 Tbsp. salt

½ tsp. cayenne pepper

2 lbs. lean ground beef

This recipe is probably close to a hundred years old! In the early 1950s, my mom, Carol Wagner, was in the Missionary Club (a group of girls waiting for missionaries), where she met Elaine Plowgian. Elaine's mother brought this recipe with her from Armenia many years ago, Elaine gave the recipe to Mom, and now, sixty years later, Mom's still making these pies.

(recipe continued on next page)

(Armenian Meat Pies, continued)

Thaw frozen rolls according to package directions and let rise until double in size. Stretch each ball of dough into a circle about 4 inches in diameter. Place dough circles on greased baking sheets. Preheat oven to 450. In a food processor, combine green peppers, onion, and parsley. Process until liquid (you can use a blender if you don't have a food processor, or you can just finely chop by hand). Pour into a large bowl. Add tomatoes, allspice, salt, and cayenne pepper. Mix well to combine. Add ground beef. Mix with hands until well combined. Spread about 2–3 Tbsp. meat mixture evenly over each dough circle (don't mound the meat, or it won't cook thoroughly!). Bake in the upper third of oven for 20 minutes. Serve warm or at room temperature—but they're also good cold! Makes 70 pies.

Nan Slaughter
Sammamish 2nd Ward
Redmond Washington Stake
Sammamish, Washington

Green Enchiladas

½–¾ lb. ground beef
½ medium onion, finely chopped
1 clove garlic, minced
1 tsp. chili powder
Salt and pepper to taste
12 corn tortillas
Vegetable oil
1 large onion, chopped

1 ½ C. American cheese or Monterey Jack cheese, grated
¼ C. margarine
3 Tbsp. flour
½ tsp. salt
2 C. milk
1 4-oz. can chopped green chiles

Brown the ground beef, ½ chopped onion, and garlic until the meat is cooked through. Add chili powder, salt, and pepper; set aside. Soften tortillas by frying in ½ inch of hot oil for only a few seconds; do not allow them to become crisp. Place a spoonful of meat mixture on a tortilla. Add a tablespoon of onion and cheese. Roll up and place seam side down in a 9 x 13-inch baking dish. Prepare remaining tortillas in the same manner. Any remaining meat and cheese may be sprinkled on top of enchiladas. Add more cheese, if desired. In a medium saucepan, melt margarine over medium heat; add flour and salt and stir until bubbly. Add milk; stir until smooth and slightly thickened. Add green chiles and remove from heat. Pour over enchiladas. Bake at 350 for 15 minutes, or until thoroughly heated. Makes 6 servings.

This is the recipe for my favorite enchiladas. I make them at least once a month. I prefer using Velveeta because it's so creamy, but this is equally good with Monterrey Jack cheese. I have made these for Linger Longer at church and have been asked to bring them after every fast and testimony meeting. These enchiladas will knock your socks off and are so incredibly easy to throw together. The cream sauce makes them *muy bueno!*

Marta McPherson
Salisbury Ward
Wilmington Delaware Stake
Selbyville, Delaware

Lasagna

1 lb. ground beef
½ tsp. garlic salt
2 6-oz. cans tomato paste
1 15-oz. can tomato sauce
1 Tbsp. whole basil
¼ tsp. salt
2 15.5-oz. cans stewed tomatoes
10 oz. lasagna noodles

2 eggs, beaten
3 C. cottage cheese
½ C. Parmesan cheese
2 eggs, beaten
1 tsp. salt
½ tsp. pepper
2 Tbsp. parsley flakes
1 lb. mozzarella cheese, shredded

In a large skillet, brown ground beef and drain. Add garlic salt, tomato paste, tomato sauce, basil, salt, and stewed tomatoes. Set aside. In a large pan, cook noodles according to package instructions. In a large bowl, combine cottage cheese, Parmesan cheese, eggs, salt, pepper, and parsley flakes. In a 9 x 13-inch pan, make the following layers: sauce, noodles, cottage cheese mixture, shredded cheese; repeat all layers. Bake at 375 for 30 minutes. Top with additional shredded cheese and bake 5 minutes longer. I always assemble my lasagna and then put it in the refrigerator or freezer; I then increase the baking time to 60 minutes if refrigerated, 90 minutes if frozen. Makes 6–8 servings.

Diana Stacey
Porters Crossing Ward
Eagle Mountain Utah East Stake
Eagle Mountain, Utah

This recipe has been passed down for three generations now. We all use the same recipe, with maybe a slight variation depending on what ingredients we have on hand at the moment. The secret about this recipe is that it always turns out different, depending on who makes it! It is the funniest thing! Whenever we have it for dinner we always ask each other for the recipe, thinking it's not the same one! We always laugh when we realize that it is the same recipe!

{ COOKIES }

Whoever wishes to keep a secret must hide the fact that he possesses one.

{ Jean de La Fontaine }

Outrageous Oatmeal Cookies

2 C. flour

1 tsp. baking soda

1 tsp. baking powder

1 tsp. kosher salt

1 C. unsalted butter, softened

1 C. sugar

1 C. packed dark brown sugar

2 large eggs

2 tsp. vanilla

3 C. oats (not instant)

1½ C. raisins

Preheat oven to 350. In a large bowl, whisk flour, baking soda, baking powder, and salt; set aside. In a separate bowl, combine butter, sugar, brown sugar, eggs, and vanilla with a hand mixer on low. To cream, increase speed to high and beat until fluffy and the color lightens. Stir the flour mixture into the creamed mixture until no flour is visible. Be careful to not overmix. (Overmixing develops the gluten, making a tough cookie.) Stir in the oats and raisins. Fill a cookie scoop with dough (use a #40 cookie scoop; it measures 2 Tbsp. of dough). Press against side of bowl, pulling up to level dough in the scoop. Drop 2 inches apart onto a baking sheet sprayed with nonstick spray. Bake 11–13 minutes on center rack until golden, but still moist beneath cracks on top. Remove from oven; let cookies sit on baking sheet for 2 minutes before transferring to a wire rack to cool. Makes 36 cookies.

Not your average oatmeal cookies, these are the best oatmeal raisin cookies you will ever try. The secret is the perfect ratio of flour, sugar, and oats. The texture is chewy instead of crispy, like some oatmeal cookies.

Helen Henwood
Kerrville Ward
Texas Hill Country Texas Stake
Kerrville, Texas

Polka Dot Macaroons

1 14-oz. bag shredded coconut

1 14-oz. can sweetened condensed milk

½ C. flour

1¾ C. miniature M&M baking bits

Preheat oven to 350. Grease cookie sheets; set aside. In a large bowl, combine coconut, milk, and flour until well blended. Stir in baking bits. Drop by rounded tablespoonfuls, about 2 inches apart. Bake 8–10 minutes or until edges are golden. Baking time may be longer depending on oven and type of cookie sheet used. You will know they are done because they won't look wet anymore; they will look dry and will be browned on the edges. Cool completely on wire racks. Store in tightly covered container. Makes 16 cookies.

The secret is the mini M&M baking bits. I love coconut and I love M&Ms, so when I found this recipe while visiting the United States, I just knew it was going to be a keeper. I baked a ton of these cookies to take home with me. They are delicious!

Nell McPhee
Invergordon Branch
Aberdeen Scotland Stake
Aberdeen, Scotland

Lemon Zucchini Cookies

2 C. flour

1 tsp. baking powder

½ tsp. salt

¾ C. butter or margarine

¾ C. sugar

1 egg, beaten

1 tsp. lemon peel, grated

1 C. zucchini, peeled and shredded

1 C. nuts, chopped (optional)

1 C. powdered sugar

1½ Tbsp. lemon juice

½ tsp. lemon peel, grated

Sift flour, baking powder, and salt; set aside. In a large bowl, cream butter and sugar until well blended. Add beaten egg and lemon peel; beat until fluffy. Slowly stir in the flour mixture until smooth; add zucchini and nuts. Drop by rounded teaspoonfuls onto a greased cookie sheet. Bake at 375 for 15–20 minutes, until lightly brown. In a small bowl, gradually stir lemon juice into powdered sugar until drizzling consistency; you may need less than 1½ Tbsp. Mix in peel and drizzle lemon glaze on slightly warm cookies. Makes 3 dozen.

Diana Day Snow
Kaysville 7th Ward
South Kaysville Utah Stake
Kaysville, Utah

The secret in this recipe is the zucchini—it makes the cookie really moist. If you peel the zucchini, no one will even know it's in the cookies. Every year my husband and I plant a garden that includes a zucchini plant, and every year we wonder what to do with all the zucchini. The abundant zucchini always brings to mind the old joke about the visiting out-of-town friends who are given a tour of the city; at each venue they are told, "There is no need to lock your car doors." But when they attend church Sunday morning, the out-of-town friends are told, "Be sure to lock all the car doors, or when you return the car will be filled with zucchini." This recipe will give you a yummy reason to plant zucchini in your garden—or better yet, to leave your car unlocked at church.

Sheilah's Kiddie Pleasers

½ C. butter

½ C. butter-flavored shortening

1 C. chunky peanut butter

1½ C. packed brown sugar

½ C. sugar

1 Tbsp. milk

½ tsp. salt (reduce to ¼ tsp. if using peanuts)

2 eggs

1½ C. flour

2 tsp. baking soda

2 C. quick oats

1 12-oz. pkg. chocolate chips

1 C. coconut

1 C. peanuts, chopped (optional)

(recipe continued on next page)

(Sheilah's Kiddie Pleasers, continued)

In a large bowl, cream butter, shortening, peanut butter, brown sugar, sugar, milk, and salt, scraping bowl several times. Mix in eggs one at a time. In separate bowl, combine flour, baking soda, and oats. Stir into creamed mixture and mix well. Add chocolate chips, coconut, and peanuts. Using cookie scoop, scoop dough and place on cookie sheet. Bake at 350 for 8–10 minutes. Do not overbake. Cool slightly on cookie sheet, then transfer cookies to cooling rack. Store in airtight container or freeze for later use. Makes about 48 cookies if using a large cookie scoop.

My five children loved having fresh-baked cookies warm from the oven when they came home from school. But someone was always a bit disappointed about which kind of cookie I made. Some liked chocolate chip, others peanut butter or oatmeal. I discovered the secret to satisfying everyone was to combine them all. After many trial batches, I finally came up with a Kiddie Pleaser! I've made them many times over the years, and now I'm making them for my grandchildren. They are always requested at our family gatherings, and bring back fond memories of when my family was all at home.

Sheilah Hurd
Vienna Woods Ward
Meridian Idaho North Stake
Meridian, Idaho

Chocolate Mint Sandwich Cookies

1½ C. packed brown sugar

¾ C. butter

2 Tbsp. water

12 oz. semisweet chocolate bits

2 eggs

3 C. flour

1¼ tsp. baking soda

1 tsp. salt

3 C. powdered sugar

⅓ C. butter, softened

8 drops peppermint extract or mint extract

2 drops green food coloring (optional)

2–4 Tbsp. milk

Preheat oven to 350. In a large, heavy-duty saucepan, combine brown sugar, butter, and water. Cook over medium heat, stirring occasionally, until butter is melted. Add chocolate bits; cook, stirring constantly, for 1–2 minutes or until smooth. Remove from heat and cool. Add eggs one at a time, beating well after each addition. Stir in flour, baking soda, and salt. Drop by rounded teaspoonfuls onto ungreased baking sheets. Bake for 6–8 minutes or until edges are set. Cool on baking sheets for 1 minute. Remove to wire racks to cool. In large mixer bowl, beat powdered sugar, butter, mint extract, and food coloring. Add milk until smooth and spreadable. Spread about 2 tsp. filling onto flat side (bottom) of 1 cookie; top with second cookie, flat side down. Squeeze together gently. Makes 15 cookies.

Geri Nakoma
Hopkinsville Ward
Hopkinsville Tennessee Stake
Hopkinsville, Kentucky

FOR YOUR EYES ONLY

Oversized Bakery Chocolate Chip Cookies

2 C. flour
½ tsp. baking soda
½ tsp. salt
¾ C. unsalted butter, melted
1 C. packed brown sugar

½ C. sugar
1 Tbsp. vanilla extract
1 egg
1 egg yolk
2 C. semisweet chocolate chips

Preheat the oven to 325. Grease cookie sheets or line with parchment paper. Sift the flour, baking soda, and salt; set aside. In a medium bowl, cream the melted butter, brown sugar, and sugar until well blended. Beat in the vanilla, egg, and egg yolk until light and creamy. Mix in the sifted ingredients until just blended. Stir in the chocolate chips by hand using a wooden spoon. Drop cookie dough ¼ C. at a time onto the prepared cookie sheets. Cookies should be about 3 inches apart. Bake for 15–17 minutes, or until the edges are lightly browned. Cool on baking sheets for a few minutes before transferring to wire racks to cool completely. Makes 32 cookies.

Tired of flat chocolate chip cookies? Your search is over! These are the best-kept secret ever. They are the best chocolate chip cookies I have been able to find. They are big and chewy and perfect. My previous Young Women's president made these for us all the time. I finally got the recipe from her and the rest is beautiful, blissful, gooey, chocolatey history. Enjoy!

Paige Buckley
Petal Ward
Hattiesburg Mississippi Stake
Hattiesburg, Mississippi

Homemade Oreo Cookies

2 boxes devil's food cake mix
2 eggs
½ C. water

½ C. oil
1 container frosting

In a large bowl, combine cake mixes, eggs, water, and oil; mix until smooth. Refrigerate for 10 minutes. Preheat oven to 350. Roll the dough into 1-inch balls and place them on an UNGREASED cookie sheet approximately 1–2 inches apart. Bake for 8–13 minutes or until cracked. Spread frosting on bottom of one cookie. Place another cookie on top and press together gently. White frosting makes them look like Oreos, but I also like to use Rainbow Chip. Makes about 24 cookies.

I got this recipe from a friend in school who wanted me to make them for her birthday. Ever since then, everyone I know wants me to make these cookies for them, and not just for their birthdays. Since I have made these cookies so many times, my dad encouraged me to put them into a competition. I won first place! That makes these not just Homemade Oreo Cookies, but award-winning, first-place cookies.

Alexandra Springgay
Novelty Hill Ward
Redmond Washington Stake
Redmond, Washington

Root Beer Cookies

Cookies:

1 C. unsalted butter

2 C. packed dark brown sugar

2 eggs

2 tsp. root beer flavoring

3½ C. flour

1 tsp. baking soda

1 tsp. salt

¼ C. water (if necessary)

Root Beer Frosting:

1 C. butter

3 C. powdered sugar

2 tsp. root beer flavoring

1–2 Tbsp. hot water

Cookies: In a large bowl, cream butter and dark brown sugar until very light and fluffy. Add the eggs one at a time, beating well after each addition. Add the root beer flavoring. In a separate bowl, whisk dry ingredients. Add a little of the flour mixture at a time to the creamed mixture. Add a little water if the dough is too dry. The dough should be slightly sticky. Chill for at least an hour. Preheat oven to 350. Lightly grease several baking sheets or line them with silicone baking mats or parchment paper. Roll dough into 1-inch balls (I like to use a mini ice-cream scoop so that the cookies are evenly sized). Place on the pan, leaving a bit of space between the cookies. Gently press the tops of the dough. (If you leave out the water, the cookies may not spread very much.) Bake for 6–8 minutes, rotating cookie sheet halfway through. Let cookies cool for a few minutes on the cookie sheet before placing them on a wire rack to cool completely.

Frosting: Using an electric mixer, beat butter on high until fluffy. Add a little powdered sugar and the root beer flavoring. Beat until smooth. Add remaining powdered sugar alternately with a little hot water until the mixture is a nice spreading consistency. Frost the cooled cookies and let stand for a few minutes to let the frosting set up. Makes 4 dozen cookies.

> The secret of this recipe: With their rich brown color, everyone who bites into a cookie expects a chocolate flavor. It is quite a surprise to find the cookies are not what you expect. With the next bite, everyone is trying to discover the flavor. No one expects root beer.

Louise Phelps
Groton Ward
Providence Rhode Island Stake
Ledyard, Connecticut

Monster Cookies

3 eggs

1 C. sugar

1¼ C. packed light brown sugar

½ tsp. salt

½ tsp. vanilla extract

1 12-oz. jar creamy peanut butter

½ C. butter, softened

½ C. multi-colored chocolate candies (M&Ms)

½ C. chocolate chips

¼ C. raisins (optional)

2 tsp. baking soda

4½ C. quick-cooking oatmeal

(recipe continued on next page)

(Monster Cookies, continued)

Preheat the oven to 350. Line cookie sheets with parchment paper or nonstick baking mats. In a very large mixing bowl, combine the eggs and sugars. Mix well. Add the salt, vanilla, peanut butter, and butter. Mix well. Stir in the chocolate candies, chocolate chips, raisins, baking soda, and oatmeal. Drop by tablespoonfuls 2 inches apart onto the prepared cookie sheets. Bake for 8–10 minutes. Do not overbake. Let stand for about 3 minutes before transferring to wire racks to cool. When cool, store in large resealable plastic bags. Makes 36 cookies.

My family is not one that likes cookies all that much; we are much more cake people. But one day while I was bored, I decided to make cookies. I thought these sounded interesting, so I made them and they knocked my socks off! I have since been converted to cookies, but only Monster Cookies. The secret is the perfect mix of all the right things. They're the best!

Holly Knickerbocker
Central Falls Ward
Providence Rhode Island Stake
Pawtucket, Rhode Island

Kadie's Kookies

1 German chocolate cake mix

2 eggs

⅓ C. vegetable oil

3 Three Musketeers mint candy bars

Preheat the oven to 350. In a medium bowl, mix German chocolate cake, eggs, and oil; the batter should be thick. Cut the candy bars into small pieces, about ½-inch thick. Use a small amount of dough to completely cover one piece of candy bar; roll into a ball shape and place it on a cookie sheet. Continue until all the dough is used. Bake for 8–10 minutes. Makes 24 cookies.

This recipe has been a lot of fun for my children, especially my four-year-old, Kadie. She loves to make these while her daddy is at work and make him guess the secret candy in the middle. Sometimes she uses Snickers, and other times she uses a Mars bar. It's a fun game for them. She enjoys trying to stump him and he enjoys getting to eat the cookies. Kadie can't eat very well—she was born without an esophagus, has heart and lung disease, and has a feeding tube. But that doesn't stop her from enjoying the thrill of baking and playing "guess my secret center" with Daddy. She may have been born with her heart on the wrong side, but it's always in the right place.

Jennifer Gossett
Springfield 1st Ward
Springfield Missouri Stake
Springfield, Missouri

Grandma's Oatmeal Chocolate Chip Cookies

1 C. butter
1 C. sugar
1 C. packed brown sugar
2 eggs
1 tsp. vanilla
2 C. flour
1 tsp. soda

½ tsp. salt
1 tsp. baking powder
2½ C. oatmeal, blended to a fine powder
4-oz. chocolate candy bar, shaved (Hershey's)
12 oz. chocolate chips
½ C. nuts, chopped (optional)

In a large bowl, cream butter and both sugars. Add eggs and vanilla; beat well. Stir in flour, soda, salt, baking powder, and oatmeal. Add shaved chocolate, chocolate chips, and nuts. Roll into balls and place 2 inches apart on a cookie sheet. Bake at 375 for 10 minutes. Makes 36 cookies.

The secret to these cookies is the shaved chocolate bar. It distributes chocolatey deliciousness throughout the whole cookie.

Heidi Kittelson
Centerton 2nd Branch
Rogers Arkansas Stake
Bentonville, Arkansas

Pumpkin Chocolate Chip Cookies

1 C. canned pumpkin
1 C. sugar
½ C. vegetable oil
1 egg
2 C. flour
2 tsp. baking powder
2 tsp. ground cinnamon
½ tsp. salt

1 tsp. baking soda
1 tsp. milk
3 drops red food coloring (these will not be
   orange without the food coloring)
1 Tbsp. vanilla extract
2 C. semisweet chocolate chips
½ C. walnuts, chopped (optional)

In a large bowl, combine pumpkin, sugar, vegetable oil, and egg. In a separate bowl, stir together flour, baking powder, ground cinnamon, and salt. In a separate bowl, dissolve the baking soda in the milk; stir into the flour mixture. Add flour mixture to pumpkin mixture and mix well. Add food coloring, vanilla, chocolate chips, and nuts. Drop by spoonfuls onto greased cookie sheet; bake at 365 for approximately 12 minutes or until lightly brown and firm. Makes 2 dozen cookies.

My secret pumpkin cookie recipe is out! Enjoy them while they last, because they vanish quickly. Adding the red food coloring is a must if you want the whole orange pumpkin effect.

Britt Beakley
Madison 1st Ward
Madison Wisconsin Stake
Madison, Wisconsin

Sour Cream Chocolate Chip Cookies

2¼ C. packed brown sugar
1½ C. butter-flavored shortening
4 eggs
2 C. sour cream
1 tsp. vanilla
6 C. flour

1 heaping tsp. baking soda
1 tsp. baking powder
1 tsp. salt
1 12-oz. bag chocolate chips
1 C. sugar
2 heaping Tbsp. cinnamon

In a large bowl, thoroughly cream sugar, shortening, eggs, sour cream, and vanilla. Add dry ingredients slowly and mix well. Fold in chocolate chips. (You can also stir in chopped nuts, if desired.) In a small bowl, combine sugar and cinnamon. Roll cookies into 1½-inch balls and then roll in cinnamon sugar. Bake at 375 for about 12 minutes, until set and lightly brown on edges. Makes 4 dozen cookies.

Jill Bridges
Bloomington 6th Ward
Bloomington Utah Stake
Saint George, Utah

The secret to this amazing cookie is threefold: 1. the sour cream (this may turn people off who don't like sour cream, but after the first bite they forget all about hating sour cream); 2. the brown sugar; and 3. the cinnamon/sugar coating! The cookies are soft and seem to taste even better the next day. This family recipe has been the "cookie heart" of our family. Just last year, my twins made these for a college family home evening cookie-baking contest—and, of course, they won first prize!

Grandma McNaughton's Soft Cookies

Cookies:
1 C. butter-flavored shortening
2 C. sugar
3 eggs
1 tsp. vanilla
1 C. buttermilk
1 tsp. baking soda
5 C. flour
½ tsp. nutmeg

½ tsp. salt
2 tsp. baking powder

Pink Icing:
1 16-oz. pkg. powdered sugar
½ C. soft margarine
A few spoonfuls of evaporated milk
1 tsp. vanilla
About ¼ tsp. red food coloring

In a large bowl, cream shortening and sugar; add eggs and vanilla. In a small bowl, combine buttermilk and baking soda. (Shh! that's a secret!) Stir in half the buttermilk mixture. Combine flour, nutmeg (shh! the nutmeg is another secret!), salt, and baking powder. Stir in dry ingredients alternately with buttermilk mixture.

(recipe continued on next page)

(Grandma McNaughton's Soft Cookies, continued)

Dough will be tender. With a rolling pin, roll dough to ½ inch thick, using generous amounts of flour. Cut out cookies with a round cookie cutter. Bake on a greased cookie sheet or, better yet, use parchment paper. Bake at 350 for about 10 minutes. The cookies will be lightly brown on top. DO NOT OVERBAKE! The cookies should be soft; they puff up almost like a cake because of the buttermilk/baking soda secret. They won't be Grandma's cookies unless you use a round cookie cutter and frost them with pink icing.

Of course, the secret to this recipe is that my grandma, Loraine McNaughton, was famous for it. She has made these cookies as long as my dad can remember. She made them for him when he was a child, and when he was in college, she mailed him shoe boxes full of these cookies. My dad had a hard time hiding them from his roommates! This recipe was my great- grandmother's but my grandma perfected it by putting her famous pink icing on the cookies. What makes it unique is the buttermilk/baking soda mixture and just the right amount of nutmeg. Whenever my grandma came to visit, she baked these cookies, and they were devoured by the end of the day. Now that she has passed, I have tried to make them just like she did. According to my dad, I've done it—so I share this special recipe in the memory of my grandmother. I love you, Grandma!

Bethany Sinks
Lake Travis Ward
Austin Texas Oak Hills Stake
Austin, Texas

Grandma's Best Orange Cookies

1 C. shortening

¾ C. sugar

1 C. carrots, cooked and mashed

2 eggs

2 C. flour

2 tsp. baking powder

½ tsp. salt

1 tsp. vanilla

¾ C. shredded coconut

1 C. powdered sugar

1 ½ Tbsp. orange juice

½ tsp. orange zest

In a large bowl, combine shortening, sugar, mashed carrots, and eggs. Mix well. Stir in flour, baking powder, salt, and vanilla. Add coconut. Drop by spoonfuls onto greased baking sheet. Bake at 375 for 8–10 minutes. While cookies cool, combine powdered sugar with enough orange juice to make a smooth icing. Stir in orange zest. Frost cooled cookies. Makes 2½–3 dozen cookies.

My grandma is a firm believer that the more stained, wrinkled, old, and used a recipe is, the better-tasting it must be! She has been using this recipe for many years, and we've had these cookies for everything from homecomings to a "just for fun" treat. Our family loves them and they have become a family staple!

Kaitlyn Rowbotham
Crescent Park 5th Ward
Crescent Park Utah Stake
Sandy, Utah

SECRET

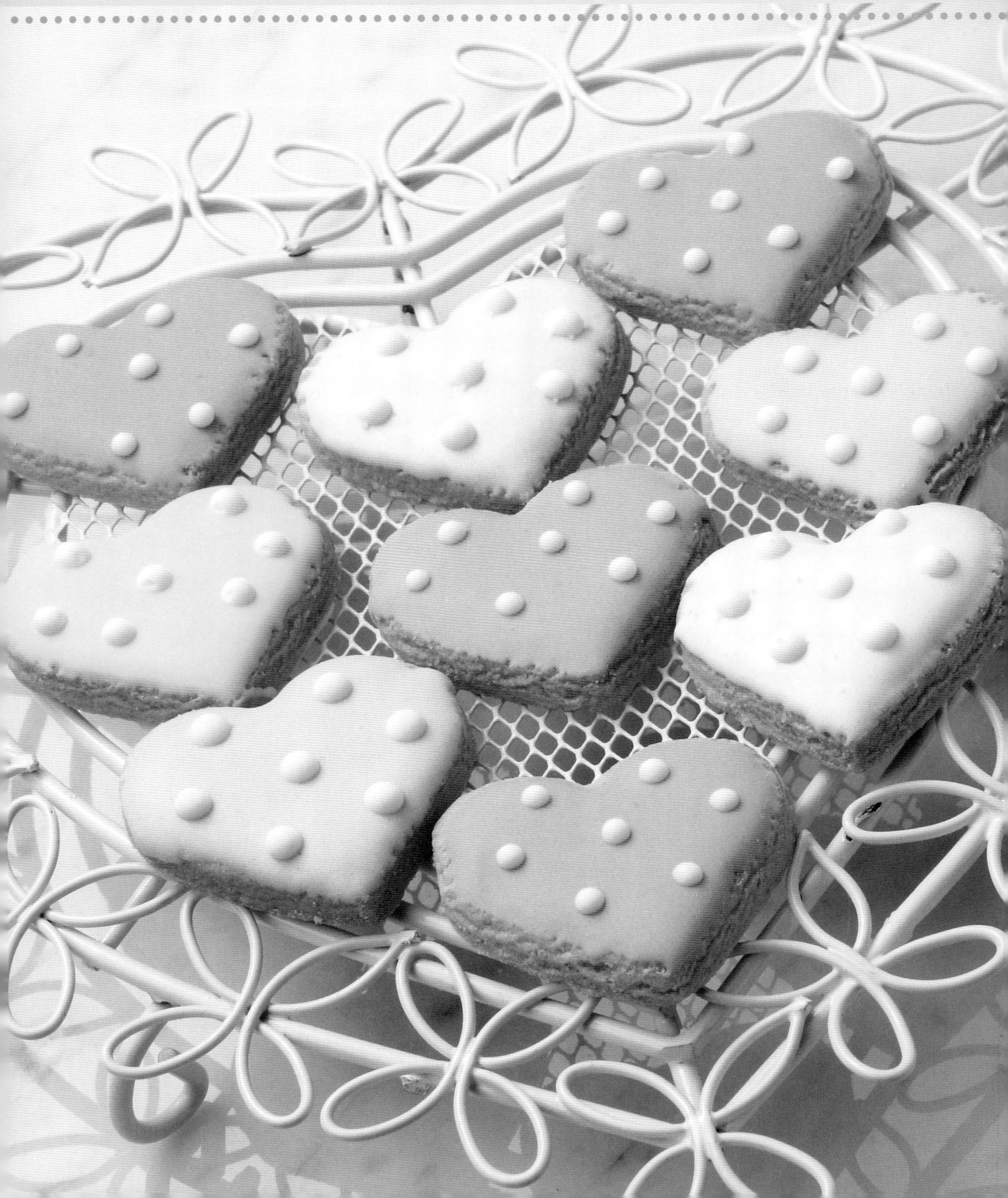

Lucy's Frosted Sugar Cookies

Cookies:

1 C. butter or margarine, softened

1½ C. powdered sugar

1 egg

1 tsp. vanilla

2½ C. flour

1 tsp. baking soda

1 tsp. cream of tartar

Lucy's Frosting:

3 C. powdered sugar

½ C. shortening

½ tsp. cream of tartar

1 tsp. almond extract

Food coloring

Water

Cookies: In a large bowl, combine butter, sugar, egg, and vanilla. Mix thoroughly. Blend in flour, soda, and cream of tartar. Cover; chill for 2–3 hours. Heat oven to 375. Divide dough in half. Roll each ball ³⁄₁₆ inch thick on lightly floured board. Cut into desired shapes. Place on lightly greased baking sheet. Bake 7–8 minutes or until light brown on edges. Makes 3 dozen cookies.

Frosting: Combine all ingredients, adding enough water to make a smooth consistency. Frost cooled cookies.

Lucy Nygaard
Spokane 2nd Ward
Spokane Washington West Stake
Spokane, Washington

The secret ingredient in this recipe is the almond extract in the frosting. We really like almond extract and I decided to try it in the frosting instead of vanilla. It makes the cookies so much better than other sugar cookies. Everyone loves these cookies and I am sure it is because of the almond! My son-in-law is my biggest fan!

Chocolate Turtle Cookies

½ C. butter, melted

¾ C. sugar

3 eggs, beaten

1 C. flour

1 tsp. vanilla

4 Tbsp. cocoa

1 container chocolate frosting

Combine all ingredients except frosting until smooth. Pour batter onto waffle iron and cook for 50 seconds. Spread chocolate frosting onto cookies. You can put the frosted cookies in the refrigerator for a few minutes to set up frosting if needed. Makes about 24 cookies.

Amanda Porter
North Ogden 15th Ward
Coldwater Utah Stake
North Ogden, Utah

FOR YOUR EYES ONLY

Just in Case Cookies

1 C. leftover breakfast or dinner (cooked cereal, pancake batter, soggy Wheaties, mashed potatoes, refried beans, etc.)

½ C. butter or margarine

1 C. something sweet (sugar, hardened brown sugar, dabs of honey, syrup, jam, etc., warmed slightly just in case it needs to be warmed to blend)

1 or 2 eggs if you have any; if not, don't worry about it

At this point, you may discover some cottage cheese, rice pudding, sweet potatoes, or some other treat; beat in just in case

2 C. sifted flour (more or less)

1 tsp. baking soda, just in case something needs soda

Flavoring to match (consider cinnamon, nutmeg, ginger, or lemon, but avoid chocolate—it's a bit much for this recipe)

Add raisins or nuts or oatmeal just in case there are lumps that need covering up

Combine all ingredients and drop by spoonfuls on a cookie sheet. Bake at 400 for 8–10 minutes. These cookies are good just in case someone comes home hungry. Makes about 3 dozen.

Duane Sartori
Hunter 2nd Ward
Salt Lake Utah Hunter Stake
West Valley City, Utah

This recipe is great when you have lots of hungry mouths to feed and want to use whatever you have. I have made these cookies hundreds of times, and never had them turn out the same twice—they're always edible, and I've used everything from refried beans to leftover mush. This recipe was given to me by our mission mom while I was serving in the California Sacramento Mission. The secret is that they were always good, no matter what they were made from, and she always had them on hand for her "boys." In several areas where I served, we had a district activity to see who could come up with the most unique Just in Case Cookies. There is another secret, too: these cookies were often shared with people who were investigating the Church, and proved many times to open doors that may not have been opened otherwise.

{ CAKES }

How can we expect another to keep our secret if
we have been unable to keep it ourselves?

{ Francois de La Rouchefoucauld }

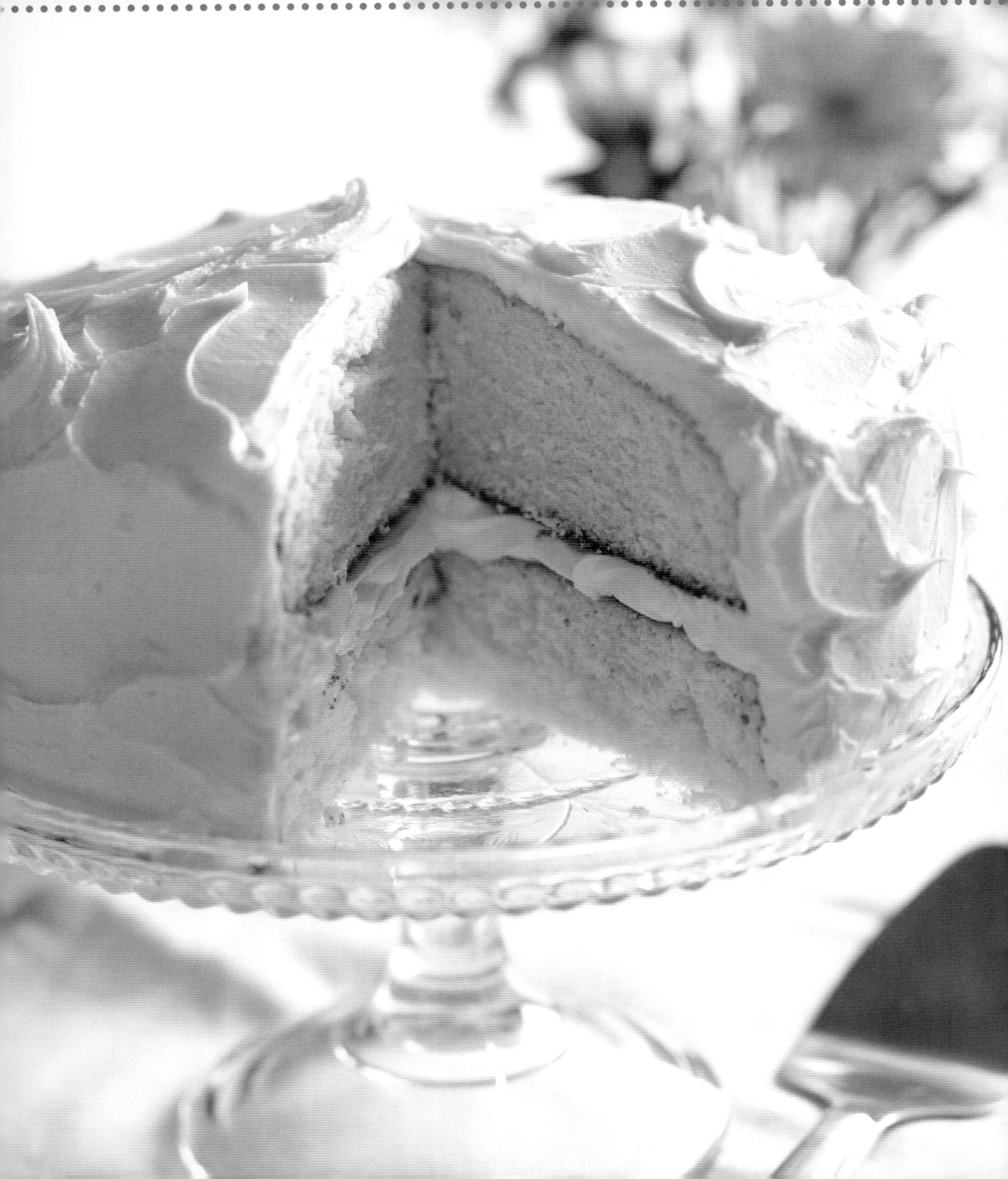

Grandma B's White Cake

1 18-oz. box moist deluxe white cake mix

⅓ C. diet lemon-lime soda

⅓ C. vegetable oil

4 large egg whites

1 C. sour cream

Preheat oven to 350 and move oven rack to second-lowest position. In a large bowl, mix all ingredients on low speed until blended (about 30 seconds). Beat at medium speed for 2 minutes more. Pour the batter into a greased 9 x 13-inch baking pan (the batter will be quite thick, so you will need to spread it out with the back of a spoon). Bake for about 30 minutes or until a toothpick inserted in the center comes out clean. Makes 12 servings.

> My grandmother baked cakes for a living for more than thirty years. This is a favorite and happens to be very simple to make. It does not taste like a boxed mix at all. Grandma B has since passed on, but we love her and her cakes. Her memory will always be kept alive through her recipes.

Sherry Colter
Boerne 1st Ward
Hill Country Texas Stake
Boerne, Texas

7s Cake

Zest from 1 lemon

2 eggs

¾ C. vegetable oil

¾ C. sugar

1¾ C. self-rising flour

¾ C. milk (approximately)

Grate the lemon zest into a mixing bowl. Add the eggs and beat. Add oil, 7 Tbsp. at a time, until you've added 14 Tbsp. (¾ C.). Beat. Add sugar, 7 Tbsp. at a time, until you've added 14 Tbsp. Keep beating. Add flour, 7 Tbsp. at a time, until you've added 28 Tbsp. (1¾ C.). Alternate adding the flour with milk so the batter is smooth. You may need to add more or less milk to make the batter a smooth consistency. Pour batter into a greased 9 x 13-inch cake pan. Bake at 350 for 60 minutes. Makes 12 servings.

Corina Ayala
Ensign 8th Ward
Ensign Utah Stake
Salt Lake City, Utah

> The secret is not an ingredient; it's a step. You MUST add the vegetable oil, sugar, and flour 7 tablespoons at a time. If you add each ingredient all at once as it is called for in the recipe, the cake will not rise properly. This is a fact—I've tried it. I started making it when I was 10. I was taught by my mother, and she was persistent in adding the ingredients 7 tablespoons at a time. Now, after many years, I make it for my children, 7 tablespoons at a time.

# German Sweet Chocolate Cake

Cake:

4 1-oz. squares German sweet chocolate
½ C. water
2 C. flour
1 tsp. baking soda
¼ tsp. salt
1 C. butter, softened
2 C. sugar
4 eggs, separated
1 tsp. vanilla extract
1 C. buttermilk

Coconut-Pecan Frosting:

1 12-oz. can evaporated milk
1½ C. sugar
¾ C. butter
4 egg yolks
1½ tsp. vanilla extract
1 8-oz. pkg. flaked coconut
1½ C. pecans, chopped

Cake: Preheat oven to 350. Line bottom of 9 x 13-inch pan with parchment paper. Microwave chocolate and water on high for 1½–2 minutes; stirring halfway through. Stir until all is melted and smooth. In a medium bowl, mix flour, soda, and salt. Set aside. In a large bowl, cream butter and sugar until light and fluffy. Add 4 egg yolks one at a time, beating well after each addition. Stir in melted chocolate and 1 tsp. vanilla. Add flour mixture alternately with buttermilk. Beat after each addition until smooth. In a separate bowl, beat egg whites on high until soft peaks form. Gently fold into batter. Pour into 9 x 13-inch pan. Bake at 350 for 30 minutes, or until toothpick inserted into center of cake comes out clean. Cool completely, then frost with coconut-pecan frosting.

Frosting: In a large saucepan, combine milk, sugar, butter, egg yolks, and vanilla. Cook, stirring constantly, on medium heat until thick and golden brown, about 12 minutes. It is done if it will coat the back of a spoon. Remove from heat. Stir in coconut and pecans. Cool to room temperature and spreading consistency. Frost cake when cool. Makes 12 servings.

Ada Bach
Pinneberg Ward
Neumünster Germany Stake
Pinneberg, Germany

My mother is a baker, and she makes the most delicious cakes. This is a favorite that I like to make. The secret is the frosting. I suggest chopping the pecans into small pieces and making the frosting first so it can be cooling while you make the cake. I get asked to make this all the time for church events, and am now known as the "lady that makes that chocolate cake." I am pretty sure you will never taste another German chocolate cake better than this one.

Watermelon Cake

1 18.25-oz. white cake mix
1 3-oz. box watermelon gelatin
1¼ C. water
2 eggs
¼ C. canola oil

2½ C. prepared vanilla or buttercream frosting, divided
Red and green gel food coloring
Chocolate chips

In a large bowl, combine the cake mix, gelatin, water, eggs, and oil; beat on low speed for 30 seconds. Beat on medium for 2 minutes. Pour into two greased and floured 9-inch round baking pans. Bake at 350 for 30–35 minutes or until a toothpick inserted near the center comes out clean. Cool for 10 minutes before removing from pans to wire racks to cool completely.

Set aside 2 Tbsp. frosting for decorating. Place 1¼ C. frosting in a bowl; tint red. In another bowl, tint remaining frosting green. Place one cake layer on a serving plate; spread with ½ C. red frosting to within ¼ inch of edges. Top with second cake. Frost top with remaining red frosting to within ¾ inch of edges. Frost sides and top edge of cake with green frosting.

Cut a ¼-inch hole in the corner of pastry or plastic bag. Fill the bag with reserved white frosting. Pipe around top edge of cake where green and pink frosting meets. For "seeds," insert chocolate chips upside down into cake top. Makes 12 servings.

This is a very unique cake that everyone loves. The secret is how I get the watermelon flavor into the cake: watermelon-flavored Jell-O! It's so simple and full of flavor. This is perfect in the spring and summer. Watermelon Jell-O is seasonal in some places, so stock up when you see it. If it's not available, you can substitute Melon Fusion Jell-O.

Trisha Garrison
Maple Grove Ward
Anoka Minnesota Stake
Orono, Minnesota

Big Beth's Buttercream Frosting

1½ C. shortening
½ C. butter
8 C. powdered sugar

½ tsp. salt
2 tsp. clear imitation vanilla extract
¾ C. heavy cream

Cream shortening and butter until fluffy. Add powdered sugar and continue creaming until well blended. Add salt, vanilla, and cream. Blend on low speed until moistened. Add additional cream, if necessary. Beat at high speed until frosting is fluffy. Frosts 3 dozen cupcakes.

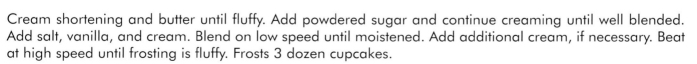

I make wedding cakes, and I get more requests for this frosting than any other. Everyone loves the way it tastes. Butter flavoring can be added if desired.

Beth Imel
Iron Mountain Branch
Green Bay Wisconsin Stake
Iron Mountain, Michigan

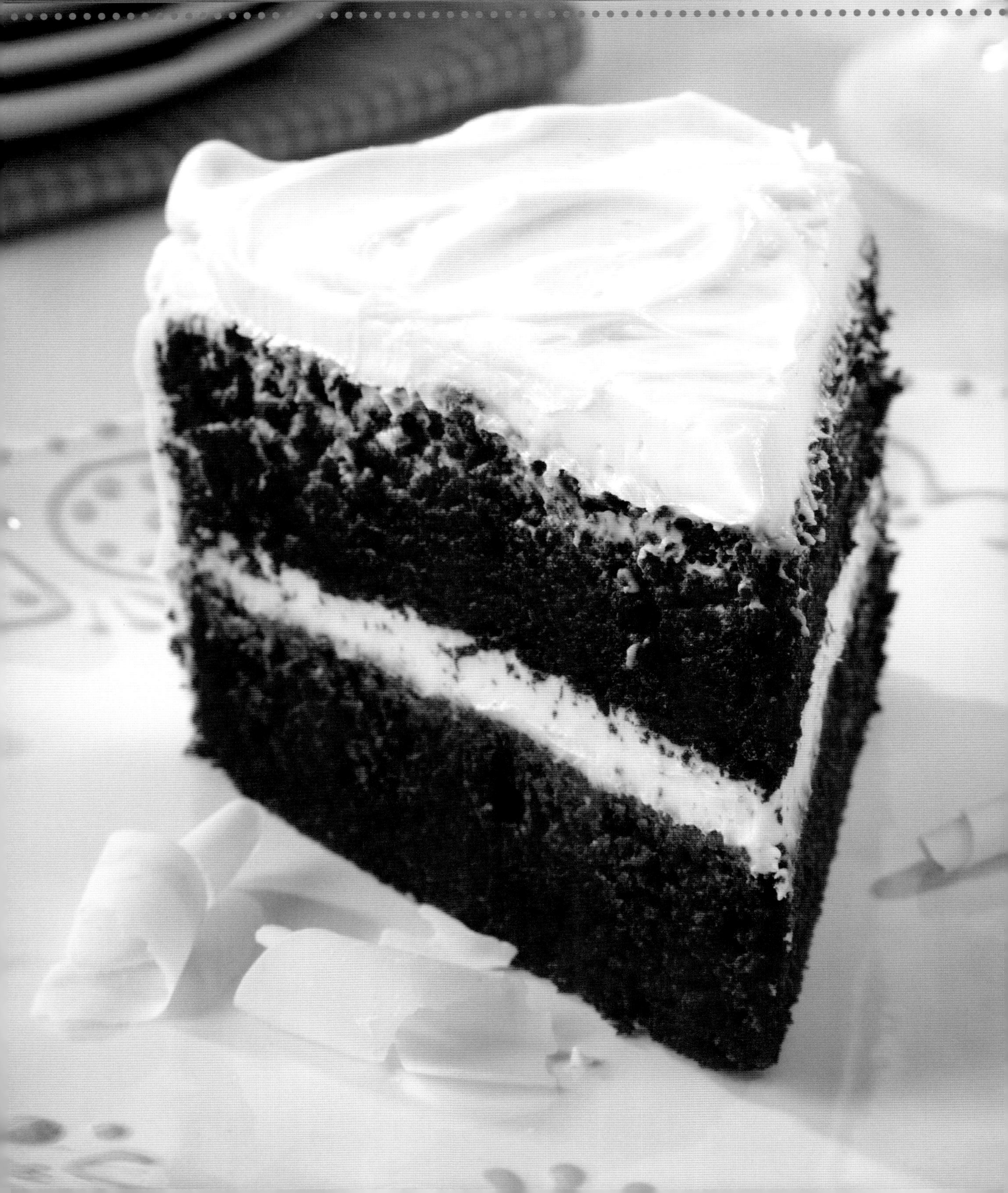

Big Beth's Red Velvet Cake

3 Tbsp. unsweetened cocoa powder

1 oz. red food coloring

1 C. buttermilk

1 tsp. salt

1 tsp. vanilla extract

1 C. oil

2 C. sugar

2 eggs

2½ C. flour, sifted

1½ tsp. baking soda

1 tsp. white vinegar

Grease two 9-inch round cake pans. Preheat oven to 350. Make a paste of the cocoa and food coloring. Set aside. In a small bowl, combine buttermilk, salt, and vanilla. Set aside. In a large bowl, combine oil and sugar. Beat in the eggs one at a time, then stir in the cocoa mixture. Beat in the buttermilk mixture alternately with the flour, mixing just until incorporated. Stir together baking soda and vinegar, then gently fold into the cake batter. Pour batter into prepared pans. Bake for 30 minutes, or until a toothpick inserted into the center of the cake comes out clean. Allow to cool completely before frosting. Refrigerate until ready to serve. Frost with desired frosting. Makes 12 servings.

This fabulous recipe came from my great-grandmother and has been passed down the family tree to me. This is my favorite cake of all time. My baking customers love it just as much as I do.

Beth Imel
Iron Mountain Branch
Green Bay Wisconsin Stake
Iron Mountain, Michigan

Wellesley Fudge Cake

⅔ C. butter

2 ⅔ C. packed brown sugar

1 whole egg

3 egg yolks, well beaten

4 squares unsweetened chocolate

⅔ C. boiling water

1½ tsp. baking powder

2⅔ C. sifted cake flour (do not use all-purpose flour)

⅔ C. buttermilk

1¼ tsp. baking soda

1 tsp. vanilla

Pinch of salt

Preheat oven to 350. In a bowl, cream butter and sugar; add egg and egg yolks. In a saucepan, melt chocolate in boiling water; stir to consistency of thick paste and add to creamed butter mixture. In a separate bowl, combine baking powder and sifted flour. In a separate bowl, combine buttermilk and baking soda. Add flour mixture alternately with buttermilk mixture to chocolate butter mixture. Add vanilla and salt. Bake in 2 greased round cake pans or a greased 9 x 13-inch baking pan. Frost with favorite frosting. Makes 12 servings.

Kestin Gruhn
Carthage Ward
Joplin Missouri Stake
Carthage, Missouri

This is a very special cake; the original recipe is from Wellesley College, where this cake was served in the Tea Room. It is very popular and the perfect chocolate cake.

Baby Food Carrot Cake

4 eggs
2 C. sugar
1½ C. oil
2 C. flour

1 tsp. cinnamon
1 tsp. salt
1 tsp. baking soda
3 medium jars baby food carrots

Mix eggs, sugar, oil, and flour. Add remaining ingredients and beat well. Pour into 9 x 13-inch greased and floured pan. Bake at 350 for 30–35 minutes (or until toothpick inserted near center comes out clean; check at 30 minutes). Frost with cream cheese frosting. Makes 15 servings.

Abbie Barnett
Bayshore Ward
Stansbury Stake
Stansbury Park, Utah

The secret to great carrot cake is baby food carrots. (I am not a fan of chunky carrot cake.) This recipe is a smooth, velvety, and oh-so-moist cake due to the baby food carrots. I make it for my coworkers, and they now request it for their birthday cake at work. They call it "the baby food cake."

Big Beth's Super Fudgy Frosting

½ C. butter
¼ C. shortening
⅓ C. unsweetened cocoa powder
2 C. powdered sugar

2 Tbsp. milk, heavy cream, or half-n-half
1 C. hot fudge topping
1 tsp. vanilla extract

Cream the butter or margarine with the shortening. Sift cocoa with powdered sugar; add to the creamed mixture. Mix, adding milk or cream 1 Tbsp. at a time, to keep the mixture smooth. Don't use more than ¼ C. milk or cream. Add the hot fudge topping and the vanilla extract. Blend until smooth and creamy. Makes 16 servings.

This is my ultimate chocolate frosting—the one I use whenever I need to impress chocolate lovers. The secret to this frosting is the fudge topping. It's sinfully rich, so prepare with caution!

Beth Imel
Iron Mountain Branch
Green Bay Wisconsin Stake
Iron Mountain, Michigan

Cream-Filled Chocolate Cupcakes

Cupcakes:

3 C. flour

2 C. sugar

⅓ C. unsweetened cocoa powder

2 tsp. baking soda

1 tsp. salt

2 eggs

1 C. milk

1 C. water

1 C. vegetable oil

1 tsp. vanilla extract

Filling:

¼ C. butter

¼ C. shortening

2 C. powdered sugar

1 pinch salt

3 Tbsp. milk

1 tsp. vanilla extract

Preheat oven to 375. Line 36 muffin cups with paper liners. In a large bowl, mix the flour, sugar, cocoa, baking soda, and salt. Make a well in the center and pour in the eggs, 1 C. milk, water, oil, and vanilla. Mix well. Fill each muffin cup half full with batter. Bake for 15–20 minutes. Allow to cool. To make filling: In a large bowl, beat butter and shortening until smooth. Blend in powdered sugar and pinch of salt. Gradually beat in 3 Tbsp. milk and vanilla. Beat until light and fluffy. Fill a pastry bag with a small tip. Push tip through the top of cupcakes and squeeze in filling. Frost. Makes 36 cupcakes.

Bricelynn Jeeter
Savannah Ward
Savannah Georgia Stake
Tybee Island, Georgia

These remind me of family gatherings because we used to make them every year at our family reunion. We love the commercial cream-filled cupcakes, and these taste very close. They remind me of the old carefree days, and I love making them for my children.

Big Beth's Cream Cheese Frosting

½ C. butter, softened

2 8-oz. pkgs. cream cheese, softened

1 tsp. vanilla extract

3 C. powdered sugar, sifted

In a medium bowl, cream butter and cream cheese until creamy. Mix in the vanilla, then gradually stir in powdered sugar. Store in the refrigerator. VARIATION: Add ⅓ C. cocoa powder to make Chocolate Cream Cheese Frosting. This recipe makes a lot, but is easily halved. Makes 24 servings.

Beth Imel
Iron Mountain Branch
Green Bay Wisconsin Stake
Iron Mountain, Michigan

Perfect for carrot cake, pumpkin cake, or spice cake.

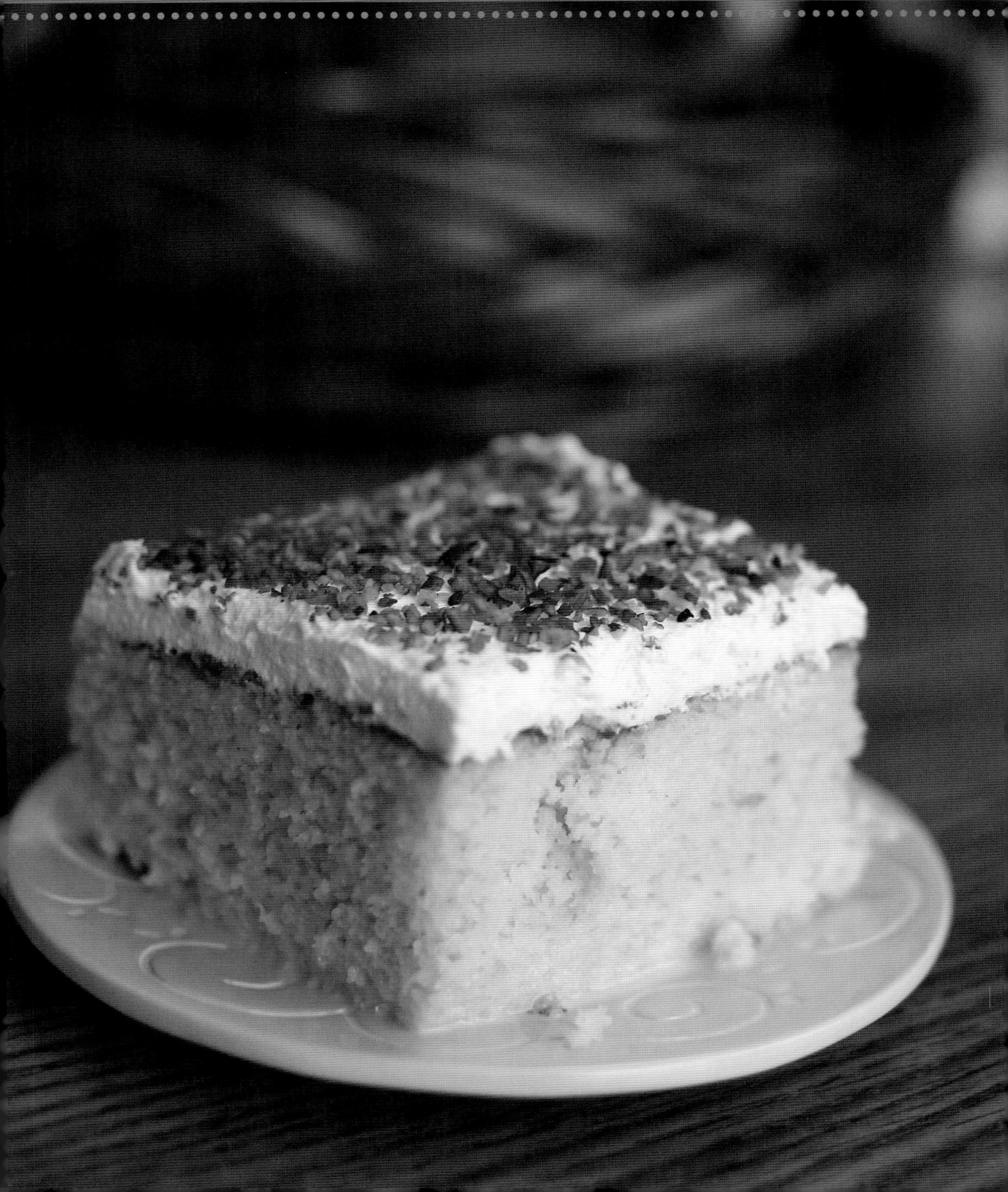

Tres Leche Cake

1½ C. flour
1 tsp. baking powder
½ C. unsalted butter, softened
2 C. sugar, divided
5 eggs

1½ tsp. vanilla extract, divided
2 C. whole milk
1 14-oz. can sweetened condensed milk
1 12-oz. can evaporated milk
1½ C. heavy cream

Preheat oven to 350. Grease and flour a 9 x 13-inch baking pan. Sift flour and baking powder together and set aside. In a large bowl, cream butter and 1 C. sugar until fluffy. Add eggs and ½ tsp. vanilla extract; beat well. Add the flour mixture to the butter mixture 2 Tbsp. at a time; mix until well blended. Pour batter into prepared pan. Bake at 350 for 30 minutes. Pierce cake several times with a fork. In a large bowl, combine the whole milk, condensed milk, and evaporated milk. Pour over the top of the cooled cake. Whip the cream with the remaining 1 C. sugar and remaining 1 tsp. vanilla until thick and stiff enough to form peaks when beaters are lifted out. Spread over the top of cake. Be sure to keep the cake refrigerated. This is best if it sits in the fridge for 24 hours before serving so all the flavors can blend together. If you eat it right away it is still good, but it's so much better a day or two after that. Makes 18 servings.

This has been my favorite cake for as long as I can remember. Don't be shy with the milk. It seems like a lot, but trust me, it all soaks in over the course of 24 hours. Be sure to keep it cool. The secret: the longer you wait to eat the cake, the better it gets. I usually make it two days before serving and keep it covered in the fridge. It's great topped with sliced strawberries, but don't put them on the cake until immediately before you serve it.

Alexia Hinkley
Palmyra Ward
Palmyra New York Stake
Palmyra, New York

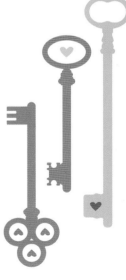

Grandma Liz's Tomato Soup Cake

1 C. sugar
1 tsp. baking soda
1 tsp. baking powder
½ tsp. ground cloves
½ tsp. nutmeg
1 tsp. cinnamon

1½ C. flour
2 Tbsp. vegetable oil
1 10.75-oz. can tomato soup
1 C. raisins
½ C. nuts, chopped

In a large bowl, combine sugar, baking soda, baking powder, cloves, nutmeg, cinnamon, and flour. Add oil and tomato soup and mix well. Stir in raisins and nuts. Bake in a greased 8 x 8-inch pan at 350 for 30 minutes. Frost with a butter or cream cheese frosting. Makes 8 servings.

Bev Qualheim
Logandale Nevada 4th Ward
Logandale Nevada Stake
Logandale, Nevada

Sunset Strip Cake

Cake:
1 18.25-oz. white or orange cake mix
1½ C. milk
1 3.4-oz. instant vanilla pudding mix
1 3-oz. orange gelatin
4 eggs
½ C. canola oil

Filling:
1 20-oz. can crushed pineapple, drained
2 C. sugar
1 10-oz. pkg. flaked coconut
1 C. sour cream
1 8-oz. container frozen whipped topping, thawed
Toasted coconut (optional)

In a large bowl, combine all cake ingredients; beat on low speed for 30 seconds. Beat on medium for 2 minutes. Pour into three greased and floured 9-inch round cake pans. Bake at 350 for 25–30 minutes or until a toothpick inserted near the center comes out clean. Cool for 10 minutes, then remove from pans and cool completely on wire racks. For the filling: In a large bowl, combine the pineapple, sugar, coconut, and sour cream. Reserve 1 C.; set aside. Place one cake on a serving plate; top with a third of the remaining pineapple mixture. Repeat layers twice. Fold whipped topping into the reserved pineapple mixture. Spread over top and sides of cake. Sprinkle with toasted coconut, if desired. Refrigerate until serving. Makes 12 servings.

This is a very delicious, moist cake. I love that it doesn't have thick, overly sweet frosting; the whipped topping and pineapple is a perfect combination.

Darcy Lind
Canyon Gate Ward
Las Vegas Nevada Sandstone Stake
Las Vegas, Nevada

Caramel Cake

Cake:
1 box butter cake mix
4 eggs
½ C. butter
¾ C. water

Caramel Icing:
2¾ C. sugar, divided
¾ C. evaporated milk
½ C. butter (do not substitute)
1 Tbsp. vanilla

Cake: Combine ingredients and bake cake according to package directions. Allow to cool.

Icing: In a nonstick skillet, melt ¾ C. sugar over low heat until brown and bubbly, but not burned. Meanwhile, mix milk and 2 C. sugar in a 3-quart saucepan. Bring to rolling boil. When most of the sugar melts in skillet, STRAIN into boiling mixture. Cook 4–5 minutes, stirring constantly. Remove from heat. STRAIN a second

(recipe continued on next page)

(Caramel Cake, continued)

time into mixer bowl to remove lumps. Straining twice is important to get a smooth texture. Add butter and vanilla. Beat with mixer until it starts to cool and thicken. Icing will be runny when spread on cooled cake, but will set up fine. I put the mixer bowl in the freezer for at least an hour so the mixture cools more quickly. Makes 12 servings.

My best friend, Julie Renfrow, has made a Caramel Cake for every family birthday for longer than I can remember; a master in the kitchen, she finally taught me how to bake this wonderful creation. The secret: Most recipes call for brown sugar to make the frosting, but Julie's recipe uses white sugar, caramelized in a skillet on the stove. It is sooo good!

Holly Knickerbocker
Central Falls Ward
Providence Rhode Island Stake
Pawtucket, Rhode Island

Milky Way Cake

8 regular-size Milky Way bars
1½ C. butter, divided
4½ C. sugar, divided
4 eggs, beaten
2½ C. flour
½ tsp. baking soda

1½ C. buttermilk
1 C. pecans, chopped
1 8-oz. can evaporated milk
1 6-oz. pkg. chocolate chips
1 C. marshmallow cream

In a saucepan, combine candy bars and ½ C. butter. Cook over low heat, stirring continuously until melted—this burns easily, so watch very carefully! Set aside. In a large bowl, cream 2 C. sugar and ½ C. butter. Beat in eggs. Sift flour and baking soda and add to creamed mixture alternately with buttermilk. Stir in candy mixture. Add nuts and mix well. Pour into greased and floured 9 x 13-inch pan. Bake at 325 for 1 hour 10 minutes or until done. For frosting: In a saucepan, combine remaining 2½ C. sugar, evaporated milk, and remaining ½ C. butter and cook to softball stage, stirring frequently. Remove from heat and add chocolate chips and marshmallow cream. Cool slightly, then beat until thick. Spread over cake. Makes 20 servings.

Emily Price
Laurel Ward
Annapolis Maryland Stake
Laurel, Maryland

This is tried and true and very, very rich—serve small pieces. My best friend begs me to make this every year for her son's birthday. My kids also request this for any special occasion that calls for food. It tastes just like a Milky Way, so this one's for you Milky Way lovers. The secret, of course, is the Milky Way bars!

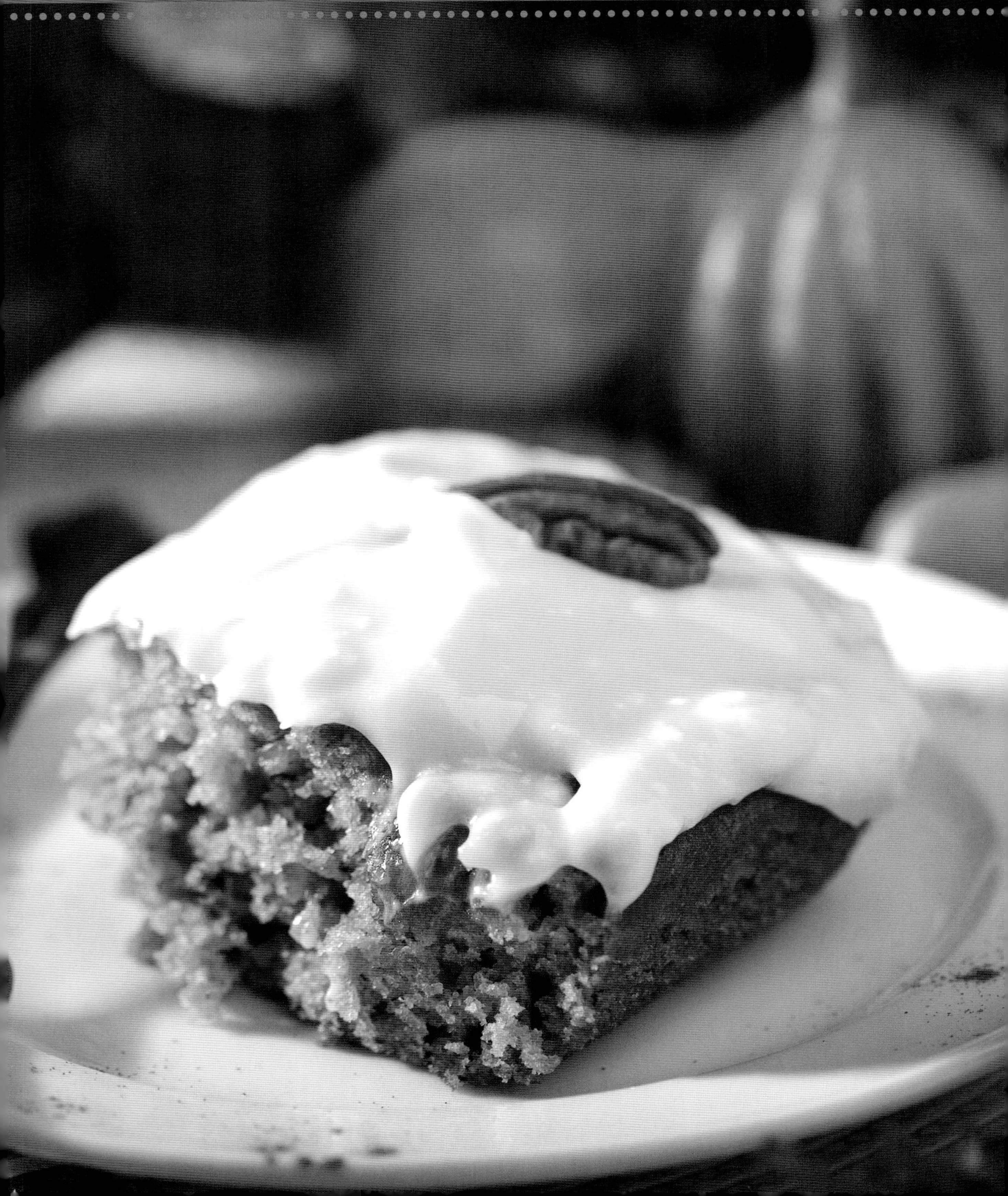

Mom's Pumpkin Cake

1 18.25-oz. box yellow cake mix
1 15-oz. can solid-pack pumpkin
3 eggs
⅓ C. sugar

⅓ C. vegetable oil
1 Tbsp. pumpkin pie spice
1 16-oz. can vanilla frosting
1 3-oz. pkg. cream cheese, softened

In a large bowl, combine cake mix, pumpkin, eggs, sugar, oil, and pumpkin pie spice; beat on low for 30 seconds. Beat on medium for 2 minutes. Pour into a greased 9 x 13-inch baking pan. Bake at 350 for 25–35 minutes or until a toothpick inserted near the center comes out clean. Cool on a wire rack. In a small bowl, beat frosting and cream cheese until smooth; spread over cake. Makes great cupcakes, too! Makes 12 servings.

My mom is the queen at finding quick, easy recipes that taste like a million bucks. This is one of those recipes. My dad's birthday is a few days before Halloween so, of course, he always gets this delicious, moist pumpkin cake. Don't be afraid to add the extra sugar; you need it to balance the blandness of the packed pumpkin. Trust the recipe—it all works out, I promise.

Gaines Jopplin
Lake Nokomis Ward
Minneapolis Minnesota Stake
Minneapolis, Minnesota

Golden Spice Cake

7 egg yolks
1 whole egg
1 C. butter
2 C. packed brown sugar
1 C. molasses
1 tsp. baking soda
5 C. flour
1 tsp. ground cloves

2 tsp. ground cinnamon
2 tsp. ground ginger
1 fresh nutmeg, ground (2–3 tsp. ground
    nutmeg)
Tiny pinch of cayenne pepper
¾ C. buttermilk
1½ C. raisins (optional)

Beat eggs, sugar, and butter to a light batter. Add molasses, soda, flour, spices, and buttermilk. Beat well. Stir a few tablespoons of flour into the raisins and add the raisins to the batter. Pour into 2 greased loaf pans. Bake at 350 for 35–45 minutes. Makes 12 servings.

Anastasia Upton
Falls Lake Ward
Raleigh North Carolina Stake
Raleigh, North Carolina

This is a true family recipe passed down for so long we don't even know where it originated. It's a timeless classic that tastes incredible.

Cranberry Cake with Liquid Gold Sauce

Cake:

3 Tbsp. butter

1 C. sugar

2 C. flour

3 tsp. baking powder

1 tsp. salt

2 C. evaporated milk

2 C. fresh cranberries

Liquid Gold Sauce:

½ C. butter

1 C. sugar

1 C. heavy cream

Cake: Cream butter and sugar. Add flour, baking powder, and salt. Stir in evaporated milk. Toss the cranberries with a few tablespoons of flour and fold into batter. Pour into greased 9 x 13-inch pan and bake at 350 for 35 minutes.

Liquid Gold Sauce: In a medium saucepan, combine butter, sugar, and cream. Cook the sauce over medium heat and bring to slow boil, stirring constantly. Cut cooled cake into squares and drizzle with Liquid Gold Sauce. You will think you are in heaven! The combination of the tart cranberries and the delicious buttery sauce go together so well. Makes a very pretty dessert. Makes 12 servings or 18 cupcakes.

A very good friend of mine gave me this recipe years ago when we got together one year for Thanksgiving. On the morning of Thanksgiving there was a huge ice storm in Dallas; the roads were so bad that not all of us could be together. We had some of the traditional Thanksgiving dishes, but not all of them. Fortunately, my friend shared this dessert with us. It has been a favorite of mine since then. I like to make it at holiday time. It is such a pretty dessert. Be careful, though; there is a secret to the sauce: Do not change the temperature on your cook top at all once you start the sauce. If you do, your butter will separate.

Leslie Owen
Coppell 1st Ward
Carrollton Texas Stake
Coppell, Texas

FOR YOUR EYES (

White Almond Wedding Cake

1 18.25-oz. white cake mix

1 C. flour

1 C. sugar

¾ tsp. salt

1⅓ C. water

1 C. sour cream

2 Tbsp. vegetable oil

1 tsp. almond extract

1 tsp. vanilla extract

4 egg whites

(recipe continued on next page)

(White Almond Wedding Cake, continued)

Preheat oven to 325. Grease and flour a 9 x 13-inch cake pan. In a large bowl, stir the cake mix, flour, sugar, and salt until well mixed. Pour in the water, sour cream, vegetable oil, almond and vanilla extracts, and egg whites. Beat with an electric mixer on low until all the ingredients are mixed and moistened but some lumps still remain. Pour the batter into the prepared cake pan, and bake until the top is a light golden brown and a toothpick inserted into the center of the cake comes out clean, about 25 minutes. Allow to cool before frosting with desired frosting. Makes 20 servings.

This recipe is special to our family because it has been the wedding cake of choice for every child in our family. We have also made it for birthdays and showers as well. It is really delicious. My mom bakes and decorates cakes, and this is one of the most popular cakes she makes. I love it, and I am so glad to share it.

Katie Sweetwater
Glenville Ward
Albany New York Stake
Niskayuna, New York

Lemon Gold Cake

Cake:

2 C. cake flour, sifted

2 tsp. baking powder

½ C. butter or shortening, softened

1 C. sugar

1 tsp. vanilla extract or ½ tsp. lemon extract

3 egg yolks, beaten until thick and lemon-colored

¾ C. milk

Luscious Lemon Frosting:

3 tsp. orange zest, grated

Dash salt

3 Tbsp. butter, softened

3 C. powdered sugar, sifted

2 Tbsp. lemon juice

1 Tbsp. water

Cake: Sift flour once, then measure 2 C. into a bowl. Add baking powder and sift 3 times. Cream butter thoroughly, gradually adding sugar. Add extract and continue creaming until light and fluffy. Add egg yolks and beat well. Add flour alternately with milk, a small amount at a time. Bake in two greased 9-inch springform pans (or a 9 x 13-inch pan) at 375 for 25–30 minutes; it's done when a toothpick inserted in the center comes out clean. Cool and spread with Luscious Lemon Frosting.

Frosting: Combine orange zest, salt, and butter. Add part of sifted sugar gradually, blending well after each addition. Combine lemon juice and water, adding alternately with remaining sugar until the frosting reaches spreadable consistency. For a deeper yellow tint, add food coloring. Makes 12 servings.

Rozlynn Peterson
Cedar Rapids 3rd Ward
Cedar Rapids Iowa Stake
Cedar Rapids, Iowa

This is actually the secret recipe of my boss's mother. He made it for my birthday and I begged for the recipe. I guess his mother doesn't give her recipe out much, but luckily it was my birthday, and my boss couldn't resist my pleas. Enjoy!

Blue Ribbon Carrot Cake with Buttermilk Glaze

Glaze:
1 C. sugar
½ tsp. baking soda
½ C. buttermilk
¼ C. butter
1 Tbsp. light corn syrup
1 tsp. vanilla extract

Frosting:
¼ C. butter
1 8-oz. pkg. cream cheese, room temperature
1 tsp. vanilla extract
2 C. powdered sugar
1 tsp. freshly squeezed orange juice
1 tsp. orange peel, grated

Cake:
2 C. flour
2 tsp. baking soda
2 tsp. cinnamon
½ tsp. salt
3 eggs
¾ C. vegetable oil
¾ C. buttermilk
2 C. sugar
2 tsp. vanilla extract
1 8-oz. can crushed pineapple, drained
2 C. grated carrots
1⅓ C. shredded coconut
1 C. seedless raisins
1 C. walnuts, coarsely chopped

Glaze: In small saucepan over high heat, combine sugar, baking soda, buttermilk, butter, and corn syrup. Bring to a boil. Cook 5 minutes, stirring occasionally. Remove from heat and stir in vanilla. Set aside until cake is baked.

Cake: Preheat oven to 350. Generously grease a 9 x 13-inch baking dish or two 9-inch cake pans. Sift flour, baking soda, cinnamon, and salt together. Set aside. In large bowl, beat eggs. Add oil, buttermilk, sugar, and vanilla; mix well. Add flour mixture, pineapple, carrots, coconut, raisins, and walnuts; stir well. Pour into prepared pan(s). Bake for 45–55 minutes or until toothpick inserted in the center comes out clean. Remove cake from oven and slowly pour buttermilk glaze over hot cake. Cool cake in pan until buttermilk glaze is totally absorbed, about 15 minutes. Frost.

Frosting: In large bowl, cream butter and cream cheese until fluffy. Add vanilla, powdered sugar, orange juice, and orange peel. Mix until smooth. Frost cake and refrigerate until frosting is set. Serve cake chilled. Makes 20 servings.

Emily Price
Laurel Ward
Annapolis Maryland Stake
Laurel, Maryland

This is my special recipe for carrot cake that is sure to make you weak in the knees. Everyone always asks what's in it; the secret is pouring the buttermilk glaze over the hot cake. You are sure to get many compliments with this dessert.

{ DESSERTS }

To know that one has a secret is to know half the secret itself.

{ Henry Ward Beecher }

Sara's Chocolate Mousse

7 oz. dark or semisweet chocolate bar
½ C. milk

6 eggs
⅓ C. packed brown sugar

Using the microwave, melt the chocolate in the milk; it takes 3–5 minutes, but stir after every 30 seconds until chocolate is melted. Let cool. Separate egg whites and yolks. In a medium bowl, mix yolks with the sugar until it starts to bubble; mix in the melted chocolate. In a large bowl, whip the egg whites to soft peaks. Fold the chocolate mixture into the whipped egg whites until the entire mixture is brown. Refrigerate for at least 8 hours. Serve cold. Makes 4 servings.

This mousse is so delicious! You can make it with milk chocolate, but anyone who makes chocolate mousse needs to know that the secret to a great chocolate mousse is to use dark chocolate.

Sara Moreira
Ermesinde Branch
Porto Norte Portugal Stake
Valongo, Portugal

 # Nanaimo Bars

½ C. butter, room temperature
¼ C. sugar
⅓ C. unsweetened cocoa
1 large egg, beaten
1 tsp. vanilla extract
2 C. graham cracker crumbs
1 C. coconut
½ C. walnuts or pecans, chopped

¼ C. butter, room temperature
2–3 Tbsp. milk or cream
2 Tbsp. vanilla custard powder
½ tsp. pure vanilla extract
2 C. powdered sugar
4 oz. unsweetened baking chocolate, chopped
1 Tbsp. unsalted butter

In a saucepan over low heat, melt ½ C. butter. Stir in the sugar and cocoa powder. Gradually whisk in the beaten egg. Cook, stirring constantly, until the mixture thickens (1–2 minutes). Remove from heat and stir in the vanilla extract, graham cracker crumbs, coconut, and chopped nuts. Press the mixture evenly into a 9-inch square pan. Cover and refrigerate until firm. Using an electric mixer, cream the ¼ C. butter. Beat in milk or cream, vanilla custard powder, vanilla extract, and powdered sugar. If the mixture is too thick to spread, add a little more milk. Spread the filling over the bottom layer, cover, and refrigerate until firm, about 30 minutes. In a heat-proof bowl over a saucepan of simmering water, melt the chocolate and 1 Tbsp. butter. Spread over the filling and refrigerate. Makes 20 servings.

This is a well-known dessert all across Canada. Our family secret: the unsweetened chocolate top makes it amazing and sets it apart from the other recipes out there. My mom came up with this and it is a winner every time.

Erin Duerichen
Braes Bayou Ward
Houston Texas South Stake
Houston, Texas

Aunt Leanna's Ooey-Gooeys

1 14-oz. pkg. caramels
⅔ C. evaporated milk, divided
1 German chocolate cake mix

¾ C. butter, melted
1 C. pecans, chopped
1 12-oz. pkg. semisweet chocolate chips

In a medium bowl, combine caramels and ⅓ C. milk. Melt in microwave; set aside. In a separate bowl, combine cake mix, melted butter, and pecans; mix well. Pat half (the less the better) the cake mixture into a greased and floured 9 x 13-inch pan. Bake at 350 for 6 minutes. Remove from oven and pour caramel mixture over the top. Sprinkle with chocolate chips. Cover with remaining cake mixture by flattening sections of the dough between your hands and laying it on top of the caramel mixture. Bake at 350 for 18 minutes. Cool before cutting. Makes 12 servings, but it's never enough.

This is one of our Rucker family recipes, but Aunt Leanna has the secret touch and makes the very best desserts. My grandmother and all of my aunts are geniuses in the kitchen—and Aunt Leanna is baking royalty, with a down-home touch.

Lacy Allphin
Weldon Springs Ward
North St. Louis Missouri Stake
St. Peters, Missouri

Chocolate Banana Peanut Butter Delight

Chocolate Cake:
½ C. butter or margarine, softened
1¼ C. sugar
2 eggs
3 1-oz. envs. liquid unsweetened baking
   chocolate
¾ C. milk
1 tsp. vanilla
2 C. flour
1 tsp. baking soda
½ tsp. salt
½ C. sour cream

Banana Cake:
½ C. butter or margarine, softened
½ C. sugar
1 egg
¾ C. mashed ripe bananas (1½ medium)

¼ C. sour cream
½ tsp. vanilla
½ tsp. banana extract
1 C. flour
½ tsp. baking soda
½ tsp. baking powder
¼ tsp. salt

Peanut Butter Frosting:
1 C. butter or margarine, softened
1 C. creamy peanut butter
4 C. powdered sugar, divided
¼ C. milk
½ tsp. vanilla

Garnish:
Peanuts (optional)
Chocolate chips (optional)

(recipe continued on next page)

(Chocolate Banana Peanut Butter Delight, continued)

Chocolate Cake: Heat oven to 350. Grease and flour three 8- or 9-inch round cake pans. In medium bowl, beat butter and sugar with electric mixer on medium speed, scraping bowl occasionally, until blended. Beat in eggs, one at a time. Beat in chocolate, milk, and vanilla. Beat in flour, soda, salt, and sour cream on low speed, scraping bowl constantly. Divide batter evenly between two of the three pans (the banana cake, below, goes in the third pan). Bake 25–30 minutes or until toothpick inserted in center comes out clean. Cool 10 minutes; remove from pans to cooling rack. Cool completely, about 1 hour.

Banana Cake: In a medium bowl, beat butter and sugar with electric mixer on medium speed, scraping bowl occasionally, until blended. Beat in egg; beat 1 minute. Beat in bananas, sour cream, vanilla, and banana extract. Beat in flour, soda, baking powder, and salt on low speed, scraping bowl constantly. Pour into remaining pan. Bake at 350 for 23–25 minutes or until toothpick inserted in center comes out clean. Cool 10 minutes; remove from pan to cooling rack. Cool completely, about 1 hour.

Frosting: In medium bowl, beat 1 C. butter with electric mixer on medium speed until fluffy. Beat in peanut butter, ½ C. powdered sugar, milk, and vanilla. Gradually beat in remaining 3½ C. powdered sugar, beating after each addition until smooth. Place 1 chocolate cake layer on serving plate; spread with ⅓ C. frosting. Place banana cake layer on frosted layer; spread with ⅓ C. frosting. Top with chocolate cake layer. Frost sides and top of cake with remaining frosting. Garnish with peanuts and chocolate chips, if desired. Store in refrigerator. Makes 10 servings.

This is made after every baptism in our family. I don't know how we got started with the tradition, but my parents made it for us and now my siblings and I have continued on the tradition for our kids. It is something special and fun they look forward to. I have handed this recipe out so many times I would hardly call it a secret, but this is absolutely a family recipe we intend on passing down through our family for a very long time.

Celine Hawkins
Fishers 2nd Ward
Indianapolis Indiana North Stake
Cicero, Indiana

Hello Dollies

½ C. margarine

1 C. graham cracker crumbs

1 C. coconut

1 C. chocolate chips

1 C. nuts, chopped

1 14-oz. can sweetened condensed milk

Melt margarine in a 9 x 13-inch pan. Sprinkle graham cracker crumbs evenly in melted margarine. Sprinkle coconut over crumbs. Next sprinkle chocolate chips over the coconut. Then sprinkle chopped nuts over the chocolate chips. Finally, drizzle the condensed milk evenly over all. Bake at 350 for 20 minutes or until browned. Cool and cut into squares. Makes 20 servings.

This is my late Grandmother Phillips's recipe. It is one of my favorites, and is so quick and easy to make. Although my grandmother is in heaven, this recipe still lives on.

Heather Whipple
Paidmont Ward
Fredericksburg Virginia Stake
Culpeper, Virginia

Maw-Maw's Xtreme Chocolate Brownies

⅔ C. butter or margarine

1½ C. sugar

¼ C. water

4 C. semisweet chocolate chips, divided

2 tsp. vanilla

4 eggs

1½ C. flour

½ tsp. baking soda

½ tsp. salt

Walnuts, chopped (optional)

Preheat oven to 325. Grease a 9 x 13-inch baking pan. In a heavy saucepan, bring butter, sugar, and water to a boil, stirring constantly until the butter is melted and sugar is dissolved, about 3 minutes. Remove from heat. With a wooden spoon, stir in 2 C. chocolate chips until melted; cool slightly, then beat in vanilla. In a large bowl, whisk eggs; gradually add the chocolate mixture, beating with a wooden spoon until completely mixed. In a small bowl, mix flour, baking soda, and salt; add to the egg/chocolate mixture and mix well to combine. Stir in the remaining chocolate chips. Add chopped walnuts, if desired. Spread into prepared baking pan. Bake for 35–40 minutes. Do not overbake. Cut into squares. Makes 12 servings.

Lorna Walsh
Tickle Creek Ward
Mount Hood Oregon Stake
Mount Hood Parkdale, Oregon

Maw-Maw, as we call her, is the best cook I honestly have ever known. She is the funniest woman. I tried to get her to submit some recipes to this book on her own, but she is much too shy with her talents. My grandmother was a baker/cook at a boarding school in Wales for more than fifteen years and has many treasured recipes from her experiences. These brownies are one of my favorites! I never thought I would taste brownies that were better than the boxed kind until she made these for me. The secret is out. Everyone will want the recipe, trust me.

Chocolate Velvet Ice Cream

⅔ C. sugar

⅓ C. unsweetened cocoa powder

3 egg yolks, beaten

2⅔ C. heavy cream

⅓ C. semisweet chocolate chips

In large bowl, stir sugar and cocoa. Add egg yolks; blend with electric mixer. Add cream a little at a time, beating well after each addition. Chill mixture in refrigerator. While cream mixture is chilling, chop chocolate chips in blender, food processor, or rotary grater until fine. Stir into cream mixture. Freeze in canister of ice cream maker according to manufacturer's instructions. Makes 8 servings.

This is my family's special chocolate ice cream recipe. We make homemade ice cream throughout the summer, and this is one of our favorites. We just can't get enough of it!

Betsy Prinze
New Haven Ward
Tulsa Oklahoma Stake
Tulsa, Oklahoma

Granola Bars

1 C. butter, room temperature

2 C. packed brown sugar

1 C. corn syrup

1⅓ C. creamy peanut butter

1 tsp. vanilla

⅔ C. wheat germ

6 C. quick-cooking oatmeal (may need ½ C. more)

1 C. mini chocolate chips

In a large bowl, mix butter, brown sugar, corn syrup, peanut butter, vanilla, and wheat germ until well blended. Add oatmeal and chocolate chips and mix well. Pour onto a cookie sheet pan and distribute with your hands. Spray a rolling pin with nonstick cooking spray and roll out the dough evenly in the pan, pushing as you roll to compact dough. Bake at 350 for 17–20 minutes. Cool completely and cut into 32 bars. Enjoy!

I found this recipe about a year ago and made my usual modifications. It has been a family favorite ever since, especially for the kids! I am asked to bring these granola bars to most of our extended family gatherings. I can't even tell you how many times I have made them—usually at least once a week for my family alone!

Amy Barton
Spring Haven Ward
Syracuse Utah Stake
Syracuse, Utah

Yummy Caramel Chip Bars

½ C. butter, cubed

32 caramels

1 14-oz. can sweetened condensed milk

1 18.25-oz. yellow cake mix

½ C. vegetable oil

2 eggs

2 C. semisweet chocolate chips

1 C. vanilla or white chips

1 1.4-oz. toffee candy bar, chopped (Heath)

In a large saucepan, combine the butter, caramels, and milk; cook and stir over medium-low heat until smooth. Cool. In a large bowl, beat the cake mix, oil, and eggs until blended. Stir in chips and chopped candy bar (batter will be stiff). Press ¾ of the batter into a greased 9 x 13-inch baking pan. Bake at 350 for 15 minutes. Place on a wire rack for 10 minutes. Pour caramel mixture over the crust. Drop remaining dough by spoonfuls onto caramel layer. Bake at 350 for 25–30 minutes longer or until edges are golden brown. Cool on a wire rack for 10 minutes; run a knife around edges of pan. Cool for 40 minutes; cover and refrigerate for at least 1 hour before serving. Makes 24 servings.

Natalie Buchanan
Harbor Hills Ward
Newport Beach California Stake
Newport Coast, California

I got the recipe for these bars out of my mother's PTA cookbook, which has recipes from all the mothers at my sister's high school. I do not even remember the lady who submitted these treats or I would give her the credit she deserves. They are a-m-a-z-i-n-g. I use them as my secret weapon to make my husband do whatever I say . . . hahaha.

Orange Creamy Surprise

1 pkg. graham crackers, crushed, OR
1 box graham cracker crumbs
½ C. butter or margarine, melted
½ gal. orange sherbet
1 8-oz. pkg. cream cheese

1 C. orange juice
1 12-oz. container frozen whipped topping, thawed

Combine crushed graham crackers or graham cracker crumbs with melted butter; press into a 9 X 13-inch glass dish. Bake at 325 for 5 minutes. Combine remaining ingredients and pour over graham cracker crust. Put in freezer until approximately 30 minutes before serving. Makes 10 servings.

This recipe was created when I lived in Stanton, California; I was experimenting with recipes before having the missionaries over for dinner. It became an overnight success and we always served it for our missionaries when they came to eat with us. My secret is adding the orange juice for extra orange flavor.

Teri Rodeman
Benton City Ward
Kennewick Washington Stake
Benton City, Washington

Banana Pudding

1 5-oz. pkg. instant vanilla pudding mix
2 C. cold milk
1 14-oz. can sweetened condensed milk
1 Tbsp. vanilla extract

1 12-oz. container frozen whipped topping, thawed
1 16-oz. pkg. vanilla wafers
6 bananas, sliced

In a large mixing bowl, beat pudding mix and milk for 2 minutes. Blend in condensed milk until smooth. Stir in vanilla; fold in whipped topping. Layer wafers, bananas, and pudding mixture in a glass serving bowl. Chill until served. Makes 12 servings.

Kierstyn Carr
High Desert Ward
Bend Oregon Stake
Bend, Oregon

This is my mom's way of making banana pudding, and it rocks! Whenever I serve it, everyone thinks I spent forever on it because it tastes and looks so great. Nobody ever believes I used instant pudding. It's true, but shhh! Keep the secret! Be ready to get a lot of praise when you make it.

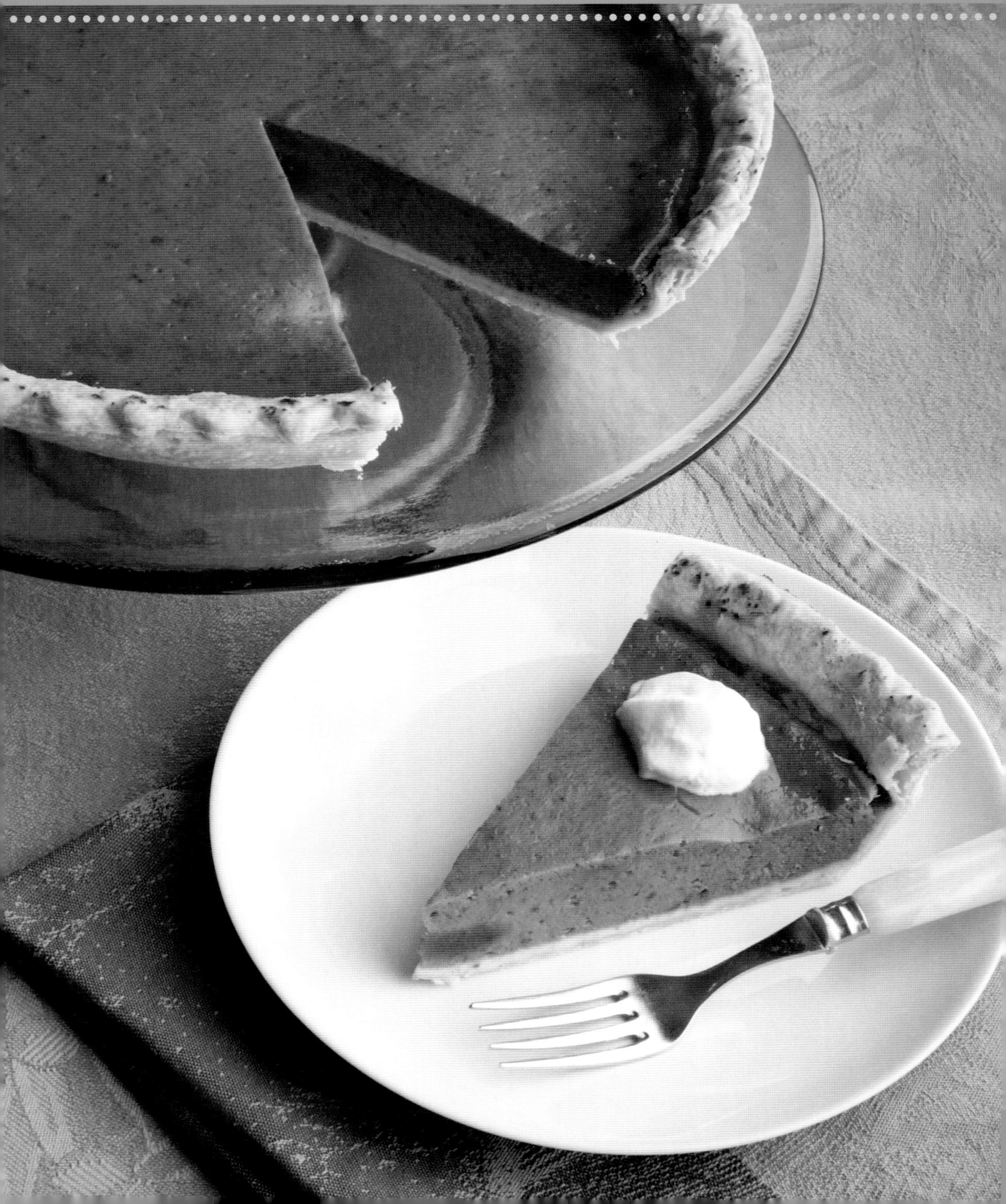

Grandma's Pumpkin Pie

Crust:
2 C. flour
¼ C. sugar
Pinch of salt
⅔ C. shortening
About ⅔ C. cold water

Pie:
2 C. sugar
Pinch of salt
2 tsp. cinnamon
½ tsp. ground cloves
1 tsp. ginger
4 beaten eggs
28 oz. evaporated milk
2 tsp. vanilla
29 oz. pure pumpkin

Crust: Sift flour, sugar, and salt into a bowl. Add shortening. Mix with a pastry blender until the dough is in very small pieces. Add water slowly, mixing after each addition, until dough looks like slightly rough playdough. Mix with your hands until smooth. Sprinkle flour on the counter and roll out half of the dough with a rolling pin. Place crust in pie dish. Fold edges under and pinch crust to make it ruffled. Repeat with second half of crust.

Pie: Mix all dry ingredients. Add wet ingredients. Pour into crusts until batter is about ¼ inch from the bottom of the pinch marks in the crust. Bake at 425 for 15 minutes; reduce the temperature to 350 and bake for 45 minutes or until a toothpick inserted near the center comes out clean. Makes 2 pies.

Marcie Davies
Taylorview Ward
Taylor Mountain Idaho Stake
Idaho Falls, Idaho

My grandma made this pie every Thanksgiving, and it was always the special finale to a fabulous home-cooked Thanksgiving dinner. Years ago, my mom asked how she made her delicious pie. My grandma replied, "It's the recipe on the pumpkin can." My mom protested, "No, it's not! I've made the recipe on the can, and it's not as good as yours!" Then my grandma spilled the secret: "Don't you know? I just add an extra half cup of sugar!" My grandma was getting older, so I went over to her house and she showed me exactly how to make her famous pumpkin pie. She sent me home with one of the pies in her pie dish. This pumpkin pie holds special memories of Thanksgiving with my grandma (and funny times drowning our pieces of the pie in whipped cream!).

Tropical Fudge

3 C. sugar

1 8-oz. can crushed pineapple

1 C. evaporated milk

¼ C. light corn syrup

¼ tsp. cream of tartar

¼ C. unsalted butter, room temperature

1 C. Macadamia nuts

In a well-buttered heavy saucepan, combine sugar, pineapple, evaporated milk, corn syrup, and cream of tartar. Bring to a boil over low heat, stirring constantly. Continue cooking, stirring occasionally, until candy reaches softball stage (235 degrees on a candy thermometer). Remove from heat. DO NOT STIR. Cool until saucepan feels lukewarm. Add butter and beat until candy begins to thicken. Add nuts and pour into a buttered dish. Cut when firm. Makes 16 servings.

Baking has always been a hobby of mine. I own a small confections shop and love making candy. I always get asked for my secrets, but the secret to making wonderful candy is practice more than anything. This is one of my favorites and is sure to please. It is pretty much a no-fail recipe.

Lynn Churchill
Frontenac Ward
St. Louis Missouri Stake
St. Louis, Missouri

Pumpkin Cream Trifle

1 18.25-oz. pkg. spice cake mix

1 3.4-oz. pkg. instant vanilla pudding mix

1 C. pumpkin, canned or mashed fresh

½ C. vegetable oil

½ C. water

3 large eggs

1 tsp. ground cinnamon

½ tsp. ground ginger

2 3.4-oz. pkgs. cheesecake instant pudding mix (can use 2 vanilla or 1 cheesecake and 1 vanilla)

2 C. cold milk

2 C. frozen whipped topping, thawed

Pecans, chopped and toasted

English toffee bits or chopped toffee candy bars (like Skor or Heath)

Caramel sauce drizzle, if desired

Preheat oven to 350. Spray a 9 x 13-inch baking pan with nonstick spray. In a large mixing bowl, combine cake mix, vanilla pudding mix, pumpkin, oil, water, eggs, cinnamon, and ginger. Blend with electric mixer on low speed for 1 minute. Stop mixer and scrape down sides of bowl with a rubber spatula. Increase mixer speed to medium and beat for 2 minutes more. Batter should look thick and well blended. Pour the mixture into prepared pan and bake for 32–39 minutes or until cake springs back lightly when touched and a toothpick inserted near the center comes out clean. Cool completely. (Cake can be frozen at this point. Thaw at room temperature before assembling trifle.) When ready to assemble trifle, cut or tear cake into 1-inch cubes. Combine pudding mixes with milk and blend with whisk until the pudding starts to thicken. Fold in whipped topping, then quickly assemble trifle. Place ⅓ of cake cubes into trifle bowl. Top with ⅓ pudding mixture and

(recipe continued on next page)

(Pumpkin Cream Trifle, continued)

sprinkle with ⅓ nuts and toffee bits. Repeat layers two more times, ending with nuts and toffee on top. Drizzle with caramel sauce, if desired. Serve immediately or refrigerate, covered, no longer than 24 hours. Makes 16 servings.

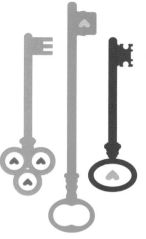

When I was first married, I really didn't think I could cook very well; more than seventeen years later, I am a cooking demonstrator and published recipe author and have won several awards for my recipes. What is my secret? My two favorites are research and variation. I love to read cookbooks from cover to cover; you get a sense of what will work and you can let your creativity fly. Then simply think up variations on something you already know works. That's how I created this Pumpkin Cream Trifle—I varied a strawberry banana trifle using the flavors of fall. It was a complete hit, and won first place at a bake-off.

Gayle Holdman
Highland 14th Ward
Highland Utah West Stake
Highland, Utah

Famous Zucchini Brownies

½ C. vegetable oil

1½ C. sugar

2 tsp. vanilla extract

2 C. flour

½ C. unsweetened cocoa powder

1½ tsp. baking soda

1 tsp. salt

2 C. zucchini, shredded

½ C. walnuts, chopped

6 Tbsp. unsweetened cocoa powder

¼ C. margarine

2 C. powdered sugar

¼ C. milk

½ tsp. vanilla extract

Preheat oven to 350. Grease and flour a 9 x 13-inch baking pan. In a large bowl, mix oil, sugar, and 2 tsp. vanilla until well blended. In a separate bowl, combine flour, ½ C. cocoa powder, baking soda, and salt; stir into the sugar mixture. Fold in the zucchini and walnuts. Spread evenly into the prepared pan. Bake for 25–30 minutes, until brownies spring back when gently touched. To make the frosting, melt 6 Tbsp. cocoa and margarine; set aside to cool. In a medium bowl, blend powdered sugar, milk, and ½ tsp. vanilla. Stir in the cocoa mixture. Spread over cooled brownies before cutting into squares. Makes 16 servings.

This is my mom's secret recipe. These brownies are to die for! The secret is the zucchini. We have a garden that gets overrun with zucchini every year, so we make these brownies a lot. They are more like cake than brownies, but they turn out so fudgy and moist. The texture depends on how you grate the zucchini—we grate ours very fine on a microplane, which turns the zucchini into mush and makes the brownies turn out cake-like. My sister grates hers on a regular grater, which makes the batter thicker and gives the finished product a more brownie-like texture. Either way, the zucchini gives off tons of moisture and the brownies end up all gooey and fudgy. Oh, and don't worry—you can't taste the zucchini . . . shhh! Nobody will ever know it's in there.

Sage Kendrick
Lakeside Park Ward
Cincinnati Ohio Stake
Villa Hills, Kentucky

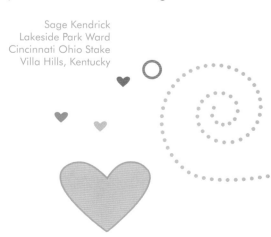

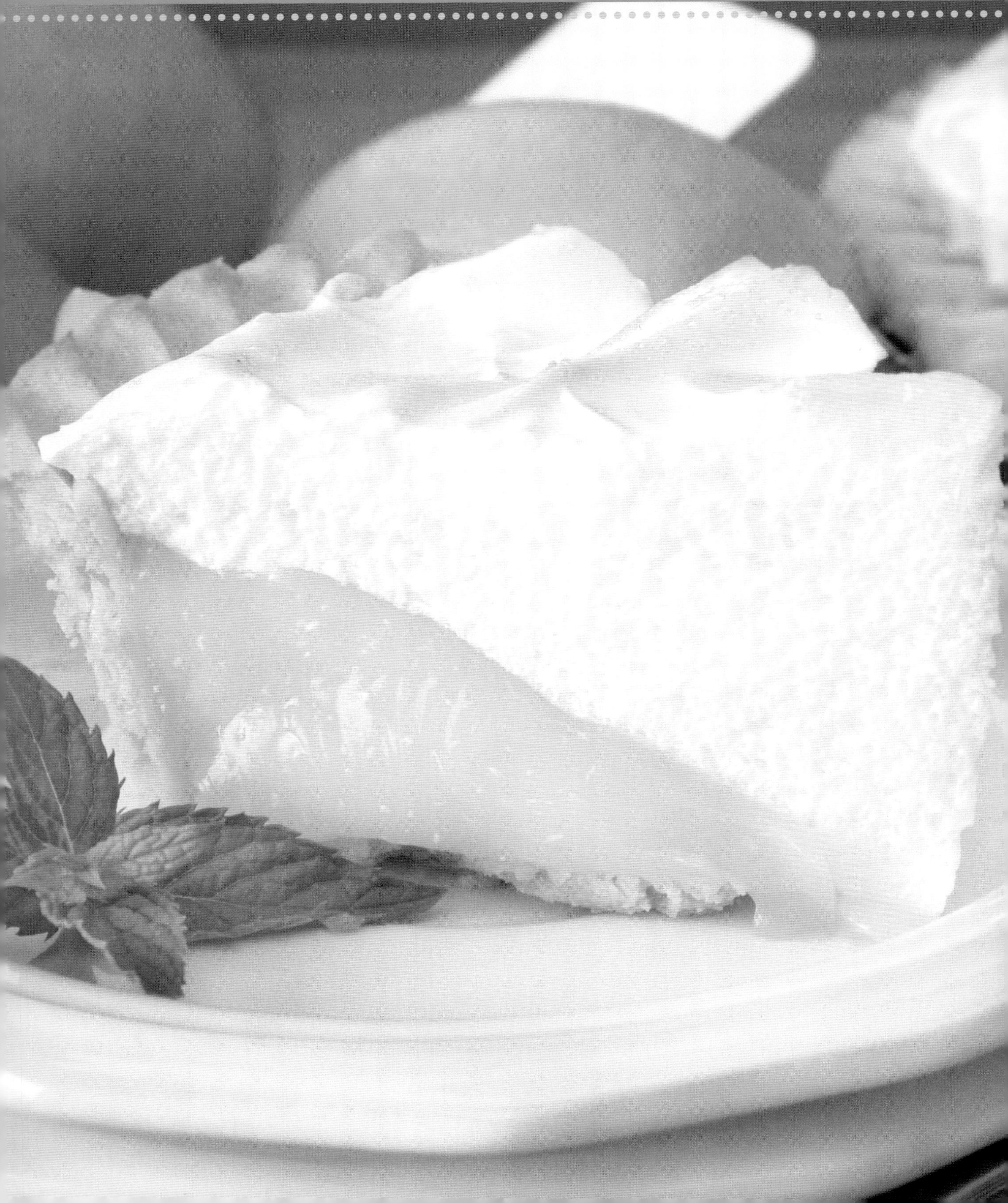

Lemon Meringue Pie

Crust:
4 C. sifted flour
2 tsp. salt
1⅓ C. shortening
¼–⅓ C. very cold water

Filling:
6 large lemons
12 egg yolks
4 C. sugar

1½ C. cornstarch
6 C. warm water
1½ C. butter

Meringue:
12 egg whites
1 tsp. cream of tartar
1 C. sugar
1 Tbsp. lemon peel, grated

Crust: Preheat oven to 475. Combine flour and salt. Cut shortening into salted flour; the dough must be cut into pieces the size of small peas. Sprinkle 1 Tbsp. water at a time over the dough, mixing thoroughly. Continue sprinkling water and stirring until dough sticks together. Divide dough in half and form into two smooth balls. Put each ball of dough between 2 sheets of plastic wrap and roll out flat into a large 10-inch circle. Put into pie pans, cut off excess dough, and crimp edge. Prick bottom and sides thoroughly with fork. Bake for 8–10 minutes or until golden brown.

Filling: Wash the lemons and grate the lemon peels to get about 6 Tbsp. zest. Set aside. Cut the lemons in half and juice them to get 2 C. juice. Set aside. Separate eggs; in a separate bowl, beat the egg yolks; save the egg whites for the meringue. In a large saucepan, combine the sugar and cornstarch; add warm water, mix well, and cook over medium heat, stirring constantly, until mixture thickens and boils, about 7 minutes. Boil and stir for 1 minute. Stir half of the hot mixture into the beaten egg yolks. Blend the egg yolk mixture into the hot mixture in the saucepan and boil and stir for another minute. Remove from heat; stir in butter, 5 Tbsp. lemon peel (save 1 Tbsp. lemon peel for the meringue), and lemon juice. Pour into two 10-inch baked pie crusts.

Meringue: Preheat oven to 400. Beat egg whites and cream of tartar until foamy and becoming stiff. Beat in sugar, 1 Tbsp. at a time. Continue beating until glossy peaks form. Add grated lemon peel. Put meringue over hot lemon filling. Make sure the meringue covers the entire pie shell and touches the crust. Bake until tips of meringue turn dark brown, 7–10 minutes. Cool for at least 4 hours. Makes 2 10-inch pies.

Stephanie Springgay
Novelty Hill Ward
Redmond Washington Stake
Redmond, Washington

When they were dating, my mom decided to make my dad dinner. People were always telling my mom what an amazing cook she was, so what could go wrong—right? She decided to make a lemon meringue pie; like her mom did, she used instant Jell-O, and the crust was hard as a plate. My dad ate it, then invited her over for dinner. His mother made a homemade lemon meringue pie from scratch. It was perfect! My mom immediately asked my grandma teach her how to make that perfect pie! Since then we have made hundreds of lemon meringue pies—you name it, we've made this pie for it!

Mint Chocolate Chip Ice Cream

2 C. 2% milk

2 C. heavy cream

1 C. sugar

½ tsp. salt

1 tsp. vanilla extract

1 tsp. peppermint extract (NOT PEPPERMINT OIL)

3 drops green food coloring (optional)

¾ C. semisweet chocolate bar, shaved

In a large bowl, stir the milk, cream, sugar, salt, vanilla extract, and peppermint extract until the sugar has dissolved. Color to your liking with the green food coloring. Pour the mixture into an ice cream maker, and freeze according to the manufacturer's instructions. About 10 minutes into the freezing, add the chocolate pieces. After the ice cream has thickened, about 30 minutes later, spoon into a container and freeze for 2 hours. Makes 8 servings.

My daughter is a mint chocolate chip fanatic; we discovered this ice cream years ago and it's very good. We usually make this at least three or four times a year.

Betsy Prinze
New Haven Ward
Tulsa Oklahoma Stake
Tulsa, Oklahoma

Beijinho

2 Tbsp. butter

2 14-oz. cans sweetened condensed milk

2 C. coconut

1 C. sugar

1 C. coconut

In a saucepan over medium heat, melt the butter; pour in milk and cook over medium heat for 4 minutes, stirring constantly with a wooden spoon and scraping the sides of the pan. Add 2 C. coconut and cook over low heat 7–10 minutes, stirring constantly, until mixture is thick and not sticking to pan. Let cool for 10–20 minutes. Place sugar in one small bowl and 1 C. coconut in a separate small bowl. Butter your hands and shape teaspoonfuls of cooled mixture into little balls. Roll each ball in the sugar or coconut. Let set in the refrigerator for an hour before serving. Makes 15 servings.

Kelly Hammons
Park View Ward
Payson Utah South Stake
Payson, Utah

This Brazilian dessert has been passed from generation to generation. I grew up in Brazil, where Beijinho was a very popular dessert for birthdays and special occasions. I remember my mom and grandma making these treats when I was little. They are easily one of my favorite desserts today, and now they are a favorite for my husband and children, too. One bite is enough to keep them coming back for more! We love them and hope you will too.

Darcy's Secret Sinfully Amazing Strawberry Banana-Split Dessert

2 C. graham cracker crumbs (about 32 squares)

½ C. butter, melted

¼ C. sugar

½ C. butter, softened

2 C. powdered sugar

1 Tbsp. milk

1 tsp. vanilla extract

3 large firm bananas, cut into ¼-inch slices

2 8-oz. cans crushed pineapple, drained

2 qt. fresh strawberries, sliced

2 C. heavy cream

¼ C. powdered sugar

1½ C. walnuts, chopped

In a medium bowl, combine graham cracker crumbs, melted butter, and sugar; press into an ungreased 9 x 13-inch dish. Chill for 1 hour. In a medium bowl, cream softened butter, 2 C. powdered sugar, milk, and vanilla. Spread over crust; chill for 30 minutes. Layer with bananas, pineapple, and strawberries. In a small bowl, beat cream until soft peaks form. Add ¼ C. powdered sugar; beat until stiff peaks form. Spread over fruit. Sprinkle with nuts. Chill until served. Makes 12 servings.

This dessert is one of the most requested desserts that I make. It really is like a banana split but better. The secret is the whipped cream; whipping the cream is so much better than anything from a container. I have made this a few dozen times and the bowl always gets licked clean.

Darcy Lind
Canyon Gate Ward
Las Vegas Nevada Sandstone Stake
Las Vegas, Nevada

Passion Fruit Mousse

1 14-oz. can sweetened condensed milk

1 8-oz. can media crema (table cream from Nestle) or 1 C. heavy cream

1 C. passion fruit juice (unsweetened)

1 env. unflavored gelatin

2 Tbsp. hot water

Semisweet mini chocolate chips

Pour sweetened condensed milk, media crema or cream, and passion fruit juice into a blender. Blend for 30 seconds. In a small bowl, combine gelatin and hot water. Add the gelatin mixture to the blender. Blend on low until light and fluffy, 30 seconds to 1 minute. Pour into a serving bowl or dessert dishes, and refrigerate at least 30 minutes. Sprinkle with mini chocolate chips and serve. Makes 4 servings.

I am so pleased to invite you all to taste this recipe! I'm from Brazil, and I love cooking great and different kinds of foods. This recipe is my creation after trying hundreds of mousses—I finally found one that is both simple and easy, and most important, delicious! Enjoy; it's a great and refreshing dessert!

Tatiana Pryor
Osage Beach Ward
Saint Robert's Stake
Fortaleza, Ceara
Brazil

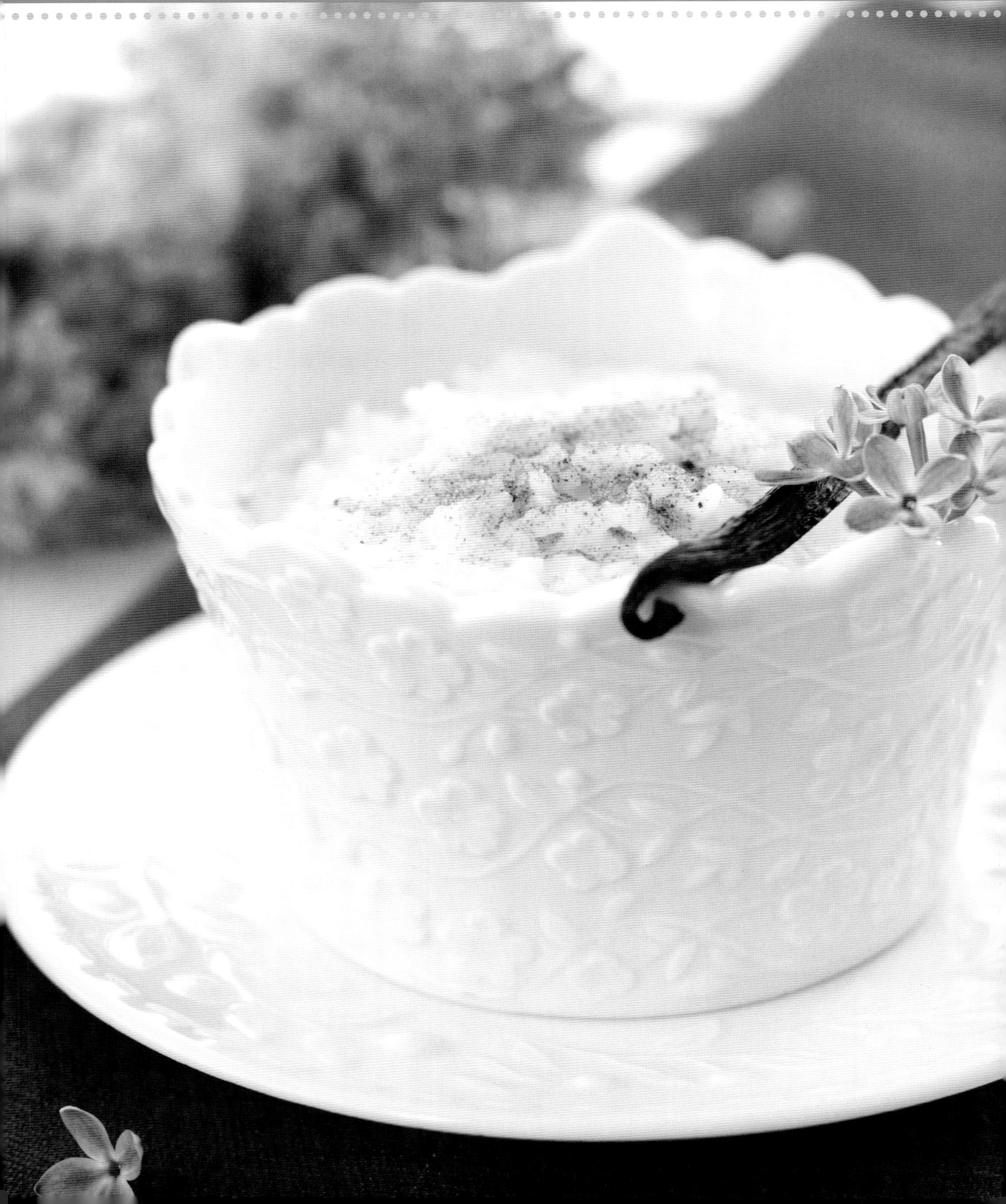

Ris a la Mande (Rice Pudding)

1 vanilla pod
4 C. whole milk
½ C. rice
Salt

½ C. blanched almonds
1 C. heavy cream
⅓ C. sugar

Split the vanilla pod and remove the beans. In a covered pot, boil the vanilla beans, milk, rice, and a little salt over low heat for about 45 minutes. Stir the pudding now and then. Remove the vanilla beans and cool the pudding. Chop the almonds but save one whole to put in the dessert. Stir the almonds into the cold pudding. Whip the cream and carefully fold it into the pudding. Now taste it to see if it is fine. Makes 4 servings. Traditionally, whoever gets the whole almond in his or her serving receives a small treat.

When my mother was a child, my grandmother asked what her secret wish was for her birthday. She answered that all she wanted was Ris a la Mande. Her wish came true: On her birthday she had a big baking dish filled with Ris a la Mande, and she was filled with joy!

Mille Norgaard
Randers Branch
Aarhus Denmark Stake
Randers, Denmark

Buckeyes

2 C. creamy peanut butter
¼ C. unsalted butter, room temperature
¼ tsp. salt
½ tsp. vanilla extract

2–2½ C. powdered sugar
2 Tbsp. shortening
9–12 oz. semisweet chocolate chips

Line a baking sheet with waxed paper and set aside. In a bowl, mix peanut butter, butter, salt, vanilla, and powdered sugar with hands to form a smooth, stiff dough. Shape into balls using 2 tsp. dough for each ball. Place on prepared cookie sheet and refrigerate. Melt shortening and chocolate in a metal bowl over a pan of lightly simmering water. Stir occasionally until smooth; remove from heat. Remove balls from refrigerator. Insert a wooden toothpick into a ball and dip the ball most of the way into the melted chocolate. Return to waxed paper, chocolate side down, and remove toothpick. Repeat with remaining balls. Refrigerate for 30 minutes to set. Makes 5 dozen.

True Ohioans are known for their commitment to the Ohio State University football team: The Buckeyes! The buckeye tree is our state tree. These trees grow nuts that look like the eye of a buck (deer). The football team got its name from the tree. Here in Ohio a football party ain't a real football party unless you're servin' up some delicious Buckeyes! These mouth-watering chocolate-covered peanut-butter balls are the secret to any great game day! True Ohioans have taken these delicious treats a step further and not only serve 'em up for football parties or games, but they are sure to prepare these little treats for almost any holiday, party, or family event!

Robert and Kimberlie McBride
Westland Ward
Columbus West Stake
Galloway, Ohio

Lemon Bar Trifle

2 C. flour
1 C. pecans, chopped
1 C. butter, melted
1½ C. sugar
¼ C. cornstarch
¼ C. flour
1¾ C. cold water
3 egg yolks, beaten

⅔ C. lemon juice
2 Tbsp. butter
4 tsp. lemon peel, grated
1 8-oz. pkg. cream cheese, softened
3 C. powdered sugar
1 8-oz. container frozen whipped topping, thawed

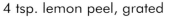

In a small bowl, combine flour and pecans; stir in melted butter. Press into an ungreased 9 x 13-inch baking dish. Bake at 350 for 18–20 minutes or until light golden brown. Cool on a wire rack. In a small heavy saucepan, combine the sugar, cornstarch, and flour. Stir in water until smooth. Cook and stir over medium-high heat until thickened and bubbly. Reduce heat; cook and stir 2 minutes longer. Remove from heat. Stir a small amount of hot mixture into egg yolks; return all egg yolks to the pan, stirring constantly. Bring to a gentle boil; cook and stir 2 minutes longer. Remove from the heat. Gently stir in the lemon juice, butter, and lemon peel. Transfer to a large bowl. Cool to room temperature without stirring. Cover surface with waxed paper; refrigerate until chilled. In a large bowl, beat cream cheese and powdered sugar until smooth. Fold in whipped topping. Crumble the baked pecan mixture; set aside ½ C. for topping. Just before serving, in a 3-quart trifle bowl, layer 1 C. each pecan mixture, lemon mixture, and cream cheese mixture. Repeat layers two more times. Sprinkle with reserved pecan mixture. Refrigerate leftovers. Makes 9 servings.

My in-laws make this for family gatherings all the time. It really is a secret recipe. My mother-in-law doesn't ever give the recipe out. But lucky for you guys, she did give it to my wife! I have never been a fan of lemon deserts but this is something on its own level. It's seriously one of the best desserts I have ever had—and is way too good a secret to keep!

Ryan Murphy
West Hills Ward
Knoxville Tennessee Stake
Knoxville, Tennessee

FOR YOUR EYES O

Grandma Ludlow's Rhubarb Crunch

4 C. rhubarb
2 Tbsp. flour
1 C. sugar
2 Tbsp. butter, melted
1 C. sugar
1 tsp. baking powder

1 egg, well beaten
1 C. flour
¼ tsp. salt
1 C. oatmeal
¼ C. butter, melted

(recipe continued on next page)

(Grandma Ludlow's Rhubarb Crunch, continued)

In a medium bowl, combine rhubarb, flour, sugar, and 2 Tbsp. melted butter. Spread in an 8 x 8-inch pan. In a small bowl, combine sugar, baking powder, egg, flour, salt, oatmeal, and ¼ C. melted butter. Mix until crumbly and sprinkle on top of rhubarb mixture in pan. Gently shake pan to settle. Bake at 375 for 30–35 minutes. Serve with a scoop of vanilla ice cream. Makes 6–8 servings.

I will never forget the night I first tasted this yummy dessert. My husband and I had just driven eight hours to Grandma's home in Montana. It was pretty late, but Grandma had dinner ready when we got there. I sat at the counter in her laundry room, the same place I had sat as a child, and devoured this dessert. My grandma amazes me. She goes and goes and goes. While she was serving a mission at the Family History Library, we loved having so many opportunities to see her while she lived close by. At the age of eighty, she wanted to hike up to Timpanogos Cave, and she did it! I don't know what her secret is, but I want to be just like her!

Teresa Riley
Oquirrh Point 1st Ward
Oquirrh Point Utah Stake
Salt Lake City, Utah

Peanut Butter Playdough

1 C. peanut butter (use the cheapest peanut butter; it is not as oily)

1½ C. powdered milk

1 C. corn syrup

1½ C. powdered sugar

The secret is to use EXACT measurements! Combine all ingredients and mix well. Make sure you level each ingredient with a butter knife to keep precise. Play and eat! Makes enough to fill about 8 small baggies with ½ C. in each.

Brianna and Alyssa Sinks
Lake Travis Ward
Austin Texas Oak Hills Stake
Austin, Texas

My name is Brianna and I am fourteen years old; my sister, Alyssa, is ten. We both love this recipe! My grandma taught us how to make Peanut Butter Playdough. She gave me my very own recipe box and this was the first recipe I put in it. My grandma was a first-grade teacher and she made this for her class every year; she also made it for my mom and uncles when they were little. My grandma got the recipe when she went to BYU in the 1960s. The secret to this recipe is to use exact measurements and to use cheap peanut butter (that's always good, right?). And who says you can't play with your food? Well you can now! The best secret is that you can eat it when you are done! How fun is that? I love to bring the peanut butter playdough with me when I go babysitting. The kids get so excited and it keeps them busy for a long time! I am so grateful to my grandma for taking the time to teach us how to make this fun and creative recipe. We love you so much, Grandma!

Chocolate Malt Cheesecake

⅓ C. unsalted butter, room temperature

¼ C. sugar

1 C. graham cracker crumbs

3 8-oz. pkgs. cream cheese, room temperature

1 14-oz. can sweetened condensed milk

¾ C. chocolate malt powder

4 eggs

1 tsp. vanilla

1 C. semisweet chocolate chips

Preheat oven to 300. In a medium bowl, combine butter, sugar, and graham cracker crumbs. Press mixture firmly into bottom of a 9 x 3-inch round springform pan. In a large bowl, beat cream cheese until fluffy. Add condensed milk and beat until well blended. Add malt powder, eggs, and vanilla; beat thoroughly. Fold in chocolate chips. Pour filling into crust. Bake 65 minutes or until cake springs back when lightly touched. Cool to room temperature, then chill in refrigerator. Makes 12 servings.

I am a newlywed, so we don't really have any secret recipes of our own yet. Instead we rely on a lot of our parents' recipes or old handed-down recipes from grandparents. This is one of our favorites. It tastes like a malted milkshake. Sometimes when I make this I use milk chocolate mini chips or white chocolate chips.

Dallin Aimes
Philadelphia 1st Ward
Valley Forge Pennsylvania Stake
Philadelphia, Pennsylvania

Kiwifruit Cobbler

12 large kiwifruit

2 Tbsp. packed brown sugar

1 Tbsp. lemon peel, grated

1 Tbsp. flour

½ tsp. cinnamon

½ 3.2-oz. pkg. corn muffin mix

1 Tbsp. additional brown sugar

½ tsp. ground nutmeg

Vanilla ice cream or cream (optional)

Heat oven to 375. Peel kiwifruit and cut into ¾-inch cubes. Place cubed kiwifruit in a greased baking dish. In a small bowl, combine brown sugar, lemon peel, flour, and cinnamon. Sprinkle on top of fruit. Mix lightly and place in hot oven for 25 minutes. Prepare ½ pkg. muffin mix as directed. When fruit mixture is hot and bubbling, spoon on prepared mix. Combine 1 Tbsp. brown sugar and nutmeg and sprinkle on top. Return cobbler to oven for another 18–20 minutes or until crust is golden brown. Remove and allow to cool. Serve warm; serve with ice cream or cream, if desired. Makes 8 servings.

I love fruit cobbler but, if you ask me, kiwifruit is definitely the secret to really great cobbler.

Francisco Olivarez
Punitaqui Branch
Ovalle Chile Stake
Punitaqui, Chile

Peppermint Fudge

2½ C. sugar
½ C. margarine
1 5-oz. can evaporated milk
1 7-oz. jar marshmallow creme (2 C.)

8 oz. vanilla chips
Red food coloring
½ C. peppermint candy, finely crushed

Line a 9-inch square pan with foil so that foil extends over sides of pan. Butter the foil. In a large saucepan, combine sugar, margarine, and milk. Bring to a boil, stirring constantly. Continue boiling 5 minutes over medium heat, stirring constantly. Remove from heat. Add marshmallow creme, vanilla chips, and desired amount of food coloring. Blend until smooth. Stir in crushed peppermint. Pour into prepared pan. Cool to room temperature. Score fudge into 36 or 48 squares. Sprinkle top with additional crushed peppermint candy. Refrigerate until firm. Makes 20 servings.

> This is a recipe from the Pace family, a special family I met on my mission while serving in New York City. They made us tons of fudge one year and this was my favorite. Luckily I married their daughter, so I still get to enjoy this every year!

Gaines Jopplin
Lake Nokomis Ward
Minneapolis Minnesota Stake
Minneapolis, Minnesota

Razzycherry Pie

Crust:
2 C. flour, plus a little extra for rolling the
  dough
1 tsp. salt
1 Tbsp. sugar
¾ C. butter-flavored shortening
¼ C. ice water
1 egg
1 Tbsp. vinegar

Filling:
1 10-oz. pkg. frozen raspberries, thawed and
  drained, juice reserved
2 C. pitted frozen cherries, thawed and
  drained, juice reserved
4 Tbsp. cornstarch
1 C. sugar
Dash of salt
½ tsp. almond extract
½ tsp. ground orange zest
Dash cinnamon
1 Tbsp. unsalted butter, chilled

(recipe continued on next page)

(Razzcherry Pie, continued)

Preheat oven to 425. To make crust, sift flour, salt, and sugar into a large mixing bowl. Cut in shortening with pastry blender or fork. In a small bowl, whisk ice water, egg, and vinegar. Sprinkle egg mixture 1 Tbsp. at a time onto flour mixture while fluffing with fork. Cover and chill. To make filling, place reserved juices in a 2 C. measuring cup. Add enough water to make 1½ C.; pour the juice into a medium saucepan. Add cornstarch, sugar, and salt. Stir to dissolve. Heat and stir until mixture thickens and turns clear. Add raspberries, cherries, almond extract, orange zest, and cinnamon. Stir gently and remove from heat. Divide chilled pastry dough in half. Roll out half the dough onto a slightly floured surface, forming a circle large enough to line a 9-inch pie plate. Place rolled dough in pie plate. Pour in filling and dot with butter. Roll out remaining pastry and place over top of pie. Trim excess dough from the rim and crimp the edges all the way around the plate. Bake 35–45 minutes, or until crust is golden brown. TIP: For a golden, glossy crust, beat 1 egg white and 1 Tbsp. cold water; brush the surface of dough with the mixture before baking. Makes 8 servings.

This is a family recipe that has won several prizes, including first place at the Utah State Fair in 2005. Our family doesn't see a holiday without this pie. It takes some effort to make, but trust me—it's worth it, especially served with a big scoop of vanilla ice cream.

Katherine Hinkley
Sheridan 1st ward
Gillete Wyoming Stake
Sheridan, Wyoming

Easy Gluten-Free Fudge

1 C. margarine
2 C. packed brown sugar
1 10-oz. can sweetened condensed milk

1 tsp. vanilla
1 C. white chocolate chips

In a large microwaveable bowl, combine margarine, brown sugar, milk, and vanilla. Microwave on high for 3 minutes; stir. Microwave for another 3 minutes; stir. Microwave for another 3 minutes. Add white chocolate chips and microwave for 2 minutes. Remove from microwave and beat with hand mixer on high speed for 2 minutes. Pour into a lightly greased 9 x 9-inch pan and place in refrigerator until hardened. Cut into squares and enjoy! Makes about 64 pieces.

Abigail Nelson
Kennebecasis Valley Ward
Saint John, New Brunswick, Canada Stake
Sussex, New Brunswick
Canada

I was diagnosed with celiac disease when I was two and a half years old. My mom experimented with a lot of recipes to find things that I could eat. I really love sweet things but I could not have any of the yummy treats my mom made for my family. I was so happy that my mom found this recipe. It is the secret to keeping my sweet tooth happy!

A Woman's Best Friend

1 3.5-oz. pkg. instant vanilla pudding
1 3.5-oz. pkg. instant banana pudding
1 pkg. strawberry glaze
1 C. fresh blueberries
4 C. fresh strawberries, quartered
1 angel food cake, cubed

6 bananas, sliced
1 9-oz. container frozen whipped topping,
   thawed (Cool Whip)
1 7-oz. aerosol can whipped cream
1 large whole strawberry, with the stem
¼ C. cinnamon sugar

Prepare pudding mixes according to package directions; combine. Set aside. Prepare the strawberry glaze according to package directions. Stir blueberries and strawberries into the strawberry glaze. Now for the fun part! Arrange a layer of cake cubes on the bottom of a glass dish (either a 6 x 12 glass casserole dish, about 4–5 inches deep, or a trifle bowl). Add a layer of pudding to cover the cake all the way to the edge. Carefully arrange a layer of bananas on top of the pudding. Spread with half the strawberry glaze mixture. Pay attention to the outside of the glass dish and how it looks, because it's all about presentation! Use ¾ of the container of Cool Whip to cover the strawberry glaze mixture. Then begin again, repeating the same layers, but leave a 1½-inch border between the glass edges of the dish and the bananas and the strawberry glaze mixture. Decorate with the aerosol can of whipped cream the way you frost a cake, filling in the 1½-inch border. Add a little whipped cream swirl in the middle of the dish. Slice the whole strawberry in ⅛-inch slices, cutting only partway to the stem. Fan the sliced berry and place in the middle of the whipped cream swirl. Sprinkle a bit of cinnamon sugar wherever you see whipped cream. Makes 10 servings.

Joyleen Williams
Abilene 2nd Ward
Abilene Texas Stake
Abilene, Texas

You know when you are just craving something sweet, but you want to still feel healthy and guilt-free afterwards? Well, a few years ago, I was thinking just that when I stumbled on this recipe. My friends and coworkers all love this! You can substitute lite Cool Whip and sugar-free pudding mixes made with skim milk to make it even healthier. Other than the glaze, everything is pretty healthy and tastes great! Although the preparation time might be a little long, it is so worth it! I usually leave the remainder as a gift when my husband and I are invited for dinner. It's a great conversation starter, and everyone loves fruits and sweets in one! Bon appetit!

Secret Eggnog Fudge

1 C. good-quality commercial eggnog (not low-fat)

2¾ C. sugar

1½ C. mini marshmallows

½ tsp. cinnamon

1 pinch nutmeg (optional)

2 Tbsp. butter (no substitutes)

6 oz. white chocolate chips

1 C. almonds, chopped coarsely

Line a 9 x 9-inch pan with aluminum foil; set aside. In a heavy-bottomed saucepan, combine eggnog and sugar; stirring constantly, bring to a rolling boil over medium to medium-high heat. Boil for exactly 2 minutes. Watch that the mixture does not boil over the pot; if it's boiling too hard, turn down the heat slightly, but continue a rapid boil. Remove from heat; stir in the marshmallows, cinnamon, and pinch of nutmeg, if desired. Return saucepan to heat; bring back to a rolling boil for another 6 minutes, stirring constantly; again, turn down the heat if the mixture threatens to boil over. The mixture will start to turn a brown color, which is normal. After boiling for the full 6 minutes; remove from heat; add the butter, white chocolate chips, and nuts. Beat until the mixture has a glossy appearance and the chips and butter are mixed in well. Pour the mixture into the prepared foil-lined pan. Cool to room temperature. Remove from pan, using the sides of foil as handles. Peel the foil away from the fudge; cut the fudge in small squares. Makes 15 servings.

Jerry McCall
Casper 6th Ward
Casper Wyoming Stake
Casper, Wyoming

This is the biggest hit. The secret is that you don't need a candy thermometer, which makes it really easy, and it tastes even better than those fudges that require you to slave over the stove. When my wife was pregnant, all she wanted was eggnog—and that's pretty much how this recipe came to be. When your wife is pregnant, you make anything happen.

Conference Caramel Crunch

8 C. popped popcorn

2½ C. pretzels

4½ C. square rice cereal (Rice Chex)

4½ C. square graham cereal (Golden Grahams)

1 C. roasted, salted sunflower seeds

2 C. packed brown sugar

1 14-oz. can sweetened condensed milk

1 tsp. vanilla

1 C. light corn syrup

½ C. margarine

(recipe continued on next page)

(Conference Caramel Crunch, continued)

In a large bowl, combine popcorn, pretzels, rice cereal, graham cereal, and sunflower seeds. Set aside. In a saucepan, combine brown sugar, milk, vanilla, corn syrup, and margarine. Cook, stirring constantly, over medium heat until boiling. IT BURNS EASILY, so keep an eye on it and KEEP STIRRING it. Using a candy thermometer, cook to softball stage (235 degrees), about a minute or two. Remove from heat, and slowly pour the hot mixture over the popcorn mixture, stirring gently to coat. It will be sticky and addicting. Makes 24 servings.

Marie Waldvogel
Bountiful 24th Ward
Bountiful Heights Utah Stake
Bountiful, Utah

Our family has determined that the secret to a peaceful general conference weekend is plenty of good food. This is one of our favorites. I make a huge batch on Saturday and we snack on it during the general conference sessions. Sometimes I try to teach a gospel message with it by associating the ingredients with gospel topics (sunflower seeds=faith is like a seed, pretzel sticks=iron rod, caramel=stick to it, and so on). But when it really comes down to it, eating it is the best part.

Cake Batter Ice Cream

1 C. whole milk, very cold
¾ C. sugar
2 C. heavy cream, very cold

1 tsp. pure vanilla extract
⅔ C. white cake mix

Place freezer bowl of ice cream maker into the freezer. (It is better to keep it in there 24/7; that way it is always ready.) In a medium bowl, whisk milk and sugar until the sugar is dissolved. Stir in cream and vanilla until well blended. Stir in cake mix, making sure there are no lumps. I like to use white cake mix, but you can use any kind you like. Pour mixture into the freezer bowl; mix until it has thickened, about 25–30 minutes. Remove ice cream from freezer bowl and place into a separate container. Place the ice cream into the freezer to further harden (and put the freezer bowl back in the freezer to be ready for next time). Makes 10 servings.

Janelle Snow
Peoria Ward
Peoria Illinois Stake
Peoria, Illinois

I don't know about you, but I thought Cold Stone had the best cake batter ice cream. I threw some ideas together and came up with this recipe—and to be honest, I think it's even better than Cold Stone's ice cream. My family couldn't believe how delicious this turned out. I get lots of praise for this ice cream. I have used all different flavors of cake and all are awesome, but I stick to the original white the most. It is so rich, creamy, and cake battery. If you like cake batter ice cream, you will LOVE this!

A Cookbook Featuring Secrets from Around the World!

Recipes in the *Worldwide Ward Cookbook: Secret Recipes* were submitted by members of the Church living in all fifty of the United States and the District of Columbia.

Recipes were also submitted by Church members living in thirty-two countries outside the United States, including:

Argentina
Australia
Brazil
Canada
Chile
China
Colombia
Denmark
England

Finland
France
Germany
Guatemala
Haiti
Hong Kong
India
Ireland
Mexico

New Zealand
Peru
Philippines
Portugal
Russia
Scotland
Singapore
South Africa
South Korea

Sweden
Switzerland
Taiwan
Thailand
Venezuela

Italicized entries in the index will help you find recipes from a specific state or country.

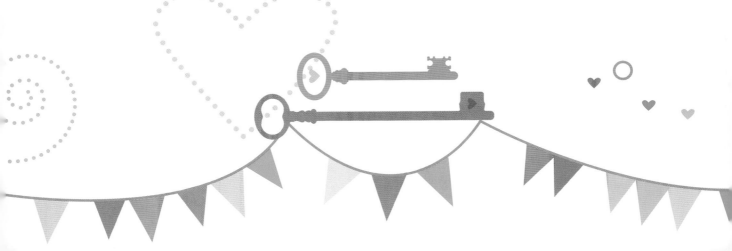

INDEX

SECRET